*"It was early morning, when I was seven years old, that I saw the angels. I am as sure of it now as I was then . . . . This, my own experience, stands both at the beginning and the end of this book . . . . The Angels have a stupendous reality. Their activity among us has become to me a vital, positive reality."*

Mother Alexandra

Mother Alexandra

# *THE HOLY ANGELS*

*"In Him was life and the life was the light of men"* (John 1:4).

**Light and Life Publishing Company**

Minneapolis, Minnesota

1987

Line drawings by Mother Alexandra.
Photo on back cover by Jerrine Habsburg.

LIBRARY OF CONGRESS CATALOGING IN PUBLICATION DATA

Alexandra, Mother, 1908-
  The holy angels.

  1. Angels—Biblical teaching.   I. Title.
BS680.A48A43              235'.3              81-5773
ISBN 0-932506-10-0                            AACR2

# Contents

# MOTHER ALEXANDRA

Mother Alexandra was born in 1909 in Bucharest, Romania, the youngest daughter of King Ferdinand and Queen Marie and was christened Ileana. She lived through the harrowing events of World War I and, being a perceptive child, fully comprehended the suffering which surrounded her and early learned to follow her mother in works of charity.

At 22 she married Archduke Anton of Austria and lived in Sonnberg, Austria, giving birth to six children, two born during the second war. In March 1944, wishing to get away from the Nazi oppression, she moved the children to Romania. Here, at the foot of her castle of Bran, she built a hospital in the memory of her mother, Queen Marie. She devoted herself to the care of the war-wounded and lovingly served the surrounding population. Subsisting and still working at the hospital, it was here she witnessed the end of the war and the Communist takeover in August 1944.

Then began the sad exile's life, the "D.P." no one wanted. She and her family went first to Switzerland, then Argentina, and finally, obtaining scholarships for most of the children, they settled in Newton, Massachusetts. Their needs were met by the sale of jewelry and Mother Alexandra's extensive lecture tours. When all the children were either married or had found sufficient employment, she fulfilled her great desire to devote her life entirely to God and became a nun. She is now abbess of the Orthodox Monastery of the Transfiguration in Ellwood City, Pennsylvania.

# Acknowledgments

This book was started before I entered the monastic life. I am well aware of its deficiencies, but at no time was I able to tap the many sources such a study requires; therefore I ask for the readers' indulgence.

Through the many years of search I was helped and encouraged by more people than I have space to name, nevertheless my warmest thanks go out to them all. I especially thank Metropolitan Anthony Bloom (of Surozh), London and Archbishop Valerian of the Romanian Diocese of the Orthodox Church in America for their continued encouragement. My very special gratitude goes to Father Regis Barwig, Prior of the Community of Our Lady, Oshkosh, Wisconsin, who patiently read and edited the manuscript and even retyped it for me. Finally, warmest thanks to Father Basil Pennington of St. Joseph's Monastery, Spencer, Massachusetts, for his kind interest and for accepting to write the foreword; also for bringing the manuscript to the attention of the Sisters of St. Bede's Publications who have so generously undertaken to print my humble effort.

My deep-felt gratitude goes out to each and every one of them.

I pray that this little book may find favor before the Lord our God to whom be all praise and glory.

Mother Alexandra, Abbess
The Orthodox Monastery of the Transfiguration

Bible quotes taken from *The Holy Bible*, translated by Ronald Knox, copyright © 1944, 1948, 1950 by Sheed & Ward, Inc., New York.

# Foreword

"Angels we have heard on high." Most of us, I suspect, have sung that popular carol at one time or another. But how many of us have ever actually heard an angel? Or even taken them seriously? They are part of the Christmas decorations. A couple fit into the Easter scene. In our younger days we might have been fortunate enough to get acquainted with our guardian angels, but they were left behind with childhood's fantasies. No one is perhaps so neglected as these constant caring companions.

But the angels are realities, very active presences in the unfolding of the drama of creation and the working out of the daily life of our world. In ignoring them, their presence, their help, their care, we deprive ourselves of a great source of consolation, strengthening and hope.

Monastic tradition has always been very much alive to the angelic hosts. A rich theology based solidly on the revelation found in the Scriptures was elaborated by that fifth century Syrian monk who is known to us as the Pseudo-Dionysius (because he adopted as his pen name the name of St. Paul's famous convert, Dionysius, the Areopagite). Bernard of Clairvaux, the great Cistercian mystic, so elaborated on Dionysius' teaching bringing it into the Western tradition, that he has been called the "Doctor of the Angels." The Angelic Doctor—note the title—St. Thomas Aquinas, the greatest of the scholastics, fully incorporated Dionysius' teaching in his masterly *Summa Theologica*.

Rich as the tradition is, and though the greatest masters and mystics have dedicated pages and treatises to the angels, I do not know of any contemporary work comparable to this magnificent and most ample anthology prepared by Mother Alexandra. A woman who has lived fully in the tradition, Mother has garnered up for us its most precious nuggets. And this is good. For perhaps in no other period of the life of the Church have the angels been so needed and so neglected. In an age when phenomenology holds sway and men and women live primarily by their senses, advocates and friends who cannot be seen and felt are not given much credence. When science seeks to master and account for all, the activity of free heavenly spirits in the cosmic sphere just does not fit into the picture.

Mother's resume of the tradition with all its fullness, balance and richness, adds much to an impoverished scientism in helping us appreciate, enjoy and collaborate with the creative order within which we must find our own meaning and work out our salvation.

I think contact with the realities this living teaching of the tradition gives us is especially important for those Christians who are trying to live a full life of prayer and praise, especially those who chant the divine office night and day. Our sacrifice of praise lacks a most significant dimension and is in danger of getting seriously earth-bound if we are not aware of how our praise is one with that of a great heavenly host who create with us a continuum that reaches to the very throne of Him Who is enthroned upon the cherubim. Those, like St. Bernard, who have had keener spiritual vision, have recounted for us how they have seen the choirs of angels one with the earthly choirs of men and women offering the divine praises. What an effective stimulus it is to our praise when we realize that we are singing and worshipping with the angels!

In these days when we stand in dread of nuclear holocaust, when we strain, struggle and weep for peace among nations and within nations, when the reports of devastating natural calamities—floods, droughts, hurricanes, earthquakes (How much of this is not natural but the effect of our disturbing nature with our atomic and nuclear blasts, underground or over?)—tear at our hearts, baffle our minds and strain our resources, it is good to know that there are angels at work in our behalf, that the nations, the regions, the globe, the cosmos, have their angelic guardians. Perhaps, in spite of man's worst efforts, the balance can be preserved, the forces for evil offset, the worst consequences be spared us. We have much reason to pray to the Lord of the angels that his holy ministers would assist us and care for us in these times.

Before concluding, I would like to say a word about the author, a most remarkable woman of the Lord. I have already written of this great spiritual mother in my book, *In Search of True Wisdom*. Mother Alexandra is a beautiful woman of regal dignity. Her lineage is impressive: great granddaughter of both Czar Alexander II of Russia and Queen Victoria of England. Her father was King Ferdinand I of Rumania. Mother married a Catholic Archduke of Austria and boasts fifteen grandchildren, of whom she is quite justifiably proud, while at the same time, as any grandmother in these times, quite concerned. Mother's life has intimately touched the three great Catholic traditions: Roman, Orthodox and Anglican. Yet it is in the Orthodox that Mother finds herself firmly rooted. After a very difficult struggle to raise six children under the duress of war, dictatorships and persecutions, Mother Alexandra finally found the freedom to give a full response to her desire to be wholly unto the Lord. She had long practiced and taught the ways of prayer, especially the Jesus Prayer. Now she was able to enter fully into a life of prayer, first in France under a renowned spiritual mother, Mother Eudoxia, and then as founder of the first English-speaking Rumanian Orthodox monastery for women in America.

The work that went into the preparation of this volume was no mere academic task. The rich teaching we are here privileged to share is the fruit of Mother's own personal communing with the reality of the Christian tradition. We have here, not a collection of historical texts, but the living and lived synthesis of a life-giving current as it has been experienced by a deeply religious and highly sensitive daughter of God and mother of His children.

We can be very grateful that this busy *Hegumena*, upon whose spiritual wisdom so many call, has taken the time to share this fruit of her reading and reflection with us in this volume. May the Lord, to Whom she has so completely given her life, reward her with His very Self. And may her sharing bear fruit in all our lives.

M. Basil Pennington

Feast of the Holy Angels

# Preface

At the present moment, the bookshelves in airports, shops, and wherever books are sold, display any amount of volumes concerning satanic cults, but we do not see anything about the holy angels who are God's messengers, and the heavenly counterparts of hell's emissaries.

Angels are of the faith, as stated in the Symbol of Faith, "Maker . . .of all things visible and *invisible*." The Holy Scriptures abound with them: they are mentioned over 230 times. Our liturgy and prayers include them in the most solemn moments. We have special prayers, canons and *akathist* hymns addressed to the angels of God. Yet, generally speaking, the faithful know very little about them. They ignore them, or what is sadder still, they disbelieve in the reality of the holy angels, thus, in so doing, they miss the vital comfort and joy of sensing their presence, and fail to participate in the Angelic Liturgy which eternally praises the Lord God: "Every creature of reason and understanding worships Thee . . . . Thou art praised by angels and archangels . . .the many-eyed Cherubim. Round Thee stand the Seraphim . . .with six wings . . . . Singing the triumphant hymn, shouting and proclaiming, 'Holy! Holy! Holy! Lord God of Sabaoth . . .' " (Prayer and hymn during the *Anaphora*).

It comes as a shock to discover that the holy angels and demons have a common origin. They were created free creatures in infinite beauty, and endowed with perfect, absolute, free will. The use they put this freedom to is what brought about the staggering dichotomy between angels and devils: variant creatures with destinies as far removed from each other as is the east from the west, as is heaven from hell.

And, until the last man is born on earth, a tremendous battle will rage in the spiritual world over mankind's final destiny. This conflict inevitably affects us all more closely than we realize. Whereas we ourselves are free agents, and the decision is always our own, neither good nor bad can force us into any issue against our will. Nevertheless, in our every act, and especially as Christians, we are either on one side or the other. Still, we must not for one moment forget that Evil is not equal to Good. Evil came by Satan's misuse of his free will. Satan cannot be a creator, being himself a created creature. God alone is Creator: "And God saw all that he had made, and found it very good" (Gn. 1:31).

This book is planned as a guide through the Holy Scriptures and the writings of the Holy Fathers, to bring the faithful to a greater knowledge and understanding of the heavenly hosts in the hope that their belief in the holy angels may stand on a firm foundation and reap a rich harvest of grace and all blessings in the heavenly ministrations of the blessed and angelic spirits.

# THE HOLY ANGELS

# Book I

**Angels in Old Testament Times**

# I

## What Are Angels?

*1. The Holy Angels*

Like the existence of God, the existence of the holy angels is presumed, not asserted. Angels in the Bible are referred to simply as accepted fact. Although they are mentioned over two hundred times, we learn nothing about their creation or when it took place, nor do we find many physical descriptions. This is not as strange as it might at first appear. The Bible does not deal with *all* mankind, even in the first few chapters, but is concerned primarily with the history of God's action toward man. The Old Testament is concerned with the development of one nation only, God's chosen people, though we do hear of other peoples because of their historical connection with the Jews. Similarly, the story of creation describes the coming into existence of our earth, the sun and stars, the appearance of plants, animals and, finally, man. It does not include an account of how, nor when, the spiritual beings were created. This remains a matter of theological conjecture. Nevertheless, from the very outset we are made aware of their presence in the existing world and their interest in us, both for weal and woe.

For a more complete knowledge of angels and their nature, we have first to examine the Bible as a whole, both the Old and the New Testaments, in order to know what has been revealed to us about spiritual beings; only then can we pick up the threads chronologically, according to the books of the Bible. But, first of all, when referring to these celestial beings we should understand that the term "angel" is loosely and inaccurately used, for in Greek it simply means "messenger" and, properly speaking, this would apply only to the two orders of angels in direct communication with man.

Angels and archangels, although spirit, are *not* supernatural. God alone is supernatural, for he alone is uncreated. Like us, the holy angels are *created*, natural beings, as much a part of our world as we ourselves. "Yes, in him all created things took their being, heavenly and earthly, visible and invisible . . ." (Col. 1:16).

An angel has character, individuality, and a will of his own, much as we have; but in other ways angels do not resemble us. When, to make himself manifest to us, an angel takes on human semblance, he never is physically *like* a human being, but only a mental image of one. If we are so little aware of them, it is because we do not as a rule see them with our mortal eyes, and our spiritual perception is either dulled or undeveloped.

In seeking better to understand the angelic nature, we should turn to our knowledge of God rather than to our knowledge of man. St. Basil says that in his eyes "their substance is a breath of air or an immortal fire, and this is why they are localized or become visible in the shape of their own bodies to those who are worthy to see them."[1] St. Basil means that they take on a visible individuality expressed in human form, though not humanly tangible. The holy angels, from the beginning of their creation, are *completed* beings, but without material form.

Angels are of a superiority all but incomprehensible to us, but they are a part of our lives: by God's boundless mercy, they are destined, in the great moments of history, to be the heralds of the Most High to man below; they are, as well, our guides, guardians, mentors, protectors, and comforters from birth to the grave.

Angels are pure integral spirits: they are not confined to time or space; they know neither youth nor old age, but life ever at its fullest. We can barely envision for ourselves even a shadowy image of their majesty, might, and power, or grasp the lightning that is their movement, "So the living creatures came and went, vivid as lightning flashes" (Ezek. 1:14). Furthermore, mortals cannot begin to understand the freedom of the holy angels and the scope of their intellects, untrammeled by physical brains. Crystal clear and faultless, knowing no pain or frustration, unhindered by doubt or fear, neither male nor female, they are beauty, love, life and action welded into individual unutterable perfection. "Thou wilt have thy angels be like the winds, the servants that wait on thee like a flame of fire" (Ps. 103:4). In a certain sense, if it can be so expressed, they are the individualized selfness of God's own attributes.

The holy angels stand in the presence of God beholding the face of the Lord. "Angels are more than the bearers of divine messages and the guides of men: they are bearers of the very Name and Power of God. There is nothing rosy or weakly poetical in the Angels of the Bible: they are flashes of the light and strength of the Almighty Lord."[2] Their being is sustained by God's goodness, and they participate in his might, wisdom, and love. They are uplifted by their perpetual praise and thanksgiving. Uplifted Godwards, from their beginning it has been the angels' greatest joy to choose freely for God and to give him their undaunted flow of life in unending love and worship. The entire heavenly host partook from the first in the execution of God's will: Seraphim (Is. 6:2), Cherubim (Ezek. 10:1), Thrones (Col. 1:16), Dominions (Col. 1:16), Virtues (1 Pt. 3:22), Powers (Col. 1:16; Eph. 3:10),

Principalities (Col. 1:16; Eph. 3:10), Archangels (1 Thes. 4:15), and Angels. All nine choirs have ever stood bent on God's intentions, unerringly fulfilling his design: "Praise him, all you angels of his, praise him, all his armies . . .it was his decree that fashioned them, his command that gave them birth" (Ps. 148:2-5).

The Lord has set up his throne in heaven, rules with universal sway. Bless the Lord, all you angels of his; angels of sovereign strength, that carry out his commandment, attentive to the word he utters; bless the Lord, all you hosts of his, the servants that perform his will; bless the Lord, all you creatures of his, in every corner of his dominion; and thou, my soul, bless the Lord (Ps. 102:19-22).

From earliest times, these angelic hosts were conceived as divided into three hierarchies; St. Dionysius the Areopagite called them "choirs." This is the most fitting term as their whole activity is like an eternal song of praise and thanksgiving to the Most High.

First come the Seraphim, Cherubim, and Thrones. These are councillors and have no direct dealings with man, but are absorbed in unending love and adoration of God. No other creature is so intensely capable of loving God.

Second come the Dominions, Virtues, and Powers. These are understood to be the governors of space and the stars. Our orb, consequently, as part of the galaxy is under their dominion; otherwise, we have no direct contact with the second choir.

Third come the Principalities, Archangels, and Angels. These have this earth of ours in their special charge. They are the executors of God's will, the perpetual guardians of the children of men, and the messengers of God. Our study will deal chiefly with this third choir of angels.

The Archangels have distinct individualities and are an order of celestial beings in themselves, partaking of the nature of both Principalities and Angels. Yet they are also messengers, like the Angels. There are seven Archangels, the first four of whom are mentioned by name in the books of the Bible.

A. Michael (*Who Is Like God?*). The greatest leader of the heavenly host. It was he who overcame the Dragon (Lucifer) and thrust him out of Paradise.

B. Gabriel (*The Man of God*). The Angel of the Annunciation.

C. Raphael (*The Healing of God*). The chief of the guardian angels, and the one who bears our prayers to the Lord.

D. Uriel (*The Fire of God*). The interpreter of prophecies.

The names of the other three archangels are not found in the Scriptures. "Like God, Man of God, Healing, Fire." Here in the utter simplicity of the interpretations of the archangelic names, we get momentary glimpses of their personalities, through which their relationship to God becomes more apparent as does their power and influence. The Areopagite gives a won-drously clear definition: "An angel is an image of God, a manifestation of the invisible light, a burnished mirror, bright, untarnished, without spot or blemish, receiving (if it is reverent to say so), all the beauty of the absolute divine goodness, and (so far as may be) kindling in itself, with unalloyed radiance, the goodness of the secret silence."[3]

The more we become aware of the angels of light, the more strengthened we are in our capacity for good, and the sharper becomes our ability to detect and resist the snares of our bitterest enemies, the angels of darkness.

> O bodiless Angels, as you stand before God's throne, and are enlightened by its rays, and with the overflow of light forever shining, pray to Christ to give our souls peace and grant us mercy (*Lord, I Call*, Tone I).

## 2. The Fallen Angels

The Church's recognized faith in angels is founded on the Holy Scriptures and Holy Tradition; the same applies to its official teaching regarding Satan as the "fallen angel." Although our primary purpose is to deal with the "good" angels, we cannot fully comprehend their role in man's destiny, unless we are familiar with the role of Satan, the "prince of this world," and his angels, the angels of darkness.

Satan, before he became prince of the netherworld, was the greatest of all the heavenly hosts. He was called Lucifer, "the bearer of light," and held his place at the very summit of created perfection. In spite of his fall, he is much closer in the order of nature to God than to man, for being pure spirit, he is deathless and ageless; he partakes of all the attributes of the angelic world, neither space nor time encumber him, and his intellect is clarity itself. We must never for a moment forget Satan's spiritual nature and the fewness of his limitations. These are only understandable when we see him—as we must see all the angels—in relationship to God.

> The angels' mastery over the physical world is not at all to be compared to God's sovereignty. The angels' is a ministerial, relative mastery, not a creative, absolute one; they can put to use the powers and principles implanted in nature by God but they cannot call those powers and prin-ciples into being. We see the devil, then, because of his angelic nature, as a pure spirit, ageless, independent, immaterial, a life-principle; complete in itself, a pure form integrally whole in itself. He is dependent on God and independent of all things else: mirroring the divine resplendence in all its purity, the created pure spirit reflecting the incandescent beauty of the uncreated pure spirit who is God.[4]

How then, and why should a perfect, powerful, resplendent being have been chosen to be the prince of the damned, or himself be damned at all? God in his perfection gave freedom to all his creation. God willed to be loved freely, without obligation. He gave the greatest and the smallest of his intelligent creatures the right to direct their love above or below.

> Caught by the undeniable beauty, perfection, goodness of his own angelic nature, fully comprehended, Lucifer loved it. That was as it should be, but his love refused to budge a step beyond this, refused to look beyond the angelic perfection to its Divine source; he insisted upon resting in that beauty to find there fullness of happiness, to be sufficient unto himself. As is the way of pride, Lucifer isolated himself, even from God . . . . Lucifer's sin consisted in loving himself (as pride insists) to the exclusion of all else; and this with no excuse: without ignorance, without error, without passion, without previous disorder in his angelic will. His was a sin of pure malice.[5]

Thus Satan fell from his high estate because he would not fulfill his role, and lost for all time the place for which he was created.

As Isaiah remarks:

> What, fallen from heaven, thou Lucifer, that once didst herald the dawn? Prostrate on the earth, that didst once bring nations to their knees? I will scale the heavens (such was thy thought); I will set my throne higher than God's stars, take my seat at his own trysting-place, at the meeting of the northern hills; I will soar above the level of the clouds, the rival of the most High. Thine, instead, to be dragged down into the world beneath, into the heart of the abyss (Is. 14:12-15).

This is Lucifer's damnation, and of all who followed him, be it from the angelic world or our own. All those who choose false goals follow Satan and thus run the risk of forever losing God. In his agony and fury, the devil seeks to destroy and so carries others with him into a misery as absolute as his erstwhile celestial joy. For him there is no error in judgment; he *knows* what he does, and that is why his name is *Satan*, the adversary, and why his power is inferior only to the power of God. Remember, however, that Satan's power equals that of the cherubim, and that he does unceasing battle with the heavenly hosts, led by St. Michael, their standard-bearer.

Jesus testified to having seen how "Satan was cast down like a lightning flash from heaven" (Lk. 10:18). Christ the Word, spoke from his divine knowledge of what was before the beginning of time. In the flash of lightning are seen Satan's two aspects: light and the zigzag movement of the serpent. Jesus, in alluding to Satan's fall, accentuated Satan's demonic mastery of *this* world only, as well as the deceiving and deceptive nature of that mastery. For this reason, we find Michael the Archangel at war with Satan. It is not a seraph or a cherub who fights the fallen one, for they do not have the care of our world as have the archangels.

Nowhere is the story of Satan's fall more splendidly depicted than in St. John the Divine's magnificent vision in the Book of Revelation. We must, at the same time, keep in mind that St. John is giving a symbolic account of the heavenly war which began long before the earth's creation, and in which the Church is still engaged:

> Fierce war broke out in heaven, where Michael and his angels fought against the dragon. The dragon and his angels fought on their part, but could not win the day, or stand their ground in heaven any longer; the great dragon, serpent of the primal age, was flung down to earth; he whom we call the devil, or Satan, the whole world's seducer, flung down to earth, and his angels with him . . . . Rejoice over it, heaven, and all you that dwell in heaven; but woe to you, earth and sea, now that the devil has come down upon you, full of malice, because he knows how brief is the time given him (Rev. 12:7-12).

Satan's fall from heaven left him with a great consuming fury for it is on earth alone that he has power. Satan is doubly angry because his power is limited to our world and he knows fully that when our world is ended, his power to deceive mankind ends with it. His time for each one of us is shorter still, as his ability to reach us as individuals is limited to the life span granted us on the earth. It is in eternity that man reaps the fulfillment of this earthly battle.

The story of Satan's fall is so dramatic that it is difficult to drag our eyes away from that bottomless pit over which he is king (Rev. 9:11), and to look up once more to those holy angels who did not fall, but turned their burning love in all its magnificence to humbly adore their Creator and fulfill his will. It is with them we are essentially concerned in these pages, and especially with their mission to us, because of which we call them "angels."

> Thou Lord of all dost clearly save the breed of mortal men by the appointment of the angels. For Thou has set them over all the faithful who sing Thy praises in right faith, Thee the God of the fathers Who is praised and passing glorious (*Monday Canon*, Tone I).

---

[1]Tixeront, *History of Dogmas*, Vol. II. p. 133.

[2]A Monk of the Eastern Church, *Orthodox Spirituality*. London: S.P.C.K., 1961, pp. 33-34.

[3]Dionysius the Areopagite, *De divinis nominibus, IV*, in Robert Payne, *The Holy Fire*. New York: Harper and Brothers, 1957, pp. 246-247.

[4]From "Devil Himself," Walter Farrell, O.P., in *Satan*, ed. by Fr. Bruno de Jesus-Marie, O.C.D. New York: Sheed and Ward, p. 6.

[5]*Ibid.*, p. 14.

# The Angels in Genesis

## 1. Angels in the Old Testament

The holy angels in the Old Testament are especially the guardians of the Law, pressing man on to obedience, chastising his disobedience, and protecting him in time of trouble. Although Satan is but seldom mentioned in the majority of the narratives where angels take a forceful hand in the affairs of men, his influence is no less difficult to detect. It is clear, then, that the Law was given in consequence of Lucifer's own fall, and of his prevailing upon man to follow him in his sin.

God, mindful of his loved creation, gave man the Law as a signpost whereby he might find his way back to the happiness of paradise. Through many of the Old Testament stories the holy angels are seen supporting man and aiding his understanding of the redeeming Law. Keeping man on the right path is, under the Old Testament, or Covenant, one of the angelic attributes.

We see the angels as "messengers," as "sons of God," as "watchers," and as the "hosts of heaven." They slip in and out of the stories of the Bible like so many strokes of light, ever inspiring and magnificent. Yet, in every way, they are strangely close and natural to those who have been permitted to see them and entertain them in their company.

## 2. The Garden of Eden

We can conjecture how Satan, jealous of man's perfect state in the Garden of Eden, enticed Adam and Eve to sin. Lucifer, who had been the most perfect of created beings, could not bear to see a creature so inferior to himself enjoying now a beatitude he had so wantonly cast away. Man, when he fell, did not lose his freedom; he remains free and keeps his right of choice between good and evil. The road back to Eden lies ever open but Satan does all in his power to prevent mankind's return.

There is an old French saying, *Les heureux n'ont pas d'histoire*, that is, "The happy have no story." This saying could well be used to explain one of the reasons why we have so little knowledge of the holy angels: they are indeed happy and the cup of their joy is forever running over. The same cannot be said of us human beings. Therefore, about us there is a story to tell; and in this story, often sad, dark, and horrible, there forever shines a light, at times but a spark, a shimmer, but always there, for the angels remain ever among us.

It seems that we can view the vexed problem of good and evil in man's earthly life as resulting directly from the influence exercised over us by the angels, both of light and of darkness. Our impulses and thoughts do not appear to be, so to speak, self-fabricated but as coming from without. Of course, it is we ourselves who decide by free will which course to pursue.

Turning to the Bible's chronological account, we can note how the angels participated in man's story. Man's narrative starts in the presence of the spiritual beings called angels, in their two roles: guardian and tempter. From the beginning we see that man is caught up by, and pulled into, a great spiritual battle. This battle is not between the forces of good and evil. This battle is not between God and the Devil, as is so often wrongly presumed; it is a war waged between the angels of light led by Michael, and the angels of darkness led by Satan (Rev. 9:15; 12:1-9).

Man, created in the image and likeness of God, was destined to move Godwards, to find union with God without depersonalization. The angels existed before man, and Satan, it is presumed, made his choice before God had placed man in the Garden of Eden.

This partly explains the presence of the tempter in the Garden of Eden prior to the fall of man, when man had all his heart could desire: a glorious destiny, beauty, peace, companionship, and perfect freedom. Freedom includes the right of choice; without this capacity man would have been a will-less, unintelligent creature. Through this power of selection he participates in the higher order of creation and enjoys the fullness of its privileges: "Thou hast placed him [man] only a little below the angels . . ." (Ps. 8:6). Man did not need to know sorrow, but he willed a taste of evil. Thus, he thought it would bring him fuller knowledge and place him next to God.

In the wondrous allegorical story of the Garden of Eden, Satan, well aware of man's ambition, couches with malicious cleverness the enticing thought: You shall be as gods, but God is jealous of his power and would not have you so endowed; come let us try it, you'll like it! In the words of St. Gregory of Nyssa: "For this was the beginning of the entire sequence of sin, the unwillingness to be ignorant of evil."[1]

He appealed to man's pride and envy—for the real temptation was intellectual, not sensual: it was not in the taste and juiciness of the fruit that the temptation lay, but in the supposed power and knowledge it would impart. It is always the mind that sins in the first place. Satan by his angelic nature could sin by intellect alone, and it is by intellect that he tempts and misuses good. There is no created evil. All that God created was good and is good. It is his creatures who first willed evil and then perpetrated it. Evil exists only where it is practiced. God permits it, in that he permits freedom. Thus man listens to the voice of the tempter who is described as "more subtle than any beast"—subtle, not repulsive as the serpent now is, for it is only after he has played his fateful role that he is cursed: ". . .thou shalt crawl on thy belly and eat dust all thy life long" (Gn. 3:14).

The characterization of the tempter becomes a loathsome thing. Satan has added to his original sin the sin of being a seducer and of making another creature fall.

When the Lord had banished Adam and Eve from the Garden to till the ground from whence he was taken, the Bible mentions for the first time one of the spiritual guardians whose attribute is not to watch over man, but to protect a principle—the Lord God "posted his Cherubim before the garden of delight, with a sword of fire that turned this way and that, so that he could reach the tree of life no longer" (Gn. 3:24). The flaming sword also is considered to be, by pious legend, one of the seven archangels and bears the name *Jophiel*, originating from the Hebrew verb "to burn."

And what of man? Man, created in the image of God? We do not know exactly what his state was in the Garden of Eden. In Adam's words: "Here, at last, is bone that comes from mine, flesh that comes from mine . . . ." (Gn. 2:23) and in so speaking of Eve he recognized her as completing his own nature.

The consequence of sin was *diabolic*, that is, utterly divisive. Following original sin, man became many nations, a race splintered and fragmented. But man did not lose his freedom, for "made in the image of God, man is a personal being confronted with a personal God. God speaks to him as to a person, and man responds."[2] Man is still under the command to be "like" God whose image he still bears, and is bound to strive for union with him. "But this commandment is addressed to human freedom, and does not overrule it. As a personal being man can accept the will of God; he can also reject it."[3]

God's purpose for man following Adam's fall is his redemption and return to his original estate. As a loving Father, he gives to the children of men, mentors in the form of prophets and great leaders, and also assigns his holy angels to assist, guard, protect, and teach them. We meet the angels all along the way of salvation until the very birth of the Redeemer himself, with whose advent the angelic attributes received a new tenor.

O ye immortal angels who most blessed, have indeed received from the original Life, from glory everlasting, life that never perishes, ye have become the holy beholders of eternal wisdom and ye are fittingly shown forth as close ranks of torches filled with light (From *Lord, I Have Cried,* Tone I).

### 3. Abraham Entertains the Angels (Gn. 18)

God in his infinite mercy sought out man and calling him out of the mire he had fallen into, began the long process of selection and purification. Abraham was the first to hear and answer the call.

The story of Abraham entertaining the three angels is lovely and full of meaning.

> He [Abraham] had a vision of the Lord, too, in the valley of Mambre, as he sat by his tent door at noon. He looked up, and saw three men standing near him; and, at the sight, he ran from his tent door to meet them, bowing down to the earth. Lord, he said, as thou lovest me, do not pass thy servant by; let me fetch a drop of water, so that you can wash your feet and rest in the shade (Gn. 18:1-4).

One can with the mind's eye see the plains of Asia Minor baking in the noonday sun, the air vibrating over the parched earth, the horizon melting in a haze of dust, no distinct line between earth and a cloudless sky, too hot to be truly blue. Abraham sits and contemplates in the cool of his large black camel's hair tent where a slight draught can be induced by open sides in the shade of an oak tree. The holy and upright man, ever seeking the way of the Lord, gazes with half-closed eyes upon the still plain before him, and then he sees three men standing there as if formed out of the stillness and the blaze. Abraham calls all three by one name: "Lord." He offers the best he has to give: to sit in the shade of a tree, water for their feet—a rare and precious gift in those parts and indicative of the touching desire of a man to offer God that which to him is the most precious.

Abraham and Sarah entertain the three holy visitors who predict the birth of Isaac, at which Sarah, who was "past her prime" (Gn. 18:11), laughed. How often do we echo that mocking laugh of incredulity when believers make a claim we cannot comprehend. Further, the visitors predict the destruction of Sodom and Gomorrah. Abraham pleads for the righteous inhabitants of the condemned cities and humbly implores mercy: "Dust and ashes though I be, I have taken it upon me to speak to my Lord, and speak I will" (Gn. 18:27). His pleading is listened to and heard.

The prophecy of the celestial visitors comes true. Lot and his family are spared the ruin of Sodom and Gomorrah. Isaac is conceived and born.

According to the interpretation of the Eastern Orthodox and Roman Catholic tradition, Abraham's visitation by the three angels was the first revealed image of the Holy Trinity, full knowledge of which the New Testament alone would unveil. That the three angelic figures were understood to be one is indicated thus: "So God finished speaking to Abraham, and left him, and Abraham turned and went home" (Gn. 18:33).

And, as such, the three angels must be seen rather as a self-revelation of God, than merely as an angelic apparition. The angels visually portrayed in their perfect unity and equal perfection the first fleeting glimpse of the great mystical doctrine of the Trinity, "admitting through the spiritual and unwavering eyes of the mind the original and super-original gift of Light of the Father who is the Source of Divinity, which shows to us images . . .in figurative symbols towards its Primal Ray."[4]

Therefore, icons of the Holy Trinity portray this meal offered by Abraham and Sarah to the three angels. It is the most pure image of the Triune God as yet revealed to man which we also find so perfectly reflected in the words of the evening hymn:

> O joyful light of the Holy Glory of the Immortal Father, the heavenly, holy Blessed One, Jesus Christ; having come to the hour of sunset, beholding the evening light, we hymn the Father, Son, and Holy Spirit: God.

> In times past, O Godhead in nature One, Thou hast plainly appeared in Three Persons to Abraham, and in symbols hast revealed the highest mystery of theology. We sing Thy praises with faith, O God, One Sovereignty and Threefold Sun (*Sunday Midnight Office*, Canticle III, Tone I).

### 4. Lot and Hagar (Gn. 19:1-17; 21:9-21)

In the story of Lot we have our first encounter with the guardian messenger angels. Faithful to his promise to Abraham to spare Lot out of the general destruction of Sodom and Gomorrah, the Lord sent two angels to Sodom, first to save Lot and then to destroy the two cities.

This tale is hardly a pretty one, dealing as it does with one of man's greatest sins called, even today, by the name of the town in which it originated. Not even the two heavenly messengers were spared the insult and abomination of lecherous attack.

Lot was sitting, we are told, in the gate of Sodom when he saw the visitors appear, and he invited them to rest within his house. The men of Sodom immediately tried to misuse the unknown visitors and surrounded Lot's house. While Lot was defending the entrance, they fell upon him. The angels dragged Lot into the house and smote the attackers with blindness, so that they could not find the door and thus departed. The angels then declared themselves to Lot and his family, and forthwith led them out of the doomed city, bidding them go and not look back. But Lot's wife did look back and was turned into a pillar of salt. One cannot help thinking that, in a sense, Lot's family was not really much better than those left behind. It was rather because of Abraham's prayers than because of his own virtues that the guardian angels protected Lot. This is one of the lessons to be drawn from the story, namely, the power of intercessory prayer. "When a just man prays fervently, there is great virtue in his prayer" (Jas. 5:16).

The further promise made to Abraham also comes true. "...old as she was, she conceived and bore a son.... To this son whom Sarah had borne him, Abraham gave the name of Isaac..." (Gn. 21:3).

\*     \*     \*

Especially moving is the story of Hagar, Abraham's bondwoman who had borne him a son during the years of Sarah's sterility. Sarah had herself advised Abraham to have a child by this bondwoman, but now she saw the other woman's son as a danger to her own boy. Therefore, Sarah talked Abraham into sending Hagar and her child into the wilderness. The words of the Bible are full of beauty as they recount this tale:

> At last all the water in the bottle was spent, and she left the boy under one of the trees there, while she went and sat down opposite where he was, at a bow-shot's distance; I cannot bear to see my child die, she said. And there, sitting opposite him, she wept aloud. But God had listened to the child's crying, and now his angel called to Hagar out of heaven. Hagar, he said, what ails thee? Do not be afraid, God has listened to the crying of thy child, where he lies yonder. Up, and take thy child with thee, hold him fast by the hand; I will make him founder of a great nation yet. With that, God gave clear sight to her eyes, and she saw a well that had water in it; to this she went, and filled her bottle, and gave the boy drink (Gn. 21:15-20).

How often are we blind in our despair, not seeing the spring close at hand! Hagar's angel was both her guardian and the messenger who revealed to her God's loving care for the outcast and the illegitimate. If they but put their trust in him, God makes a place in the world for all men, and cares for them in their distress, no matter how rejected they are in their society.

Abraham, who had sacrificed Hagar and the child of his natural love, believed that God asked of him the supreme sacrifice of Isaac, his son born in wedlock. It was an angel who stayed Abraham's hand when, according to the lights of those times, he believed he was obeying God's command. He felt that his offering to his God should surpass that of the heathen surrounding him. Therefore he was ready to sacrifice Isaac, the son whom he loved (Gn. 22:1-12). The angel enlightened Abraham's understanding, that true worship of the true God requires no human sacrifice. This was a sacrifice that God had reserved for himself, namely, to offer his only-begotten Son for the redemption of all mankind.

A further example, which is neither exactly that of the guardian nor of the messenger, but an instance in which inspiration is transmitted through an angel, is the story of Abraham's sending forth his faithful servant to find a wife for Isaac. When instructing him how to proceed, Abraham told his servant that there is nothing to fear for God will arrange that "his angel will go before thee, enabling thee to find a wife for my son there" (Gn. 24:7).

In this story the angel does not appear visibly, but directs through inspiration. The servant's prayers were of course always addressed to God directly. The guardianship of God's angel made a perilous journey safe, and assured the success of the servant's mission. This concept of the angel who protects the traveller we will find developed later on in the story of Tobias. It is a thought piously carried on into the Christian tradition and of great comfort to travellers, especially to those who undertake long and lonely journeys.

> Let us faithfully who earnestly desire to sing the praises of the angelic lights through which our help from God is ministered, beg that with clearness of mind and most pure lips, we may also attain their brightness (*Monday Canon*, Canticle III, Tone I).

### 5. Jacob (Gn. 28; 32; 48)

It is most interesting to follow through the Bible and see how the general conception about angels changes as men advance in their knowledge of God. At the beginning, they seem not to have distinguished clearly between God's self-manifestation and his messengers. (Or, perhaps, is it we who can no longer distinguish?) Jacob's vision of the angels ascending and descending upon a heavenly ladder appears to be the first clear picture given to men of the heavenly hosts. Nevertheless, even Jacob seemed somewhat confused. From the following verses it is difficult to know if he came to wrestle with a self-manifestation of God or with one of his created angels:

> Meanwhile Jacob had left Bersabee, and was on his way to Haran. There was a place he reached as nightfall overtook him, so that he must lie down and rest; so he took some of the stones that lay around him, to make a pillow of them, and went to sleep. He dreamed that he saw a ladder standing on the earth, with its top reaching up into heaven; a stairway for the angels of God to go up and come down. Over this ladder the Lord himself leaned down, and spoke to Jacob, I am the Lord, he said, the God of thy father Abraham, the God of Isaac; this ground on which thou liest sleeping is my gift to thee and to thy posterity . . . . So it was that, when he rose in the morning, Jacob took the stone which had been his pillow, and set it up there as a monument and poured oil upon it . . . (Gn. 28:10-14; 18).

Jacob turned his stone pillow into a pillar and blessed it by pouring oil on it and called it God's house. He was the first man probably to have understood, if but hazily, that the Lord was surrounded by a heavenly host.

It is notable too, that in Orthodox hymnology, the Virgin Mary is likened to this very heavenly ladder that binds heaven and earth together.

As for Jacob, after further wanderings, and working fourteen years for his father-in-law out of love for the beautiful Rachel, he started for home, as the

Lord bade him. Nevertheless, the thought of meeting Esau, his brother from whom he had bought the birthright for a mess of pottage (Gn. 25), and stolen the blessing of their father Isaac, rather naturally bothered Jacob, so he sent messengers and gifts to propitiate Esau. While he anxiously awaited the result of the mission, Jacob had his second great experience with the spiritual world and wrestled with an angel throughout the entire night.

> And now he had set down all that was his on the further side, and he was left there alone. And there one appeared to him who wrestled with him until the day broke. At last, finding that he could not get the better of Jacob, he touched the sinew of his thigh, which all at once withered; then, he said, Let me go, the dawn is up. But Jacob answered, I will not let thee go until thou givest me thy blessing (Gn. 32:23-26).

One is hard pressed to interpret this story unless it is viewed as Jacob's honest struggle with his bad conscience in the lonely watches of the night. The angel seems to force him to see himself in his true colors, and finally, wounds him in his thigh, that is to say in his presupposed strength, that is, his self-justification. When Jacob at last comes to grip with the truth, he begs this angel to bless him.

Humbled and strengthened, Jacob goes out to meet his brother, to whom he is reconciled—a wonder brought about, no doubt, not only by Esau's generosity, but also by Jacob's new understanding.

When as an old man, Jacob blessed Joseph's sons, he was not confusing God with his angel. In his prayer Jacob was calling upon God, and the angel of God. His words are clear:

> May that God, in whose presence my fathers, Abraham and Isaac, once lived and moved, that God who has guided me like a shepherd from my youth till now, that angel of God, who has rescued me from all my troubles, bless these sons of thine (Gn. 48:15-16).

It is not always easy to distinguish between a messenger of God and God's self-manifestation. Our knowledge regarding the nature of the angels is incomplete, but from the very outset of the biblical narrative there are two easily recognizable attributes belonging to heavenly beings: that of messenger and guardian. The Old Testament writers clearly comprehended what we have long failed to do, that the angels are far more like God than like man. Only after the Renaissance did people begin to see angels rather as earthly than heavenly, and finally, relegated them to the realm of the myth where, if we imagine them to be disembodied souls, they would belong. We can only truly comprehend the angels when we see them as the true servers of God, perfectly fulfilling his command, executing their mission in fullest reflection of God's will. But we must not confuse the created angel with

God's manifestation of himself in his uncreated energies, as for example, the angel of the burning bush on Mount Horeb.

The Seraphim directly approach the divinely working light and often filled with it they plainly shine with the first gifts of radiance (*Monday Canon*, Canticle III, Tone I).

[1]St. Gregory of Nyssa, *From Glory to Glory* (ed. Jean Danielou and Herbert Musurillo). New York: Charles Scribner's Sons, 1961, p. 117.

[2]Vladimir Lossky, *The Mystical Theology of the Eastern Church*. London: James Clarke and Co., Ltd., 1957, p. 124.

[3]*Ibid.*

[4]Dionysius the Areopagite, *Mystical Theology and the Celestial Hierarchies*. Surrey: The Shrine of Wisdom.

# III

## Angels and the Early Leaders

### 1. Moses and Joshua

Man's real conception of God as the Creator and source of all law came through Moses who delivered to us the Ten Commandments in which subsist the moral essentials of life, dealing with pure fundamentals and upon which civilization as we know it today has been built. Man needed endlessly to be guided, reminded, and encouraged to keep these laws, and to be punished when he did not. It took many generations of discipline until a way of life could be perfected, even in a few.

As we know, the Lord gave Moses the Ten Commandments, the Laws and Ordinances, and finally, a guardian angel, in this interesting sequence, knowing that Moses would need his help and could not fulfill his commands without the aid of a "percepter," to use St. Cyril of Alexandria's word to describe his angel.

> And now I am sending my angel to go before thee and guard thee on thy way, and lead thee to the place I have made ready for thee. Give him good heed, and listen to his bidding; think not to treat him with neglect. He will not overlook thy faults, and in him dwells the power of my name (Ex. 23:20-21).

The fact that the angels are the very bearers of God's name often escapes us. The angel, though a created being, because of his closeness to God by the perfect way in which he does God's will, discloses God himself to us.

We must ever and again simply keep in mind the spiritual substance of all the angels because of which their proximity and nearness to us surpasses that of any physical presence, however perceptible. Dionysius calls them "Divine Intelligences." Rightly understood, this expression takes note of the fact that they communicate directly with our own intelligence. Moses, who was so highly spiritualized and transfigured, easily understood God's message and trusted the promised angel. And, consequent to the deliverance of the Ten Commandments on Mount Sinai, Moses once more in the midst of his people was instructed by God to build a Holy Tabernacle and Ark in which to place the sacred tablets of the Law. He was given specific commands as to their size, design, and material. What is more, he was bidden to construct a mercy seat.

> Make me an ark of acacia wood, two and a half cubits long, with a breadth and height of one and a half cubits. Give it a covering and a lining of pure gold, and put a coping of gold all round the top of it; a ring of gold, too, at each of the four corners, two on either of the longer sides. Then make poles of acacia wood, gilded over, and pass them through the rings on the sides of the ark, so as to carry it; these poles are to remain in the rings, never take them out. In this ark thou wilt enshrine the written law I mean to give thee.
>
> Make a throne, too, of pure gold, two and a half cubits long, one and a half cubits broad, and two cherubs of pure beaten gold for the two ends of this throne, one to stand on either side of it; with their wings outspread to cover the throne, guardians of the shrine. They are to face one another across the throne. And this throne is to be the covering of the ark, and the ark's contents, the written law I mean to give thee. Thence will I issue my commands; from that throne of mercy, between the two cherubs that stand over the ark and its records, my voice shall come to thee, whenever I send word through thee to the sons of Israel (Ex. 25:10-22).

The mercy seat was not the lid of the Ark, but had an independent significance. It symbolized the throne of God to which the people would carry their sins for forgiveness and expiation. The throne of God is to be understood in the sense that today we speak of the "seat of government." The cherubim figuratively bear and uphold the throne of God. Being the highest of the "Divine Intelligences," they are the closest to God, the first to participate in his glory, and, thus, shown as upholding his throne. The Tabernacle is called the "tent of meeting" because it is the holy focal point where the Lord meets his people in the presence of his angels, and not merely the place where worshippers assemble.

When we pray today in our Christian churches, focusing our thoughts upon the altar, the cross, or upon a sacred image or icon, we are doing so in the presence of the holy angels. Around the cupola, upholding the image of the *Pantokrator*—the Creator of all things—we find the holy angels in solemn array. Thus, we pray more fervently as we glorify God in the company of the heavenly hosts. The icons of the angels depicted on the deacon's doors of the iconostasis do not exist simply to pinpoint our thoughts (much less for the purpose of ornament!) but are the very material center where a spiritual power and divine energy rest, and which identifies itself to man's art.

It comes as a surprise to find that the Jews who were rigidly iconoclastic, in obedience to the second commandment, nevertheless portrayed in hammered gold the semblance of the cherubim on either side of the mercy seat.

It should be noted, too, that the reverence for the holy angels was not limited solely to the fashioning of the semblances of the cherubic spirits on the mercy seat.

There was, as well, the figures of the cherubim that were very beautifully embroidered upon the sacred veil that was designed to be hung before the very Holy of Holies. This was done in obedience to God's direct and specific command.

> Make a veil, too, out of twisted linen thread, embroidered with threads of blue and purple and scarlet twice-dyed, and let it hang down from four posts of acacia wood, gilded and with gilt capitals . . . (Ex. 26:31-32).

Evidently, the closeness of angels—both to God and to man—needed to be emphasized, for was not the Most High Lord to choose very often in the future to communicate his holy will and providence by the messengering of the heavenly spirits? And does he not, perhaps, today as well?

Is it not a most glaring need in our own day, in the midst of a secularized society and desacralized civilization, to emphasize the hieratic role of the angelic choirs, and to learn from them anew? We need the freshness of this outlook to restore the spirit that humbly adores its Lord.

Moses never reached the Promised Land: it was Joshua, his great follower, to whom this privileged achievement would be granted. As he led the Israelites into Canaan, Joshua was deeply aware of help from the angel that had been portended to Moses. The Lord had already caused a miracle to occur, by parting the waters of the Jordan as the Ark neared its banks, so that the children of Israel could cross over dry-footed. But now another obstacle stood in the way of advance: the fortified town of Jericho.

> There in the plain by Jericho, Joshua looked up and saw a man who stood with drawn sword in his path. Coming close to him, he asked, Art thou of our camp, or of the enemy's? Nay, said he, it is the captain of the Lord's army that has come to thy side. And with that Joshua cast himself down, face to ground; What message hast thou, my Lord, for thy servant? he asked. But first he was commanded to take the shoes off his feet, as one that stood on holy ground; so he did as he was bidden (Jos. 5:13-16).

We all know how Jericho was taken, how at the sound of the priests' trumpets and the shouts of the people, the great fortified walls collapsed, "fell flat" as the Bible has it. We are not told whether St. Michael (if it was he) was seen again, but of a certainty he was close to Joshua at all times, for this soldier and leader embodied those characteristics which the great archangel Michael personifies in the Judeo-Christian Tradition.

> O Princes of the leaders of God's hosts, servants of the Divine Glory, instructors of men and commanders of angels, intercede for us, praying

for our good and for bountiful mercy, O Princes of the leaders of the angels (*Kontakion of Synaxis of the Archangels Michael and Gabriel*).

## 2. *The Conception of Samson (Jgs. 13)*

The story of Samson's conception is one of the most human and touching of the Old Testament narratives. It seems that the Lord's angel came especially to those poor distraught women who were humiliated by their barrenness. The best known, of course, are Sarah, wife of Abraham; Elizabeth, mother of the Baptist; and the nameless wife of Manoah, mother of Samson.

Manoah was of the tribe of Dan and lived during a time when "...once again, the sons of Israel defied the Lord, and for forty years he left them at the mercy of the Philistines" (Jgs. 13:1). Manoah's wife, we are told, was barren. And it was to her, a sad and humiliated woman, that the angel appeared and promised her a son, mighty in strength and in deeds. How joyful must such a foretelling have sounded in her ears and quickened the beat of her heart! To be barren in the East was a very real disgrace and, not infrequently, would lead to the woman being "put away" by her husband. That a deliverer of Israel should have been promised just at such a time, and to such a woman, must have been all but incredible! What a sense of destiny there is in the story of Samson. Even before his birth he is singled out to become one of Israel's greatest heroes, who, in spite of his very human weaknesses, was to wage war against the Philistines almost entirely on his own, as it were, single-handed.

Samson's story begins with a quite unexpected visitor to his mother. It is, indeed, a lovely story, and for our purposes, deserving of verbatim recounting:

> To her the Lord's angel appeared, and said, Poor barren one, poor childless one, thou art to conceive, and bear a son. See to it that no wine or strong drink, no unclean food passes thy lips, for this son whom thou art to conceive and bear is to be a Nazarite from his birth; even when he is a child, no razor must come near his head. And he shall strike the first blow to deliver Israel from the power of the Philistines. So when she met her husband she told him, I have been speaking with a messenger from God, who might have been an angel, such awe his look inspired in me. Who he was, his home, his name, he would not tell, but the message he gave me was that I should conceive, and have a son. And I must abstain from wine and all strong drink, and from all unclean food, because this son of mine was to be a Nazarite from his childhood up, bound to the Lord by his vow from the day of his birth to the day of his death (Jgs. 13:3-7).

The most touching side of this story is the manner in which the parents receive this message, the way they share their common joy and concern. The naturalness of the relationship between Samson's parents-to-be and the angel is delightfully and refreshingly simple. Manoah is anxious to hear this good news at first hand; perhaps he was a bit jealous of his wife, and so he entreats God to send his messenger once again.

> Thereupon Manoah entreated the Lord to send his messenger again, and tell them how this child, once born, should be nurtured. And the Lord granted his prayer; once more the angel of God appeared to his wife, as she sat resting in a field. Her husband was not with her, and she, upon sight of the angel, ran off to fetch him; He has come back, she told him, the man I saw a few days since. So he rose and followed her, and asked the angel whether it was he that had brought the message to his wife; Yes, he said, it was I. Tell me, then, said Manoah, when thy promise is fulfilled, what life is the boy to lead, what things are they he must shun? But the angel of the Lord answered, Enough that thy wife should observe the warnings I gave her ... (Jgs. 13:8-13).

The father's deep desire to be guided by God in the rearing of his child is one which all parents might do well to imitate. It is good when a parent becomes aware of his need for God as he is faced by the long and loving task of bringing up his sons and daughters. Today, as in those days so long ago, the angel of God is close to us and our children, even if we often are unaware of the fact.

> Detain me if thou wilt, said the angel, but of thy food I must not eat; offer burnt-sacrifice, if thou wilt, to the Lord. And still Manoah did not recognize that it was the Lord's angel; What is thy name? he asked. If thy words come true, we would fain give thee some token of gratitude. My name? said he. Do not ask my name; it is a high mystery. So Manoah brought the kid, and a bread-offering with it, and laid it on the rock, presenting it before the Lord; and mystery indeed there was, before the eyes of Manoah and his wife; as flames went up to heaven from the altar, the angel of the Lord went up too, there amid the flames. At the sight, Manoah and his wife fell down face to earth. Now that he had disappeared from their view, Manoah knew him for what he was, and said to his wife, This is certain death; we have seen the Lord.... It was at the Encampment of Dan, between Saraa and Esthaol, that the spirit of the Lord first visited him [Samson] (Jgs. 13:16-25).

The revelation of the angel's true personality came to them like a flash: indeed, a flame burning with pure love of God. Though the angel did not divulge his name, we may presume that he was Gabriel, "the man of God," the Lord's special messenger. For, as we progress, we shall realize that we never can know an angel's name, but rather find their identity in accord with distinction of their function.

It is not surprising that the humble and simple couple who were called by God to witness such mystery were filled with terror and fear, but beyond the terror and the fear—in itself wholesome—the woman's logic and, above all, her deep faith, prevailed over all undue solicitude for further revelation, and she implicitly threw herself upon the mercy of the God who revealed himself.

Manoah had thought they would surely die as a result of the vision, as we have noted, but again his wife is quick to reassure him thus:

> Nay, answered his wife, if the Lord meant us harm, he would not have accepted our sacrifice and our bread-offering; he would not have shown us this marvellous sight, nor told us what is to befall. And so she bore a son, and called him Samson. As the lad grew, the Lord's blessing was on him (Jgs. 13:23-25).

And, as noted, the spirit of the Lord first visited the son of this nameless woman at the Encampment of Dan.

Reflecting on Samson's conception and vocation, one might ask how long it must be before man understands that God desires our good at all times: that his angels are always close at hand to help and guide, to inspire and sustain.

> Apart from God, I have thee, Holy Angel, a gift from the Lord, to be my provider, advisor, helper and defense. Therefore, I pray thee, do not cease to advise, admonish and direct me, teaching me to act worthily, enlightening my mind until thou bring me redeemed unto Christ (*Canon to the Guardian Angel*, Canticle VIII, Troparion I).

### 3. Gideon (Jgs. 6:2-24)

Following Moses and Joshua, Israel for a long while had no great or outstanding figure to guide them, only local leaders called Judges. Unsettled, tasting of an affluent life, and regaling in self-complacency, they lost the staunch solidarity and vigor of their desert days. Their enemies no longer respected and feared them as a God-protected people. Worse, the Israelites themselves gave in to unmindfulness of God, of all he had done for them. They began to turn to the worship of false gods. Thus, for about two hundred years they suffered war, invasion, persecution and oppression, with but few periods of peace.

When Israel was enduring one of these numerous invasions, namely, of the Madianites, it was an angel that stirred up courage in the heart of Gideon, the hero destined to liberate his people.

To tell the story in other words than those of the Bible would be foolish. It is a tale strikingly familiar. Put other names in substitution and we have the picture of any oppressed land in our own day:

. . .he left them at the mercy of the Madianites, who crushed them down without mercy; so that they were fain to take refuge in caverns and shafts and mountain fastnesses. The men of Israel would sow their lands, and then Madian and Amalec and the tribes east of them would invade the country; encamping there, they destroyed all the growing crops right up to Gaza, till there was no food left in the land of Israel for ox or sheep or ass. Carrying their tents and driving their cattle before them, they came in and spread over the countryside, hordes of men everywhere and trains of camels, like a swarm of locusts, destroying all that lay in their path. Thus Madian brought the Israelites into great need, and they cried out to the Lord for redress. But he, through a prophet, sent them this message from the Lord God of Israel: I recalled you from Egypt, rescued you from your prison there, defended you, not only against the Egyptians, but against all the hostile nations that were dispossessed of their lands to make room for you. And I told you, I am the Lord your God; you must pay no reverence to the gods of the Amorrhites, in whose land you dwell; but my command went unheeded.

And now an angel of the Lord came and waited by the oak-tree at Ephra, which then belonged to Joas, of the family of Abiezer. His son Gideon had gone out to the wine-press, so as to thresh his wheat there unobserved by the Madianites, and suddenly the Lord's angel appeared to him, and said, The Lord be with thee, courageous heart! Ah, Sir, replied Gideon, but tell me this; if the Lord is with us, how is it that such ill fortune has overtaken us? Not for us, now, these miracles of his that were on our father's lips, when they told us how he rescued them from Egypt. The Lord has forsaken us now, and lets the Madianites have their will with us. Then the Lord looked at him, and said, Thou has strength; go and set Israel free from the power of Madian. Such is the mission I have set for thee. What, Lord! said he, I deliver Israel? Why, my clan is the poorest in all Manasse, and in all my father's house none counts for so little as I. I will be at thy side, the Lord told him, and thou shalt smite Madian down as though but one man stood in thy path.

Hereupon Gideon answered, As thou lovest me, give me some proof this is thy word that comes to me. And first, do not leave this spot till I come back here with a sacrifice to offer thee. I will await thy coming, he said. So Gideon went in and cooked a goat, took a bushel of flour and made unleavened bread, put the meat in a basket and the broth from the meat into a pot, and brought them all out, there beneath the oak, to make his offering. Take the meat and the loaves, the angel of the Lord said, and lay them down on yonder rock, and pour out the broth over them. So he obeyed, and with that the angel of the Lord held out the staff he carried, and touched the meat and unleavened bread with the tip of it; whereupon fire blazed out from the rock, and all was consumed. And he looked, and the angel of the Lord was there no longer. Then Gideon knew that this was an angel of the Lord, and he cried out, An ill day for me, O Lord my

God; I have seen the Lord's angel face to face. But the Lord's word came to him, Be at peace and have no fear; thou shalt not die. So Gideon built an altar there and called it the Peace of the Lord; it stands there to this day (Jgs. 6:2-24).

And, as we know, Gideon went forth to battle and by the power of the Lord was enabled to free the Israelites. In their enthusiasm the Israelites responded by asking Gideon to be their king, but in his vast modesty and deep humility, Gideon gave the only true and wise reply: "Neither I, he said, nor any son of mine shall bear rule over you; the Lord shall be your ruler" (Jgs. 8:23).

But, as the story goes, the children of Israel did not hearken to the sage advice of Gideon, but instead "They had a covenant now with Baal, that he should be their god, and thought no more of the Lord, their own God, that had rescued them from the power of the enemies who lived round about them" (Jgs. 8:34).

So continued their tragic history as prey to the enticements and allurements of the evil adversary.

You who are secondary lights of the Original Light, O Holy Angels, bodiless partakers of enlightenment's wealth, I cry to you: "Illumine my mind darkened by earthly passions" (*Canon to the Heavenly Hosts and All Saints*, Canticle VII, Troparion I).

# IV

## Angels and the Prophets

### 1. Balaam and His Ass (Num. 22)

The prophets of the Old Testament, from Amos to Zechariah, cover a span of some six hundred years. They were no glorified soothsayers, but seers, men of vision who could clearly envisage God ruling over the universe. "God is in his heaven and his Kingdom must and will prevail," was the gist of their message.

Great and yet humble men, the prophets heard and obeyed the word of God when he spoke to them directly or used the medium of dreams or of his angels. They questioned not the ways of the Lord of Hosts, but hearkened willingly to his messengers.

Frequently, when embarking upon some difficult enterprise in which we honestly mean to fulfill God's will, we find ourselves bargaining with him and trying to do his will according to our own prescription. We may then find ourselves unsuccessful, and indeed, hampered at every turn. We do not always stop to consider the reason for our difficulties—or whether possibly they are blessings in disguise. It is often God's way of indicating to us that we have taken the wrong turn, for he has occasionally to shut the door in our face before he opens another.

In Numbers (22:23-35), we have the example of Balaam, a minor prophet, who, when called upon by the King of Moab to come to curse the Israelites, at first refused to obey the king's command. Balaam was not an Israelite. He knew but little of the Lord, the one God, yet he believed in him. Hence, he would not curse God's people. Later, tempted by the rich rewards being offered him, he started out on his journey in the hope of satisfying both God and the king. He wanted to believe that his will was indeed God's will. How often we do the very same thing, and thus give in to the will of Satan. These verses from the Bible clearly illustrate one of the instances in which God deals with man through his angels:

And the ass, seeing an angel standing there with drawn sword, edged away from the road and took to the open fields, so that Balaam must needs beat her, to force her into the path again. Next, the angel stood in a narrow entry between two vineyard walls; and at the sight of him the ass cowered close against one of the walls, crushing her rider's foot, and he must beat her forward again. But still the angel of the Lord would have his way; he moved on to a narrow defile, where there was no room to pass right or left, and stood there to intercept them. And now the ass, seeing him standing there, lay down under her rider; so that Balaam fell into a rage, and beat her flanks harder than ever. Hereupon the Lord endowed the ass with the power of speech, and she said, This is the third time thou hast beaten me; what have I done to deserve it? Thou hast deserved it, answered Balaam, by playing me false; if I had but a sword in my hand, I would kill thee. Why, said the ass, am I not thy own beast, that thou hast ridden these years past? And did I ever play thee such a trick before? Never, said he; and with that the Lord opened Balaam's eyes, to make him see the angel standing there with drawn sword, and he fell to the ground in worship.

How comes it, asked the angel, that thou has thrice beaten thy ass? I came to intercept thee, because this errand of thine is headstrong and defies my will; if the ass had not turned aside, yielding to my ban, I would have taken thy life and spared hers. I have been at fault, said Balaam, little thinking that thou were standing in my way; if thou art displeased with my errand, I will go home again. No, said the angel, go with them, but be sure thou utterest no word save what I bid thee. So he went on with the chiefs; and at the news of his coming Balac went out to meet him . . . (Num. 22:23-36).

As an aside it might be noted, that in the light of modern research in the field of extrasensory perception, it is a proven fact that animals also possess extraordinary faculties, thus the story of Balaam's ass can be taken seriously, even by our modern-day skeptics. But, at the same time, it must be sharply noted that we are not concerned with the animal world, but with man who, at times, can and does behave, not unlike an ass himself!

Balaam had been determined on his own course; he was visibly aggravated by his beast of burden, seemingly as pig-headed as his master and rider. Indeed, the visible intervention of an angel was necessary to make him aware of the uselessness of going against God's will, or of seeking to deceive him. Like Saul, he found it hard to kick against the goad (Acts 9:5; 26:14). It is not easy in his story to know if it was Balaam's guardian angel making himself manifest or a special emissary of the Lord sent specifically for the occasion. It must be remembered that in Balaam's day the people did not yet know about personal guardian angels, a strictly Christian concept. We who now possess hindsight should at all times read the Scriptures with Christian eyes, and in proper consideration of the historical development of the time. Reading the passages in the light of Christ they acquire their true meaning and integrity. Note that they can illustrate parallels in our times and help us solve present problems. When beset by contradictory currents and plagued by hindrances of every sort, we often do not know how in reality to interpret them. Are they a sign that we have taken the wrong turn, or are we simply being tempted to give in and take the line of least spiritual resistance as we seek the easy way out? At such times, we should confidently turn to our guardian angel to counsel us. He will answer our prayer.

> Having gained you, O Holy Angel, to be my companion, I have you to converse with, who are ever guarding me when I travel, and also abide with me in my habitation at all times; counsel me and pray to Christ, Our Lord for me (*Canon to the Guardian Angel*).

## 2. Elijah (1 Kgs. 19)

Elijah was a great man, powerful, clear-sighted, and faithful. Still, even he tasted despair. Elijah had dared to challenge the gods of the wicked Jezebel and her priests. Jezebel was the wife of Ahab, king of Israel. She was a woman of masterful temperament who easily overruled her weak husband. She was fanatically devoted to the god, Baal. To please her Ahab had a temple built to Baal, and gave her leave to slay as many of the prophets of the true God as she could conveniently lay her hands upon. But in Elijah she met her match. To unquestionably and publicly prove whose god was the strongest they agreed that each group should bring a burnt offering to their god, but the fire was to be kindled by no human hand. When Elijah called upon the Lord, fire fell down from heaven setting ablaze his offering which he had soused with water beforehand, whereas the pagan offering remained unconsumed in spite of all the prayers of the priests of Baal. The point was proved. Jezebel, one of Satan's elect if there ever was one, swore vengeance and planned the death of Elijah who had to flee into the desert as no man had sufficient courage to help him. The humiliated and saddened prophet, sick to death of this world, found safety and solace in the wilderness. One feels that he was seeking to get away not so much from the executioner's hand as from his deep disgust with his own people who he could not recall to their own true God.

Elijah threw himself down under a juniper tree and in despair longed for the release of death. "I can bear no more, Lord, he said; put an end to my life; I have no better right to live than my fathers" (1 Kgs. 19:4). What a familiar echo these words have for many of us when we are weary of this world! But God answered Elijah's prayer otherwise than in keeping with his pleading. Instead of death he gave new courage: "...he lay down and fell asleep under the juniper tree; but all at once an angel of the Lord roused him, bidding him awake and eat. Then he found, close to where his head lay, a hearth-cake and a pitcher of water..." (1 Kgs. 19:5-6). The angel visited him again, once more making Elijah eat and strengthen himself so that he might again receive God's message and start out to do God's bidding. There is a deep meaning in this record that may well hearten us if we recall it in our hour of weakness. God stands by all those who do his bidding, and his angel brings strength, both physical and moral. It was Elijah who first called the Lord: *God of Hosts.* He saw God as Master of the angelic world, a world high above our own. Thus, the prophet knew God to be within, yet uncontained by creation. He looked for God in all things and found that nothing comprised him, not even the greatest storm or cataclysm. Elijah found him in "a sound of gentle stillness." According to St. Isaac the Syrian, the angels were created in silence, and it was in that same silence that Elijah found God.

Elijah was not to know death, but was translated to heaven, even as Enoch was said to have been: " . . .a flaming chariot appeared, drawn by flaming horses, and Elijah went up on a whirlwind into heaven" (2 Kgs. 2:11).

Elijah is recognized as one of the greatest of the Hebrew prophets and the Eastern Church has him in her calendar of saints. His feast day, July 20th, is celebrated with much piety and many churches bear his name.

After his fiery departure, Elijah was succeeded by Elisha who had not the strength of character or individuality of Elijah. He appeared as head of a band of enthusiasts called the "sons of the prophets." Still, he was granted a rare momentary vision of heavenly hosts. Israel was under threat of Syria and Elisha rose early in the morning, went out, and noted the wonder of a town surrounded by horses and chariots. Elisha's servant cried out: "Alas, alas, master, what shift will serve us now? Do not be afraid, said he; we have more on our side than they on theirs" (2 Kgs. 6:15-16). Elisha prayed that his servant's eyes be opened and they were. What he saw was the mountain covered with horses and chariots of fire surrounding Elisha.

Indeed, "we have more on our side than they on theirs." The prophet knew without needing to see, but he prayed that his servant might *see* physically, what he saw spiritually. Much later Judas Maccabeus would be similarly protected by a vision.

And, too, Jesus would one day say that he could call upon the heavenly host, were he so minded, but he chose to win victory alone upon the Cross.

> He who was sanctified before he was conceived of angelic body and flaming intelligence, the heavenly man, the herald of the second coming of Christ, the glorious Elijah . . . . Through his intercessions, O Christ God, guard your people in safety of body and soul (*Aposticha*).

## 3. Isaiah (Is. 6:1-13)

Isaiah, one of the greatest prophets, equal to Moses and Elijah, was a preacher of righteousness. He spoke fearlessly in the name of God. God's call to him constitutes a unique chapter in religious literature and experience. It stands apart, by its vivid and detailed account, from any other visionary description. It is so genuine that the authenticity of the experience has never been seriously questioned.

Was Isaiah alone, or was it during a religious ceremony that he had his greatest vision? We do not know, but, unquestionably, an awareness of the divine reality behind symbolism came to him in that ultimate solitude that always accompanies great spiritual experiences.

All surroundings faded from his consciousness, and he "saw the Lord sitting on a throne" (Is. 6:1). But no words of ours can compare with those of the sacred writer himself:

> ...I saw the Lord sitting on a throne that towered high above me, the skirts of his robe filling the temple. Above it rose the figures of the seraphim, each of them six-winged; with two wings they veiled God's face, with two his feet, and the other two kept them poised in flight. And ever the same cry passed between them, Holy, holy, holy, is the Lord God of hosts; all the earth is full of his glory. The lintels over the doors rang with the sound of that cry, and smoke went up filling the temple courts.
>
> Alas, said I, that I must needs keep silence; my lips, and all my neighbours' lips, are polluted with sin; and yet these eyes are looking upon their King, the Lord of hosts. Whereupon one of the seraphim flew up to me, bearing a coal which he had taken with a pair of tongs from the altar; he touched my mouth with it, and said, Now that this has touched thy lips, thy guilt is swept away, thy sin pardoned. And now I heard the Lord say, Who shall be my messenger? Who is to go on this errand of ours? And I said, I am here at thy command; make me thy messenger (Is. 6:1-8).

As one interpreter notes:

> In reading this chapter, we participate imaginatively in Isaiah's vision and feel the same pang of conscience in the presence of the unutterable and sovereign glory of the goodness of God. It was brought home to the prophet with startling clarity that, however well he might have purified himself according to cultic requirements, however well he might have kept the customary rules of morality, in the presence of a holiness exalted in righteousness, he and all men were unclean. But with this recognition of creatureliness and unworthiness there came also a cleansing by a sovereign act of grace, and a commission to speak a word which was not his but God's.[1]

Isaiah alone of all Scripture writers speaks of having seen the seraphim—which literally means the "burning ones"—in the transitive sense. They, of all beings, are the closest to God. Isaiah witnessed the seraphim give voice to the joy and wonder of being close to God, so great a joy that even they had to cover their faces in humble adoration as they chanted the thrice holy song—a song we poor mortals to this day echo in our Liturgy in the *Sanctus* and as the Deacon crosses his stole during the Lord's Prayer to remind us that the angels ever bow before the Lord.

There is a deep connection between Isaiah's vision and that of Moses, as St. Gregory of Nyssa avers:

> And the sacred text, in describing the cherubim as hiding the mysterious contents of the ark with their wings, confirms our interpretation of the tabernacle. For cherubim, we know, is the name given to those powers who surround the Godhead in the vision seen by Isaiah and Ezekiel. Nor should our ears be surprised at the fact that they cover the ark with their wings. We find the same symbol of wings in Isaiah: only in Isaiah is the Lord's face covered (Is. 6:2), and here it is the ark of the covenant. But in each case the meaning is the same: it suggests, in my view, that the contemplation of the divine mysteries is inaccessible to our minds.[2]

It is little wonder that Isaiah, beholding so great a glory, should have fallen to the ground. The searing, purifying grace came to him by the ministering hand of a seraph of the Lord. This is the only record we have, that one of the highest choir came into direct contact with man. Yet we know not if such a one may not always be present at every divine act of forgiveness toward us. So profound had been this vision of Isaiah's, so true his consciousness of human guilt and unworthiness and the need to be cleansed, that his words are paraphrased during the most solemn moment of the Liturgy when the priest, upon partaking of Holy Communion and wiping his lips, prays: "Lo, this has touched my lips; my iniquity shall be taken away, and my sin purged." Only then is the remission of sin made possible, when we, like Isaiah, become aware of our dreadful moral uncleanness before the King, the Lord of hosts. But God desires not humble uselessness: no, he needs men and women of action to send out upon his mission. How many of us would be humble enough to trust God's appreciation of us, and go forth and do whatever his will for us might be, responding with Isaiah: "Here I am, send me!"

What we must not forget in reading over this vision, is that Isaiah is describing not the angelic host, but is rather portraying God's glory, much as we would describe the coronation of the kings of England, mentioning the different attendant nobility, not for their own sake, but because their splendor enhances that of the whole scene, while the event itself gives purpose to their splendor and presence. So Isaiah depicts the magnificence of the court of heaven. What he saw was beyond speech, yet he struggled with inadequate words so that we too might have a glorious glimpse of his ineffable vision. He is trying to throw a ray of light our way to illumine us in the midst of our darkness.

It is frequently stated that the Old Testament has no reference to the fallen angel; yet we find Isaiah gives a most striking description which may well be taken for such a reference.

> What, fallen from heaven, thou Lucifer, that once didst herald the dawn? Prostrate on the earth, that didst once bring nations to their knees? I will scale the heavens (such was thy thought); I will set my throne higher than God's stars, take my seat at his own trysting-place, at the meeting of the northern hills; I will soar above the level of the clouds, the rival of the most High. Thine, instead, to be dragged down into the world beneath, into the heart of the abyss. Who that sees thee there, but will peer down at thee and read thy story: Can this be the man who once shook the world, and made thrones totter; who turned earth into a desert, its cities into ruins; never granted prisoner release? (Is. 14:12-17).

This dramatic description is a mocking dirge which was sung at the overthrow and death of a mighty monarch who had terrorized the world. How often have we not seen this repeated! But this passage has a far deeper meaning.

Isaiah may be using words of an ancient myth, but what he is symbolically putting before us is an image of that proud will so desirous of mastering the world. Indeed, primarily, it is an assault upon the throne of God. The Fathers, especially St. Jerome, connected this passage with Christ's words: " . . .I watched, while Satan was cast down like a lightning flash from heaven" (Lk. 10:18), and interpreted this dramatic poem as a vision of the angel's fall. Whether Isaiah was referring to an earthly potentate turned oppressor, or to an angel perverted against his Creator, his words remain a powerful indictment of self-will and a clear prophecy of the ultimate destiny of those who abuse power entrusted to them.

Isaiah was not alone in this description of Lucifer's fall. We find one quite similar in Ezekiel. The verses are highly symbolic and communicate a powerful lesson for all who indulge in vainglory and, in whatever capacity, misuse the authority given them by God.

Above all, the song Isaiah heard the angels sing re-echoes in our own hymn of praise at each Holy Liturgy:

> Holy, holy, holy, Lord of Sabbaoth, heaven and earth are full of thy glory. Hosanna in the Highest! Blessed is He that comes in the Name of the Lord; Hosanna in the Highest!

### 4. Ezekiel

Ezekiel is one of the prophets and writers of Israel who was carried into captivity by the Babylonians. Like so many of us in this age, he was an exile, a displaced person. He lived among unhappy and uprooted people, many of whom had lost their faith, much like many have today. Amid this distress he saw heaven open and unfold its promise to a troubled generation.

Like Isaiah when he received his call to prophesy, Ezekiel also had a vision of the glory of God. His description of what he saw is much more complex and far harder to understand than that of Isaiah. Once more we must keep in mind that it is the glory of God, and not the heavenly hosts as such, that he is describing. Nonetheless, the picture he seeks to convey of the greatness and the power of these angelic beings is illuminating; we are made to see them in their proper setting where, as part of God's glory, they appear in their appropriate proportion. The whole description fills one with a feeling of immensity, of a deploying movement that fills all space.

Ezekiel all but fails to put his great vision into adequate words. He speaks in symbols of creatures beyond symbols, in what could almost be clumsy earthbound comparisons. Still he paints an unbelievably stirring picture that fires while it staggers the imagination. He is careful to explain that, of course, he is speaking in symbols, and he clearly remarks: "their likeness was . . .like the appearance of . . . ." Ezekiel sees God in a storm of glory and we, like him, must not fear to face that storm; rather, unflinchingly, we must look into its midst so as to see the saving truth. One commentator remarks that, "It is important to remember that we have in this narrative one of those forces which have made history. The writer of this chapter saw God in the disaster which had overtaken his nation, and so he was able to redeem that disaster."[3]

Let us have Ezekiel speak for himself:

I looked round me to find that a storm-wind had sprung up from the north, driving a great cloud before it; and this cloud had fire caught up in it, that fringed it with radiance. And there in the heart of it, in the very heart of the fire, was a glow like amber, that enclosed four living figures. These were human in appearance, but each had four faces, and two pairs of wings. Either leg was straight-formed, yet ended in a calf's hoof; they sparkled like red-hot bronze. On each of the four sides, human arms shewed beneath the wings; faces and wings looked outwards four ways. Wings of each were held touching wings of other; and when they moved, they did not turn round, but each kept an onward course. As for the appearance of their faces, each had the face of a man, yet each of the four looked like a lion when seen from the right, like an ox when seen from the left, like an eagle when seen from above. So much for their faces; each had two wings spread out above him, those two which met his neighbor's wings; with the other two he veiled his body. Each of them marched straight forward, following the movement of a divine impulse, never swerving as he marched. There was that, too, in the appearance of the living creatures which put me in mind of flaming coals, or of torches; that was what I saw going to and fro in the midst of the living figures, a glow as of fire, and from this glow lightning came out. So the living creatures came and went, vivid as lightning-flashes.

And as I watched the living figures, all at once wheels appeared close to them, one at each of the four sides, of strange color and form. All four were alike, the color of aquamarine, and each looked like a wheel within a wheel. Moved they, it was ever one of the four ways the living figures looked; and they did not turn round in moving. As for their size, their height was terrible to look upon; and the whole frame of them, all round, was full of eyes. Onward the wheels moved, when the living figures moved onward, at their side; rose above the earth when the living figures rose above it. They too had a living impulse in them, they too, whenever that impulse stirred them, must rise up and follow the way it went; with the living figures, whose vital impulse they shared, the wheels too moved, and halted, and rose.

Over the living creatures a vault seemed to rise, like a sheet of dazzling crystal resting on their heads; under this vault each held two wings erect to meet his neighbor's. Each had two turned upwards to overshadow him, and two turned downwards to veil his body. When they moved, the sound of their wings reached me, loud as waters in flood or thunders from on high, incessant as the hum of a great throng or an armed camp; only when they came to rest did they lower their wings. A voice would come from the firmament over their heads; then they would halt, then they would lower their wings. Above this vault that rested on them, sapphire blue towered up into the form of a throne, nor did that throne seem to be empty; a shape was there above it, as of one enthroned, and all about him it was filled with amber-colored flame. Upwards from his loins, an arch of light seemed to shine, like rainbow among the clouds on a day of storm; there was brightness all about him.

So much I saw of what the Lord's glory is like; and seeing it, I fell down face to earth. And now I heard a voice, which said to me, Rise up, son of man, I must have speech with thee (Ez. 1:4—2:1).

Fantastic as these descriptions are, we must seek to see beyond them for fear of misunderstanding the whole purpose of Ezekiel sharing his vision with us. In the words of Dionysius, that we

> ...like the many, should impiously suppose that those Celestial and Divine Intelligences are many-footed, or many-faced beings or formed with the brutishness of oxen, or the savageness of lions, or the curved beaks of eagles, or the features of birds, or should imagine that they are some kind of fiery wheels above the heavens...or whatever else the symbolic description has been given to us in the various sacred images of the Scriptures.
>
> Theology, in its sacred utterance regarding the formless Intelligences, does indeed use poetic symbolism, having regard to our intelligences....
> For it might be said that the reason for attributing shapes to that which is above shape, and forms to that which is beyond form, is not only the feebleness of our intellectual power which is unable to rise at once to

spiritual contemplation . . .but it is also because it is most fitting that the secret doctrines, through ineffable and holy enigmas, should veil and render difficult of access for the multitude the sublime and profound truth of the supernatural Intelligences. For as the Scripture declares, not everyone is holy, nor have all men knowledge.[4]

When we read these passages, it is hard to understand how the great cherub could have come to be depicted as a naked and frisky little boy, difficult to distinguish from Cupid, or even to be represented as a bodiless baby face supported by fluffy wings in an azure sky! The only explanation can be that the word cherub was mistakenly understood to be the diminutive instead of the singular of cherubim, as seraph is the singular of seraphim.

Although the greatness of God's glory, the splendor of the heavenly hosts, may make us feel very small and insignificant, we must remember that God called to Ezekiel to stand up and face his God and hear the words spoken directly to him. God spoke to Ezekiel as to a rational, free, responsible creature, worthy of trust and respect. So, too, God addresses all men who stand upright and obey his call to confess him before the world:

> Never fear them, son of man, never let rebuke of theirs dishearten thee; with the unbelieving and the unruly thou must learn to live, scorpions ever at thy side; rebels all, they must not frighten thee . . . (Ez. 2:6).

Could we but remember these words when we are harassed by a world that will not understand! We ought to know neither fear nor discouragement because God in all his glory notices and cares for each of us, his children.

If we read the entire twenty-eighth chapter it is apt to be confusing, for in verses one to eleven Ezekiel is alluding to some wicked potentate of his time. Reading simply verses twelve to nineteen the wise prophet is clearly depicting Satan in stunning similitudes, from the heights of his initial perfection, beauty, wisdom and power, down to his catastrophic fall and utter destruction. But let us listen to Ezekiel and picture for ourselves the images his words conjure up:

> This be thy message to him from the Lord God: The token, thou, of my considerateness. How wise thou wast, how peerlessly fair, with all God's garden to take thy pleasure in! No precious stone but went to thy adorning; . . .all of gold was thy fair fashioning. And thy niche was prepared for thee when thou wast created; a cherub thou shouldst be, thy wings outstretched in protection; there on God's holy mountain I placed thee, to come and go between the wheels of fire. From the day of thy creation all was perfect in thee, till thou didst prove false; all these traffickings had made thee false within, and for thy guilt I must expel thee, guardian cherub as thou wert, from God's mountain; between the wheels of fire thou shouldst walk no longer. A heart made proud by beauty, wisdom ruined through its own dazzling brightness, down to

earth I must cast thee, an example for kings to see. Great guilt of thine, all the sins of thy trafficking, have profaned thy sanctuaries; such a fire I will kindle in the heart of thee as shall be thy undoing. Leave thee a heap of dust on the ground for all to gaze at. None on earth that recognizes thee but shall be dismayed at the sight of thee; only ruin left thee, forever vanished and gone (Ez. 28:12-19).

Though at one time he was good and beautiful, it does not count, for in the end Satan is consumed by his own pride, destroyed by the fire of his own heart until only dust and ashes remain. Dare we at this point lift up our own eyes and picture the burning bush which was not consumed by the Angel of God who stood in its midst leading our understanding to the pure Virgin who, circumscribing the uncircumscribed God remained unchanged?

> Revealing to thee the pre-eternal counsel, Gabriel came and stood before thee, O Maid; and greeting thee, he said: "Hail, thou earth that has not been sown; hail, thou burning bush that remains unconsumed; . . .hail, thou bridge that leads to heaven . . .hail, thou deliverance from the curse; hail thou restoration of Adam, the Lord is with thee" (From Vespers of the Annunciation, *Lord I Cried*).

### 5. Zechariah (Zech. 1-4)

Zechariah prophesied about the year 520 B.C., when Darius Hystaspis was king. In 536 B.C. a body of Jewish exiles was allowed, by edict of Cyrus, a rather merciful and tolerant monarch, to return to Palestine and to rebuild their temple. This reconstruction became Zechariah's chief preoccupation to which he devoted all his energies. The times were still anxious and troublesome, the Jews needed continual encouragement and bracing. Moreover, many of them were lax and selfish, concerned more with rebuilding their own homes rather than the House of the Lord. Zechariah spurred them on with earnest appeals to repentance and the promise that in due course heathenism would be vanquished, and God's kingdom would triumph.

Zechariah was given eight visions at the outset of his ministry and, it seems they all came to him the very same night. He lays tremendous emphasis upon the transcendental nature of God and gives greater prominence to the angelic presences, than we shall see in Daniel. We see the angels busy about the affairs of men, traveling the length and breadth of the world, keeping in sight how things stand. We see "the angel of the Lord" attended by other angels who carry out his behest.

Zechariah also makes specific mention of Satan, defining him quite distinctly. There are three instances in the Old Testament in which Satan stands out and is identified by his personal name. In 1 Chronicles he bears directly upon David to sin: "And Satan stood up against Israel, and provoked David to number Israel" (1 Chr. 21:1). In Zechariah and in the Book of Job, Satan appears in the role of false witness and accuser, as well as tempter. What is common to all three accounts is that the ultimate result is good, for each temptation is an occasion for the men being tried either to stand fast or to repent, reaching spiritual heights hitherto unattained. As the Book of Common Prayer would have it: "O Almighty God, who canst bring good out of evil, and makest even the wrath of men to turn to thy praise . . . ."

As we have noted, the main preoccupation of Zechariah was the rebuilding of the temple in Jerusalem. It was at this time that he had the vision which strengthened him in his purpose:

> A vision appeared to me in the night, of one that was mounted on a sorrel horse, at a stand among the myrtle trees, down in the Valley; and never a horse in all his company but was sorrel, roan or white. Scarce had I asked, My Lord, what be these? when the angel that inspired me promised he would show me the meaning of it; and, with that, my answer came from him who stood among the myrtle trees. These have gone out on the Lord's errand, patrolling the earth. And to him, now, the angel of the myrtle-wood, those others made their report: All earth we have patrolled, said they, and everywhere is safety, everywhere is rest.* Ah, Lord of hosts, my angel monitor said, wilt thou never relent, never take pity upon Jerusalem . . . . The Lord answered him; gracious his words were; gracious and full of comfort . . . . And now, the Lord says, I am for Jerusalem again, bringing pardon with me . . . .
>
> When next I looked up, I saw a man there that carried a measuring line; so I asked him, whither he was bound? For Jerusalem, said he, to measure length and breadth of it. And at that, my angel monitor would have gone out on his errand, but here was a second angel come out to meet him. Speed thee, said he, on thy way, and tell that people of thine: So full Jerusalem shall be, of men and cattle both, wall it shall have none to hedge it in; I myself, the Lord says, will be a wall of fire around it, and in the midst of it, the brightness of my presence (Zech. 1:8—2:5 passim).

Although Zechariah was given direct vision, he evidently did not understand what he saw without the help of the angel who "speaks in him." His monitor came and went between heaven and earth, as we see when another angel intercepts him as he is about to measure Jerusalem. The monitor is given a revelation to impart, superior to the one of measuring the city; he is told to show that the size does not count nor are the walls needed where faith encompasses: for, where God is, no enemy can enter. This is the New Jerusalem of the spirit, one in which we may dwell secure and unafraid:

> Sion, poor maid, break out into songs of rejoicing; I am on my way, coming to dwell in the midst of thee, the Lord says. There be nations a many that shall rally that day to the Lord's side; they, too shall be people of mine . . . (Zech. 2:10).

*Historically, this corresponds to the peace in the Persian Empire under Darius, c. 522 B.C.

What a glorious promise for all nations and races to rejoice over—then, now, and in years to come.

Next, we come to the interesting passage regarding Satan where he stands as one opposed to God's loving design to save Israel; again, he is the unfair accuser.

> Another vision the Lord shewed me; here was an angel of his, and before this angel stood the high priest, Joshua, with the Accuser at his right hand bringing accusation against him. But to the Accuser the divine answer came, The Lord rebuke thee, Satan; the Lord, that makes choice of Jerusalem, rebuke thee! . . . . Then, for he saw Joshua standing there in his presence very vilely clad, the angel gave it out to his attendants they should take away these vile rags from him; Guilt of thine, said he, I have set by; thou shalt have new garments to wear instead . . . (Zech. 3:1-4).

The Lord's angel rebukes Satan, but also Joshua has to change his vile clothes, as his guilt is set aside. This means that Joshua had to get rid of his sinfulness as of a dirty cloth and put on a new nature clean and pure. Reform was asked of the High Priest as it is asked of us. We must be ready to cast off all earthly ties that trammel us, if we would be free of the Accuser's power. Perhaps we do not always see that our clothing is unclean and in need of a change, but our good angel is ever ready to clothe us anew the moment we see ourselves as we really are. At such a moment we, too, might hear the angel say, as he did to Joshua:

> My beckoning follow thou, my commands keep thou, people of mine thou shalt govern, house of mine thou shalt have in thy charge, and in their company, that here stand about thee, shalt come and go . . . (Zech. 3:7).

Does this not mean, perhaps, that he will always stand in the presence of the heavenly hosts? The angel draws his charge's attention never to forget that the spirit alone transcends all: "By arms, by force nothing canst thou; my spirit is all, says the Lord of hosts" (Zech. 4:6). Also, the angel warns the prophet not to doubt his mentor, or despise the small and insignificant things of everyday life: "No more you shall doubt that I come to you on the Lord's errand. Humble fortune of yesterday who dared belittle?" (Zech. 4:10).

It would appear that after his eight visions Zechariah was able to hear God's words without the angel's interpretations. The angel had played his role of mentor until the prophet understood and was able to act on his own. But, at first, willingly did he recognize his lack of knowledge and humbly made himself receptive to both vision and instruction.

> Encompass us with Thy Holy Angels, that through their mediation, guarded and advised, we may reach unity of faith and the knowledge of

Thy unapproachable Glory, for blessed art Thou unto ages of ages (*Orarion*, Prayer of the Hours).

[1]*Interpreter's Bible*, Vol. 5. New York: Abingdon Press, 1956, p. 207.
[2]St. Gregory of Nyssa, *From Glory to Glory*, p. 134.
[3]*Interpreter's Bible*, Vol. 6. New York: Abingdon Press, 1956, p. 69.
[4]Dionysius the Areopagite, *Mystical Theology and the Celestial Hierarchies*, pp. 31-32.

# V

## Angels in Poetry, Tales, and Apocalypses

*1. Esdras and the Psalms*

Second Esdras is a very difficult book belonging to what some consider to be the apocryphal writings of the Old Testament, though portions were probably composed in the beginning of the Christian era. It is, in fact, an amalgamation of several writings. The hero of the book is represented as deeply concerned about the question of God's justice. He acknowledges original sin in the fall of Adam: in whose sin we have all sinned. But it is the question of those who suffer innocently for the cause of justice that worries Esdras in a particular way, and it is to this problem that he seeks solution. In three successive visions the angel Uriel, whose name means "God is my Light," comes to Esdras to enlighten him and help him arrive at an answer to his query.

Actually from our viewpoint in the study of angelology, Esdras does not add much to our knowledge of the angelic nature but does give us the personal name of Uriel, one of the seven archangels (2 Esdras 4:1, 36; 5:20; 10:28). He also provides us with an indication of their place in the order of creation in describing God as the primary cause that exists before all times.

> Before it thundered and lightened, or ever the foundations of paradise were laid, before the fair flowers were seen, or ever the moveable powers were established, before the innumerable multitude of angels were gathered together . . . . And ere the present years were sought out, and or ever the inventions of them that now sin were turned, before they were sealed that have gathered faith for a treasure . . . (2 Esdras 6:2-5).

Esdras further exemplifies how when arguing some weighty question in our own mind, we might hear if we truly listened, an angel's voice helping us to think and smooth out our problem.

The angel Uriel, made it clear to Esdras that man cannot readily comprehend God, for God moves in his own mysterious ways.

> Thy heart hath gone too far in this world, and thinkest thou to comprehend the way of the most High? . . .I asked thee but only of the

fire and the wind, and of the day where through thou hast passed . . .yet canst thou give me no answer of them . . . . How should thy vessel then be able to comprehend the way of the Highest . . .? (2 Esdras 4:2-11).

These arguments between angel and prophet are full of depth and beauty. Those who care to plumb these matters, many of which still trouble the modern mind, should read carefully through this remarkable work. Through Esdras' words we too, might perchance hear Uriel or our own personal mentor clarifying our own questioning.

*         *         *

The Psalms, better than any other hymns or prayers, have voiced for generation after generation the worship of millions. What a picture this is for one who looks beyond!

The chariots of God are twenty thousand, even thousands of angels: the Lord is among them, as in Sinai, in the holy place (Ps. 67:18).

Then, how comforting to pass from the grandeur of this vision to the very gentle assurance that in all his glory God does not despise us, but that those very same beings who encompass him with majesty surround us with loving care:

. . .He shall give his angels charge over thee, to keep thee in all thy ways. They shall bear thee up in their hands, lest thou dash thy foot against a stone (Ps. 90:11-12).

What tremendous confidence rings through this psalm, what security for those who dwell "in the secret places of the most High." Psalm 33 is said to have been written by David after his escape from Achis, the King of Geth, as described in 1 Samuel 21:10-15. This hymn is a summons to all men to join the psalmist in his gratitude to the Lord who has "saved him out of all his trouble." Because David spoke out of his own experience, the words carry a deep and moving sincerity.

This poor man cried, and the Lord heard him, . . .the angel of the Lord encampeth round about them that fear him, and delivereth them (Ps. 33:6-7).

How positively the great king, soldier, and poet feels the presence of the Lord's angel who settled down to watch and to guard! No modern doubts or speculations such as would worry us trouble his mind; indeed, why should they, for David *knew!*

In contrast to other writings of the Old Testament, which primarily deal with God's words to men, the Psalms are composed of man's words addressed to God. They echo with a call for help, they express thanks and trust, they are prayers of confidence, praise, penitence and thanksgiving.

Bless the Lord, ye his angels, that excel in strength that do his commandments, hearkening unto the voice of his word (Ps. 102:20).

In many psalms the angels are called to witness, to join in the triumphal hymns. The psalmist is aware that without the voices of the angels to swell the choir, men's poor human tongues would be too insignificant truly to do justice to their praise:

Praise ye him, all his angels: praise him all his hosts!

Humbly do we join our prayers to theirs in praise of him who has chosen to make us a little less than the angels!

## 2. Job

The story of Job is a very remarkable book in which the problem of human suffering is faced for the first time in the Old Testament. But it is above all a treatise on Faith, in which the answer to all problems is found in God. It makes but little mention of angels except in the prologue where they are described as the sons of God who come before the Lord to give and present an account of their activities. "Satan came also among them" to accuse Job, that good and religious man, of being virtuous only because he possessed all the world's goods, claiming that if Job were to lose all, he would curse God. God believes in Job's essential goodness and faith, and lets Satan have his way with him. It is not God, but Satan who thinks up the trials and tribulations by which he puts Job's faith to the test.

Though the story of Job is well known to us, its moral may escape us. Namely, that God permits Satan's activities for ends we do not entirely comprehend but which lead, if we are faithful even unto death, back to God. God our Father trains and disciplines his children, and even uses evil unto final good.

Satan, let us not forget, is one of God's creatures, one of his children who misused his freedom. Satan hates God and all that is good because he chose to love himself above God. Satan fights the angels of light and, hating man, he tried by all means to tear us out of the hands of the Father. Satan cannot conceive of disinterested love; he expects us, as he expected Job, to fall. Satan rejoices over sin. But God trusts us as he trusted Job, and may show Satan even through us how hopeless are his efforts. In this regard we may be God's instruments for the triumph over the powers of darkness. Who can tell? We can answer as little as Job could when God asked him, "From what vantage-point wast thou watching, when I laid the foundations of the earth? Tell me, whence comes this sure knowledge of thine? ...was it thou or I designed earth's plan...? who laid its corner-stone? To me that day...all the powers of heaven uttered their joyful praise" (Job 38:4-8). The "powers of heaven" are the angels who share in the divine nature and present themselves before the Father and Creator of all, as is described elsewhere: " . . .I had a vision of the Lord sitting on his throne, with all the host of heaven waiting on his pleasure, to right and left" (1 Kgs. 22:19).

Satan in the story of Job seems to have come "among" these sons but is not one of them. He comes as an instigator of trouble, an accuser. When God asked him where he had been, Satan replied, "Roaming about the earth . . .to and fro about the earth" (Job 1:7). There is about this response an impudence, an offhandedness of one who does not "belong." It is interesting that in Arabic the verb *shatana* means "to be remote," and is close to the Latin *Satana* (Satan). Evil is the most distant thing from God, so distant that the end will be to evolve into the remoter and more satanic, into the nothingness and darkness of the bottomless pit of despair.

The angels of light personify all that God is; the angels of darkness personify all that God is not.

To listen to evil and despair is to stray from God. Job's struggle was to stand fast; he fought and won. Nothing prevents us from doing so, too, aware that thinking and acting rightly is the only reality for us.

Like Job, we can trust God through all our trials. At the end of them all, if we have endured, we shall then find the loving Father.

> The choir of Angels, rejoicing as befits them by their very rich participation in Thine own Mystery, flash forth with their light of the fairest gifts of grace (*Canon of the Angels*, Canticle I, Tone III).

### 3. Daniel

The Book of Daniel, it is believed, was written during the Maccabean revolt, in the second century B.C. It has as its hero a legendary figure of the seventh century B.C. who had lived in exile in Babylon. It is not so much the proper dating of this remarkable book that should preoccupy us, but rather its message, as significant today as it was many centuries ago.

Daniel, like all the prophets, was less concerned with writing history than in proclaiming a faith. He calls for courage, hope and patience; his words were written in times peculiarly like our own. Fear of the future loomed as largely for people then as, alas, it does for many of us now. Our chief dread appears to be destruction by thermonuclear devices, theirs was of a power equally capable of annihilating their little Israel. The Word of God that came to Daniel at that time was such as we also need to live by today. The essential doctrine consisted in an unswerving loyalty to the Lord, a day by day nobility of life, a trust that the morrow is, indeed, in God's loving care.

To our study of angelology, the Book of Daniel is especially interesting, because his account is a great step forward from the earlier writings in which the angels are the anonymous messengers of God and without distinct character of their own. Daniel gives them personal names and defines their functions as patrons or guardians of nations. He had direct contact with them, both in the practical as well as the mystical order.

Daniel, the story tells us, was carried away to Babylon and lived at the court of Nebuchadnezzar and survived until the days of Cyrus, the Persian conqueror of Babylon. Hence, he would have been a contemporary of Isaiah 2. The Book of Daniel falls into two parts: the narrative and the visionary; in both sections do we encounter angels.

The first narration of interest to us, from the angelological vantage-point is that of the fiery furnace (Daniel 3). Three friends and followers of Daniel—Shadrach, Meshach, and Abednego—refused to obey Nebuchadnezzar's order to worship a golden image and were consequently bound, and by the king's order, thrown into a furnace stoked to seven times its usual heat. But the three faithful young men, undaunted, put their faith in God and prayed for deliverance.

> Meanwhile, their tormentors were not idle; naphtha and tow, pitch and tinder must be heaped on the furnace, till the flame rose forty-nine cubits above the furnace itself . . . . But an angel of the Lord had gone down into the furnace with Azarias [Abednego] and his companions; and he drove the flames away from it, making a wind blow in the heart of the furnace, like the wind that brings the dew. So that these three were untouched, and the fire brought them neither pain nor discomfort (Dn. 3:46-51).

The gratitude of the three young men found expression in that beautiful hymn of thanksgiving which has been used for centuries in the Christian Church, known as the *Benedicite*, or *Song of the Three Children.**

> Blessed art thou, O Lord God of our fathers: and to be praised and exalted above all for ever . . . . Blessed art thou that beholdest the depth, and sittest upon the cherubim: and to be praised and exalted above all for ever . . . . O all ye works of the Lord, bless ye the Lord: praise and exalt him above all for ever . . . . O ye angels of the Lord, bless ye the Lord: praise and exalt him above all for ever . . . . O all ye that worship the Lord, bless the God of Gods, praise him and give him thanks: for his mercy endureth for ever (*Song of the Three Children* 29, 32, 35, 37, 68).

The miracle of the fiery furnace made so deep an impression on Nebuchadnezzar that he desisted from further persecuting the Jews for their religious practices. One can well imagine that the king was astonished when going to gloat over his victims' charred remains, he found the three Jewish boys walking unbound and unharmed in the midst of the flames in the company of a heavenly being!

---

*Not included in all versions of the Bible.

Who of us has not loved the story of Daniel in the lions' den? It is a beautiful religious illustration, not history, which purports to answer the question: What must man surrender in exchange for his integrity? Daniel responds by this story of steadfast faith and courage, now a favorite for generations, of both young and old.

Nebuchadnezzar died, and now it was Darius the Midian who, having conquered Babylon, sat upon the throne. He evidently had not heard of the three children of the fiery furnace, and the old trouble over religious practices broke out anew. Daniel continued to worship God in the Jewish manner, in defiance of a recent decree. Darius, more to please his advisors than out of any deep personal conviction, threw Daniel to the lions. After a sleepless night, Darius looked into the lions' den and there to his amazement, he saw Daniel sitting peacefully with the wild beasts at his feet. When the astonished (and to do him justice) delighted king questioned him, Daniel replied: "My God hath sent his angel, and hath shut the lions' mouths, that they have not hurt me: for as much as before him innocency was found in me, and also before thee, O king, have I done no hurt" (Dn. 6:22).

The writings in the second half of the Book of Daniel are what is known as apocalyptical, a form of composition which the Jews used during times of oppression, and which "unveiled" hope and assured the righteous of ultimate vindication.

Daniel was accorded many visions which he was at a loss to interpret, until the archangel Gabriel was ordered by God to interpret them for him. This is the first time a personal name is given to an angel in the Old Testament. His name means *Man of El*, that is, Man of God. *El* is the ancient Canaanite word for God, and *gabr* means *man*. Others interpret it as "*El* is my champion," or "*El* has shown himself valiant."[1]

Daniel perceived that each nation had a guardian angel and, specifically, that St. Michael was the protector and patron of Israel (Dn. 10:21). He also saw the glory of God, yet his words somehow do not reflect the power of Isaiah and Ezekiel. Daniel's descriptions seem to be more conventional, borrowing terms that have been used before; but still there is a ring of truth in his account that leaves no doubt that he did have a true and profound spiritual experience and that he did see the heavenly host. "Thousand thousands ministered unto him [God] . . ." (Dn. 7:10), he tells us.

Much of what Daniel saw and strove to put into words remains nebulous for those wanting in specific knowledge in this field, but there is one intimate moment of contact between the visionary and the Archangel Gabriel which is easy to grasp and brings his experience down to our own level.

Daniel relates that it occurred one evening when he was deeply concentrated and steeped in prayer.

Thus prayed I, thus did I confess my own sins...pouring out supplication, there in the presence of my God...when the human figure of Gabriel, as I had seen it at the beginning of my vision, flew swiftly to my side; it was the hour of the evening sacrifice when he reached me. And with these words he enlightened me: Daniel, my errand is to instruct thee and give thee discernment (Dn. 9:20-22).

How often, I wonder, does our angel touch us and seek to give us the gift of discernment—that skill of understanding and deep perception? But, alas, we are often too dull, impassive, or in too great a hurry to hear the voice of the Spirit.

Thou who art good hast shown the choirs of the Angels pouring forth streams and rivers of goodness, and shining through and through with the radiance of Thy secrecy (*Canon of the Angels*, Canticle III, Tone III).

*4. Tobit*

One of the most charming of the Old Testament narratives is that of Tobias and the Archangel Raphael. It is a religious tale, cast in pleasing form, almost like a novel. The scene is laid in Nineveh, in the time of the Assyrian captivity, and the story is about a devout family of Jewish exiles. Tobit, the father, a pious, God-fearing man, lived according to the law of his fathers, in spite of the strangers that surrounded him. He was full of good works, among which was the burying of the dead according to the custom of the Jews. Doing these acts of mercy he lost his eyesight, and his wife, "Anna did take woman's work to do" to help keep the family going. What a familiar experience of refugees in every time and clime!

At this juncture Tobit recalled having left in Media with a kinsman of his, Gabael, ten talents of silver. He resolved to send his son Tobias to recover the much-needed money. Tobit hired a stranger to accompany Tobias on the journey. This stranger was the Archangel Raphael in disguise. During their journey, the two travelling companions went fishing and the angel advised the boy to preserve the fish's liver, heart and gall as they would be of use later on. In reaching Ecbatana they lodged with Raguel, whose daughter Sara was in great distress and desirous of death. Her unhappiness was owing to the slaying, by the evil spirit Asmodeus, of her seven successive husbands on their very wedding night. Tobias fell in love with Sara and married her, notwithstanding the curse that was upon her. Raphael, protecting the young couple, burnt the fish's heart and liver which produced a smoke. "With that, the evil spirit fled; it was overtaken by the angel Raphael in the wastelands of Upper Egypt, and there held prisoner" (Tb. 8:3).

Herewith is the perfect example of the clash of the good and bad angels in which we can see the role that man's own attitude plays. The good angel was able to defend his charge because Tobias was obedient and courageous and because of his true love for Sara.

Tobias, faithful to the purpose of his journey, recovered the ten talents of silver and returned home with his bride. He was able to cure his father's blindness with a salve made from the fish's gall as the angel had instructed him.

The reunited and grateful family wished to recompense the hired stranger who had proved himself so staunch and wise a friend, pressing upon him many gifts. But the stranger refused, saying:

> Bless God, praise him and magnify him, and praise him for the things he has done unto you . . . . It is good to keep close the secret of a King, but it is honourable to reveal the works of God. Do that which is good, and no evil shall touch you . . . . A little with righteousness is better than much with unrighteousness . . .they that sin are enemies of their own life . . .when thou didst pray and Sara thy daughter-in-law I did bring the remembrance of your prayers before the Holy One: and when thou didst bury the dead I was with thee likewise. And when thou didst not delay to rise up, and leave thy dinner, to go cover the dead, thy good deed was not hid from me: but I was with thee . . . .
>
> I am Raphael, one of the seven angels, which presents the prayers of the Saints, and which go in and out before the glory of the Holy One . . . (Tb. 12, passim).

The Archangel Raphael is the angel of prayers, good deeds, and healing; he is also the protector of all wayfarers, and today especially revered by those who travel by air.

Raphael's name in Hebrew means "God heals." Of all God's emanations, how singularly transcendent is that of healing. In our pains and struggles how helpful to know that he who carries our prayers to God is the selfness of God's healing power.

Let us often keep this in mind and repeat this ancient prayer for those who travel:

> O Christ, Who art the Way and the Truth, send now Thy Guardian Angel to go with Thy servants, as once Thou didst send him to Tobias, and for Thy Glory keep them safe and sound from all harm and evil . . ." (*Prayers for Orthodox Christians*).

### 5. 2 Maccabees

In both books of the Maccabees we find the story of Jerusalem in about the years 176 to 136 B.C. The first book is a strictly historical record of the Jewish revolt from under the Syrian yoke and as led by the Maccabees. The second book, with which we are concerned, centers about the heroic figure of Judas Maccabeus, the liberator of Jerusalem. The first part of this book relates the events which lead up to, and caused the famous uprising.

"Now when the holy city was inhabited with all peace, and the laws were kept very well, because of the Godliness of Onias, the high priest . . ." (2 Mc. 3:1). Thus begins the story, but soon intrigue enters upon the scene. One Simon, quarreled with Onias the good High Priest, and because his local machinations did not bear fruit, he had it whispered into the king's ear that there was a great treasure horded in the temple which did not "pertain to the account of the sacrifices" and could be had for the asking. The king charged his treasurer Heliodorus to go and confiscate the money. Heliodorus, under pretense of visiting the cities of Celosyria and Phenice, came to Jerusalem where he was courteously welcomed. He at once demanded of Onias the surrender of the property. The High Priest protested, explaining that the money was destined to the relief of widows and fatherless children, and had been entrusted to the Temple's good keeping. Moreover, Simon had grossly exaggerated its amount. Heliodorus paid no heed to these words and set forth to appropriate the treasury. The distress of Onias and the people is indeed a moving narrative. In their despair they addressed themselves to God to save their venerated Temple from defilement.

> And all, holding their hands toward heaven, made supplication . . . . Nevertheless Heliodorus executed that which was decreed. Now as he was there present himself with his guard about the treasury, the Lord of spirits, and the Prince of all power, causes a great apparition, so that all that presumed to come in with him were astonished at the power of God, and fainted, and were sore afraid. For there appeared unto them a horse with a terrible rider, and adorned with a very fair covering, and he ran fiercely, and smote at Heliodorus with his forefeet, and it seemed that he that sat upon the horse had complete harness of gold. Moreover two other young men appeared before him notable in strength, excellent in beauty, and comely in apparel who stood by him on either side, and scourged him continually . . . . Heliodorus fell suddenly unto the ground, and was compassed with great darkness . . . (2 Mc. 3:24-27).

Heliodorus lay gravely ill. The grateful people gave thanks to God for the salvation of the Temple from defilement, but the High Priest prayed

> . . .for the health of the man . . . . Now as the high priest was making an atonement, the same young men in the same clothing stood beside Heliodorus, saying, Give Onias the high priest great thanks, inasmuch as for his sake the Lord hath granted thee life . . . (2 Mc. 3:33-34).

What comment should we make about this, other than say: Great are the works of the Lord! Both to the vanquished and the delivered God's hand was plainly seen in the guise of heavenly warriors; nor was this the last time they were to appear during those troubled and heroic days when a small, sorely oppressed nation threw off singlehandedly the yoke of a great power.

Shortly after these events, the good Onias was murdered, the old King died, and in his place ruled the unjust and cruel Antiochus Epiphanes, who finally captured and defiled the Temple. The Jews rose in revolt under the courageous and wise leadership of Judas Maccabeus, who overcame the Syrians, delivered the Temple out of the hands of the infidel and rededicated it to the use of the One and True God. The struggle was, nonetheless, not over; there remained the successors of Antiochus and other hostile neighbors. In two of his battles the day for Judas was saved by the miraculous intervention of angelic horsemen.

The Jews were being threatened by a great armed force under the command of a general named Timotheus, who thought he could overcome that small tenacious nation by the force of arms, but they as usual set their trust in God:

> Now the sun being newly risen, they joined both together; the one part having together with their virtue their refuge also unto the Lord for a pledge of their success and victory: the other side making their rage leader of the battle. But when the battle waxed strong, there appeared unto the enemies from heaven five comely men upon horses, with bridles of gold, and two of them led the Jews. And took Maccabeus betwixt them, and covered him on every side with their weapons, and kept him safe, but shot arrows and lightnings against the enemies; so that being confounded with blindness, and full of trouble, they were killed (2 Mc. 10:28-30).

Another time, Lysias, the king's "protector," set out to lay seige of the fortified town of Bethsura with a great display of footmen, horsemen, and even four score elephants, the terrifying secret weapon of those days:

> . . .Maccabeus himself first of all took weapons, exhorting the others that they would jeopard themselves together with him to help their brethren: so they went forth together with a willing mind. And as they were at Jerusalem there appeared before them on horseback one in white clothing, shaking his armour of gold. Then they praised the merciful God all together, and took heart, insomuch that they were ready not only to fight with the men, but with most cruel beasts, and to pierce through walls of iron. Thus they marched forward in their armour, having an helper from heaven: for the Lord was merciful unto them (2 Mc. 11:7-10).

What, above all, stands forth in these stories is the remarkable faithfulness and trust of these people. Judas Maccabeus was a real person who really did fight these battles against tremendous odds, and did win them. We have a most telling verse: "the one part having together with their virtue their refuge also unto the Lord . . ." while "the other side making their rage leader of their battle" (10:28). Herein lies the answer to any question we may have. The faith and courage of the Jews and the corresponding grace of God were visualized, for those who had the eyes to see, in the celestial horsemen. Their faith made them feel safe, and they *were* consequently safe, for the angel of the Lord was with them in very truth. So, too, with all those who put their trust in God, they too fight in the thick of the fray with us and for us.

Except for the riders of the Apocalypse, this is the most striking description of angels on horseback to be found in the Scriptures. There is a clear ring of truth about these passages which takes them out of sheer legendry and brings them into the realm of true, authentic spiritual experience.

### 6. The Book of the Secrets of Enoch

It is difficult to ascertain where one should place Enoch in a study like the present. These writings, of course, do not belong to the canonical books, but rather to pseudo-apocryphal literature. The historical personage of Enoch as well as the passages from the books that bear his name, are referred to in the New Testament and have influenced its writers. The Books of Enoch were also highly regarded and much quoted in the early centuries by both orthodox Christians and heretics.

Enoch himself is identified in the genealogy of Noah as the son of Jared and the father of Methuselah. We are further informed that "Enoch walked with God: and he was not; for God took him" (Gn. 5:24). Tradition has it that Enoch was so close to God that even while on earth he visited heaven and ultimately did not die, but was transmuted as St. Paul says:

> When Enoch was taken away without the experience of death, when God took him and no more was seen of him, it was because of his faith; that is the account we have of him before he was taken, that he pleased God (Heb. 11:5).

Around the name of Enoch many legends grew up, among such that he discovered writing, arithmetic, and astrology, but especially he was believed to have seen heaven. His records of this even were supposedly carried by Noah into the ark. It is not surprising, therefore, that anthologies describing heaven should bear his name, even though collected long after the real Enoch lived. This was a common procedure in Old Testament times, and even in the first centuries of our Christian era. Many writings would be assembled under the name of a prophet or wise man who stood for a particular line of thought as, for example, Solomon or Isaiah.

There are two books related to Enoch: The Book of Enoch and The Book of the Secrets of Enoch. Both disappeared from circulation around the third or fourth centuries of the Christian era. The first of these, written in Ethiopic, was rediscovered in 1773 in Abyssinia, and originally dates from the second and first centuries B.C. The latter, which is of particular interest to our present purpose, The Book of the Secrets of Enoch, has come down to us in a Slavonic version, evidently made from a Greek original, somewhere between 30 B.C. and 70 A.D. Its author was a Hellenist Orthodox Jew who lived in Egypt, but nothing further of him is known. He hides behind the name of Enoch. Although the very knowledge that such a book even existed was lost for some twelve hundred years, a few of its phrases, though not the book as such, as already noted, are quoted in the New Testament, as well as in the apocryphal literature, where it is freely cited. The book is referred to by Origen, Clement of Alexandria, and Irenaeus. Enoch surely must have influenced Dionysius the Areopagite, and through him St. Thomas Aquinas, Dante Alighieri and John Milton. The Slavonic text was translated into English by Morfill in 1896, and edited by R.H. Charles. It is this book we cite.

The Book of the Secrets of Enoch opens by telling how Enoch had a dream in which he was informed that he would be taken to visit heaven.

> There was a very wise man and worker of great things: God loved him, and received him, so that he should see the heavenly abodes, the king-doms of the wise, great, inconceivable and never-changing God, the Lord of all, . . .and the degrees and manifestations of the incorporeal hosts, and should be an eye-witness of the unspeakable ministrations of the multi-tude of creatures, and of the varying appearance, and indescribable singing of the host of Cherubim, and of the immeasurable world.[2]

While he was alone in his house, Enoch dreamed that he was visited by two heavenly messengers whom he described as very tall:

> And their faces shone like the sun, and their eyes were like burning lamps; and fire came forth from their lips. Their dress had the appearance of feathers: their feet were purple, their wings were brighter than gold; their hands whiter than snow. I awoke from my sleep and saw clearly these men standing in front of me.[3]

Notice that Enoch was no more dreaming for his visitors woke him. They are later identified by the names of Samuel and Raguel. They carried Enoch upon their wings and took him successively into the seven heavens. This is, perhaps, the origin of our expression "in seventh heaven."

Enoch tells us in chapter four to chapter six that the angels carried him above the air into ether, and there in the first heaven he saw two hundred angels, the rulers of the stars and the guardians of the snow and ice, of the clouds, dew, and the holy oil for anointing.

In the second heaven (chapters six and seven), he saw the fallen angels, "they who had apostatized from the Lord," and whose appearance was gloomy beyond words, "more than the darkness of the earth." Enoch was saddened by the sight and troubled by the fallen creatures asking him, a mere mortal, to pray to God for them.

In the third heaven (chapters eight to ten), the two accompanying angels showed Enoch Paradise, "a place such as has never been known for the goodliness of its appearance." Here is the Garden of Eden kept by three hundred angels, here also is the tree of life. They showed him the Place of Prayers, the eternal and blissful inheritance of the righteous and of those who endure and are faithful to the end. To the North of Eden the angels showed Enoch a "terrible place" of "savage darkness and impenetrable gloom, . . .prepared for those who do not honour God; who commit evil deeds on earth . . . ."[4] This is the eternal inheritance of the wicked where they suffer and are tortured, they are surrounded by fire and by ice, as the atmosphere both scorches and freezes.

In the fourth heaven (chapters eleven to seventeen), Enoch was shown the courses of the sun and the moon, with their strange and wonderful creatures, the phoenixes and chalkadri, who defy description. He was carried east of the gates of the sun and to the north; then to the east of the course of the moon. And then, just before being carried yet further, Enoch got a glimpse of the glory of God.

> In the middle of the heavens I saw an armed host serving the Lord wth cymbals and organs, and unceasing voice. I was delighted at hearing it.[5]

Thence, Enoch came to the fifth heaven (chapter eighteen) where he saw the Grigori, known also as the watchers. These are the brethren of those angels who rebelled under their prince, Satanail, and who were consequently confined to the second heaven.

Enoch was then carried on in to the sixth heaven (chapter nineteen), and there he saw the seven bands of angels,

> very bright and glorious, and their faces shining more than the rays of the sun. They are resplendent, and there is no difference in their countenance, or their manner, or the style of their clothing. And these orders arrange and study the revolutions of the stars, and the changes of the moon, and revolutions of the sun, and superintend the good or evil conditions of the world. And they arrange teachings, and instructions, and sweet speaking, and singing, and all kinds of glorious praise. These are the archangels who are appointed over the angels! They hold in subjection all living things both in heaven and earth. And there are the angels who are over rivers and the sea, and those who are over the fruits of the earth, and the angels over every herb, giving all kinds of nourishment to every living thing. And the angels over all souls of men, who write down all their works and their lives before the face of the Lord. In the midst of them are seven phoenixes and seven cherubim, and seven six-winged creatures, being as one voice and singing with one voice: and it is not possible to describe their singing, and they rejoice before the Lord at His footstool.[6]

From here Enoch passed on into the seventh heaven (chapters twenty to thirty-six), where he saw the full glory and spoke to God.

> ...and I saw there a very great light and all the fiery hosts of great archangels, and incorporeal powers and lordships, and principalities, and powers; cherubim and seraphim, thrones and the watchfulness of many eyes. There were ten troops, a station of brightness . . .they showed me the Lord from afar sitting on His lofty throne. And all the heavenly hosts having approached stood on the ten steps, according to their rank: and made obeisance to the Lord. And so they proceeded to their places in joy and mirth, and in boundless light singing songs with low and gentle voices, and gloriously serving Him.
>
> They leave not nor depart day or night standing before the face of the Lord, working His will, cherubim and seraphim, standing round His throne. And the six-winged creatures overshadow all His throne, singing with a soft voice before the face of the Lord: "Holy, Holy, Holy: Lord God of Sabaoth! heaven and earth are full of Thy glory!"[7]

How reminiscent these words are, both of Isaiah and Ezekiel, although they have a striking individuality of their own which made St. Paul use Enoch's words when speaking of the heavenly hosts (Eph. 1:21 and Col. 1:16). The picture drawn by Enoch has more detail, is less impressionistic than the descriptions made by those two first great prophets. But once more, let us not forget that we are dealing with symbols. Enoch clothes the visions of his spiritual conceptions in semblances of things perceptible to the eyes of the flesh. "Who am I," he asks,

> to tell of the incomprehensible existence of the Lord, and His face wonderful and not to be spoken of . . .and the throne of the Lord very great and not made with hands: and the choir standing around Him, of the hosts of cherubim and seraphim![8]

Nonetheless, Enoch tries to put into words that which had been revealed to him: "I also saw the Lord face to face. And His face was very glorious and marvelous and terrible, threatening and strange."[9]

Enoch was filled with awe and fear, but Gabriel said to him, "Be not afraid." Beautiful words, those: "Be not afraid, fear not!" We hear them repeated again and again throughout the Scriptures whenever the angel appears. They are the same words that were spoken to Mary in Nazareth.

In standing before the face of the Lord, Enoch was sustained by the Archangel Michael, the chief captain of the heavenly hosts. He also mentions Vretil as one of the archangels, a name we do not come across in any other literature. Vretil explained to Enoch "all the works of the heaven and the earth and the sea, . . .all about the souls of men . . . . For every soul was created eternally before the foundation of the world."[10]

Then the Lord called Enoch to be seated at his left hand with Gabriel and God revealed many secrets to him. Such secrets as had not yet been told even to the angels. The Lord disclosed how from nothing he had created all things, how from the Lowest Darkness he brought forth the visible and the invisible, how he established water and surrounded it with light and made firm the circles of the heavens.

> And for all the heavenly hosts I fashioned a nature like that of fire . . . . And from the brightness of My eye the lightning received its wonderful nature. And fire is in the water and water in the fire, and neither is the one quenched, nor the other dried up . . . . And from the fire I made the ranks of the spiritual hosts, ten thousand angels . . .I ordered them to stand each in their ranks.
>
> One of these in the ranks of the Archangels, having turned away with the rank below him, entertained an impossible idea, that he should make his throne higher than the clouds over the earth, and should be equal in rank to My power. And I hurled him from the heights with his angels . . . . And so I created all the heavens, and it was the third day. On the third day I ordered the earth to produce . . . .[11]

From the above we can assume that the angels were created on the second day, and also fell in that period. We must bear in mind that in Biblical terms the word "day" has the cosmological interpretation of an age. The Lord further describes creation up to the sixth day when he created man, richly endowed in every way:

> I purposed a subtle thing: from the invisible and visible nature I made man. From both are his death and life, and his form . . . . And I placed him upon earth; like a second angel . . .ruler to rule upon the earth, and to have My wisdom . . . . And I gave him his will, and I showed him the two ways, the light and the darkness . . . .[12]

Then God created Eve as in Genesis out of Adam's rib and set them in the Garden of Eden from whence they could see the angels singing in heaven.[13] However,

> . . .the devil took thought as if wishing to make another world, because things were subservient to Adam on earth . . . . The devil is to be the evil spirit of the lowest places; he became Satan, after he left the heavens. His name was formerly Satanail. And then, though he became different from the angels in nature, he did not change his understanding of just and sinful thoughts. He understood the judgment upon him, and the former sin which he had sinned. And on account of this, he conceived designs against Adam; · . .and deceived Eve . . . . But I cursed him [Satan] for [his] ignorance . . .nor man did I curse, nor the earth, nor any other things created, but evil fruit of man, and then his works.[14]

God forever remained, and remains, merciful to man. Only man's evil works and their fruits are cursed because God has removed his blessing from them. All things else are hallowed from their creation. We bring on our own bane by our misdeeds, the responsibility is entirely ours, even if the influence under which we act has its source in the spiritual world surrounding us. It should be encouraging to know that all good action is already blessed from the very beginning. The Lord further revealed many wonderful things to Enoch and, finally sent him back to earth in care of a guardian angel to record all he had seen until he was taken back again on high.

What is the value and authority of Enoch? The Church has made no definitive pronouncement, yet we know that he was highly regarded by the early Church when the canonicity of the Scriptures was less meticulously sifted. Though lost for twelve centuries, he has, nonetheless, through tradition greatly influenced religious thought up to the present time, and unfortunately at times, led to heresy.

We can say with truthfulness that the reading of Enoch is unquestionably interesting, that we hold in our hands the record of a truly inspired visionary. One who hides behind anonimity so that his message may be all the stronger, Enoch opens doors for our own mental images and perceptions, helping us to climb Jacob's ladder, reaching spiritual realms as yet unexplored.

Our study of angelology, as it has come down to us, would loose a connecting and clarifying link, were we to ignore this truly notable book, even though, on the other hand, we may not regard it as biblically canonical.

## 7. Summing-Up

It is significant that angels appear chiefly to the strong: the warriors, builders, lawgivers and teachers. Indeed, how could it be otherwise? People without vision cannot be leaders. The true "doers" among the children of men have always had broad horizons and have been able to see further and beyond those of the common run.

The truly great have never been ashamed to give honor to whom honor is due. Then, we see why the men of the Bible were not fearful of being considered "queer, an odd lot" because they confessed to having seen, and even to being guided by, angels. On the contrary, to them it was proof that they indeed had a mission. It gave them confidence in their undertakings and crowned them with the perseverance so necessary for the success of good works.

The angels are characterized by greatness, **swiftness**, strength, beauty, wisdom and love. Their activities are to worship and glorify God whose commands they execute; their mission to man is to protect, guide and admonish him. They are present at the hour of prayer and in battle. There is nothing weakly sentimental nor spooky about them, nor do they have feminine characteristics. They are always referred to as "he," the Man of God. They protect nations and individuals, they personify virtues, true wisdom, and authentic love.

Angels do not commonly make their presence visually known, nor do they appear because they are called, or because someone is in a trance. Nay, rather, they appear unexpectedly and fill the beholder with awe, although it is, more often than not, the message they bring rather than their presence that makes the beholder tremble.

In Genesis the angels are strange, inexplicable, full of light—and unpredictable. They teach often with a heavy hand, they bring promise and give hope. In Eden, Satan tempts, the Cherub guards.

Abraham is visited, and is given the first spark of a more penetrating comprehension of the world of the spirit, and through it, also of the most unfathomable and thrice-sacred mystery of the Most Holy Trinity. Obeying the command of the angel, he entreats him for his kinsman Lot. Hagar, whom he abandons, is specially protected by the Angel of the Lord.

Jacob is led from a selfish, grasping man to become the father of a great people through his vision of the angels.

And, Balaam, who was full of the power of the spirit would yet have taken the wrong turn had not an angelic spirit stood in his way to block him and to deal with him in a most insistent manner.

Moses, the greatest of all lawgivers, the intermediary between man and the Law of God, had an angel to guard and direct him along his way of encountering the Most High. He saw that God's Mercy Seat is supported, upheld and sustained by the heavenly cherubim, the selfness of God's greatest and most sublime powers.

Joshua, Moses' chosen and loyal follower, a soldier, leader and priest, was led in battle and heartened by the Archangel Michael.

And Samson, the perennial strong and mighty fighter for his people, was a man who had the extraordinary privilege of being cared for, looked after, and so to speak "governed" even before birth by the angel who instructed his parents as well.

Gideon, the liberator, soldier, man of wisdom and humility, took upon himself the very difficult and exacting charge that was his, only at the bidding of "the Man of God," the angelic visitor.

Elijah, prophet, reformer, man of action, was led and sustained physically and morally, encouraged, spurred on, built up to the full stature of his special calling by an angel of the Lord.

Job, in deepest philosophical speculation about life and living, was no abstractionist. A man who witnessed in his own life how angelic creatures come to play their part in the great saga and mystery of man's triumphs and trials.

And, what of Isaiah and Ezekiel, those two great prophetic figures whose words still thunder down the ages? They were indeed very brave men, intrepid sons of God who feared no one, who dared to stand up and unequivocally to speak their minds—and their hearts—to the rulers, despots and dictatorial potentates of their day. They set out upon their mission with courage simply because an angel had made it clear to them that such was the will of God. Once that was established there was no turning back, and they averred the message of the Lord in season and out of season.

Zechariah, who was so preoccupied by such down-to-earth things like building and reinforcing walls, was encouraged in his endeavors by an angel who revealed to him the world of the spirit and made him see beyond stone and mortar, beyond this material world of the unreal, to the spiritual world of the authentically real and true.

David and Solomon, kings of valor, power and unsurpassed wisdom, saw the angels as worthy of reverence and, as is a matter of permanent and blessed record, sang of the heavenly spirits in those most profound of all religious poems and hymns, the psalmody.

Daniel, the unique visionary, could not comprehend or apply his vision to the reality he had to face, but was aided with the indispensable assistance given by the interpretation of Gabriel himself.

The charming story of Tobit, so close to the humanity of each of us; the wisdom of holy Esdras: it all speaks to us of angels, of God intervening in human affairs through the medium of heavenly spirits.

And in time of military engagement, why even Judas Maccabeus was given the assistance of his heavenly warrior.

Of Enoch, as it is, we only know that he had a clearer vision of heaven than anyone else, and though veiled in anonimity, his influence was far-reaching. And yet *we* doubt! We doubt the existence of angels, basing our naive disbelief upon what seems to us to be a very reasonable sort of logic! Simply because the angels belong to a portion of creation not within our immediate and palpable ken, and because we cannot see them at will. Yet, on the other hand, how much of everyday life do we really know and comprehend? We know many "hows" but the ultimate "why" has still remained scientifically unexplained and unanswered on every side of life. We have no more reason for doubting the existence of angels than we have for questioning any inexplicable force of what we term "nature."

To find the angels, to discover them, to come into intimate contact with them requires the transcendent knowledge—and spirit—of mystical theology, not so much in terms of abstract and speculative expertise, but in the humility of a Christian soul that is governed by the simplicity, the directness, the guileless curiosity of the unsophisticated child. Indeed, we ought not be simple-minded, but we must needs be humble-minded. We need to free ourselves of theories and preconceptions, and with a fresh mind see above and beyond, and yet, still, very close at hand, for he stands by our side: the Guardian of our souls.

It is in this frame of mind that we should meditate, reflect and ruminate over what we have read, and gather within our hearts the impetus of a hope and a confidence that was given to the prophets of old because of their deep faith in God's promise, that what he said would surely come to be. Thus, we shall the easier understand how the fulfillment of that promise in the New Testament changes the role of the angels and brings them into a much closer relationship with us.

If we are genuinely honest, we must recognize that the role of the angels in the Old Testament was an important one, full of significance and unerring directness. They assisted in preparing for the Redemption. From the very outset of man's religious history, which we call indeed the "history of salvation," the angels are present, they shepherd man and prepare the way of the Lord.

And so, from the threshold of the New Testament and right into the modern world, the angels of light gleam and flash in attendance upon their only King, Jesus Christ Our Lord, and so forever intermingle with us, his faithful.

Serving Thee in trembling, the Angelic splendors stand by and ever sing of Thy measureless power, O Christ (*Canon of the Angels*, Canticle III, Tone III).

---

[1]Daniel, *The Interpreter's Bible*, Vol. 6. New York: Abingdon Press, 1956, p. 478.
[2]*The Book of the Secrets of Enoch*, trans. from the Slavonic by W.R. Morfill, M.A., ed. by R.H. Charles, M.A. Oxford: The Clarendon Press, 1896, p. 1.
[3]*Ibid.*
[4]*Ibid.*
[5]*Ibid.*
[6]*Ibid.*
[7]*Ibid.*
[8]*Ibid.*
[9]*Ibid.*
[10]*Ibid.*
[11]*Ibid.*
[12]*Ibid.*
[13]According to St. Ephrem (1, 1239) Adam and Eve lost their angelic vision at the time of their fall from grace.
[14]*The Book of the Secrets of Enoch.*

# Book II

### Angels in the New Testament

# I

## The Angel of the Annunciation

The mighty captain of the companies drew near to the city of Nazareth
and announced to thee, O Undefiled, the coming of the King and Lord of
the ages, saying to thee: "Hail, blessed Mary, thou wonder past speech and
beyond understanding, who art the restoration of mortal man" (Sessional
hymn, *Matins of the Annunciation*).

In the New Testament the angels really come into their own with their
personalities defined, their place in creation made clear. They are beings
endowed with intellect and free will, specifically distinct from and superior
to man, but essentially inferior to God. The New Testament confirms and
supplements the teaching of the Old Testament.

In reviewing the role of the holy angels in the Old Testament, we see them
as "messengers" (Gn. 24:7); "Sons of God" (Job 1:6); "Spirits" (Ps. 103:4);
"Holy Ones" and "Watchers" (Dn. 4:13); "Host of the Lord" (Jos. 5:14); and
their numbers are myriad. Their functions were and are to praise God, to
attend upon his throne, to execute his commands here on earth, to protect
the faithful, to punish the wicked, and to drive away evil spirits. In the Old
Testament they assisted in preparing the road for the advent of Jesus the
Savior, leading men along the path of virtue and righteousness.

In the New Testament, the angels adore Jesus Christ who is their King.

For above every principality, and power . . .and every name that is named,
not only in this world, but also in that which is to come . . . (Eph. 1:21; Phil.
2:10).

The duties of the angels with regard to men are to manifest and execute the
divine will. We will reflect upon all these manifestations in the four Gospels,
the Acts of the Apostles, and in the Epistles. The angels offer up prayers of
the faithful and intercede for them as revealed in the Book of Revelation.
They incite men to good, and serve them in times of peril. Each child is given
a guardian angel.

Satan, who in the Old Testament was a malevolent, superhuman being,
distinct from the angels, in the New Testament is chief of the fallen angels or

demons. He is also called "The Devil," "The Accuser," "The Calumniator," and his followers are "demons and devils."

In the New Testament and in the further writings of the Fathers of the Church, the battle between good and evil, between the Angels of Darkness and the Angels of Light, becomes ever clearer and more distinct.

Man, redeemed by Jesus Christ from the serfdom of his original sin, is a free agent and capable of joining in the battle between good and evil, to which, by the very nature of things, he cannot remain indifferent.

It is, then, with real awareness, with the fear of misinterpretation that we approach the mission of the holy angels in Our Lord's Gospel. Here the angels become much more intimate, their relationship to man, much closer. They are no longer simply meeting man as messengers and guides, but coming to fulfill a task of serving and ministering to Jesus, the Perfect Man. They become "deacons," the prototype of the deacon of the priesthood, for the word "deacon" comes from the Greek word *diakonos*, a servant and minister.

With the advent of Jesus Christ, the holy angels walk the earth firmly and mix fraternally with us men. Jesus makes it clear that each man has his own guardian angel, and these angels are an integral part of our earthly life. Because Jesus Christ, the Son of Man, became one of us, he purified humanity, through his Passion, unto the very throne of God. Thus the relationship, that of preceptor to learner, is transformed into a spiritual brotherhood and we are emboldened to regard the holy angels as our wise and protective "Elder Brethren."

Through numberless generations the Chosen People had been guided, protected, punished, coerced, instructed, and prepared, as one prepares the soil by patient sifting and care until it is ready to receive a precious seed. As a gardener finds the perfect loam tucked away in a corner of his potting shed, so God found one human being living in a small, very seldom mentioned, even despised hillside village of Galilee, whence no one expected anything worthwhile, much less extraordinary: "Can anything that is good come from Nazareth?" (Jn. 1:46).

God did not come to redeem his people in a clap of thunder, or with great pomp and display. He came quietly at night, and only a very few knew and rejoiced—an old priest and his wife, a lowly maiden and her betrothed, a few humble shepherds, and some wise men. Over and over again the story of Christ's birth moves our hearts with wonder and delight.

But if God did not come with great fanfare, neither did he come unannounced. He sent his angel before him to warn his servants that he was drawing nigh. They had been expecting him for a very long time, hoping against hope, joyfully keeping the house swept and garnished as they awaited the good news of his arrival.

St. Luke, who is considered by scholars to be a careful and exact historian, begins his story of Christ's earthly life with the appearance of the Lord's angel to Zachariah in the days when Herod the Great was King of Judea. Now Zachariah was a priest of the Temple in Jerusalem. David had divided the priests into twenty-four courses, each of which in rotation was responsible for the Temple services for a week. Zachariah belonged to the Abijah section, and he had been chosen by lot to burn the incense, a procedure employed to avoid disputes. Incense was burned twice a day, morning and evening. The daily sacrifice of the lamb was offered on the great altar of burnt offerings outside the Temple proper. The incense was offered inside the Temple on the golden altar of incense which stood before the veil of the Holy of Holies. Upon this veil the image of the cherubim was embroidered. "And he made the veil of blue, and purple, and crimson, and fine linen, and wrought cherubim thereon" (2 Chr. 3:14). The officiating priest was alone within the Temple while offering the incense; the other priests and the people worshipped without. Only once in a lifetime could a man enjoy this privilege, and he was ever after accounted "rich." It was the most solemn part of the day's service, symbolizing Israel's accepted prayers.

The humble and righteous priest was filled with fear and astonishment as well as disbelief. The whole thing seemed incredible to him; this is what happened: In performance of his priestly duty, Zachariah stood alone, deeply engrossed in prayer, watching the perfume-laden incense slowly ascending heavenward. As he worshipped, an angel became manifest on the right side of the altar and spoke to him, telling Zachariah that his prayers for the Messianic salvation were about to be fulfilled and that, as a first sign, he, Zachariah, and Elizabeth, his old and barren wife, would become parents of the Lord's forerunner.

The sign itself was the most improbable of all: "Whereby shall I know this? for I am an old man, and my wife well stricken in years?" (Lk. 1:18). The message more than the presence of the messenger perturbed Zachariah. It may well be that he was conversant with the story that the high priest Simon the Just, who had performed the same office and that an odd three hundred years before, had seen an angel clothed in white coming into the Holy Place on the Day of Atonement. Also, he knew, of course, of Daniel's visitation at the hour of the evening oblation. The angel, to reassure him gave his name and explained his office: "I am Gabriel, that stands in the presence of God; and am sent to speak unto thee, and to show thee these glad tidings" (Lk. 1:19).

This is reminiscent of Raphael's explanation of himself to Tobias. Gabriel and Raphael both stand in the presence of the Lord, and both are sent as messengers to man below. We see here two of the principal roles of the holy angels. They stand before God and at the same time come down to man.

They are worshippers and servers. Primarily, they stand in the Presence; they are part of the heavenly choirs, but they are also servers, messengers bent upon a mission from God to man. They fulfill their role of deacons. We can also see here, as in the Old Testament, that the heavenly beings are not vague and nebulous, but are separate and distinct personalities singled out by name.

The "name" plays an essential and illuminating part in our thinking and understanding. Nothing concrete or abstract has real meaning to us without a name. Our first question is: What is that? or, what is its name? This defining by an appellation gives all objects and thoughts concreteness. In fact, without a name, whatever it is remains an undefined "thing" without form, and void. There is a close and inseparable relationship between a name and a person, as the name of Jesus was, from the first, synonymous with Jesus himself. No ancient name was meaningless, all had an interpretation: Raphael means "God heals," Gabriel signifies "Man of God," and so on. It is, of course, not given to us to know the real names of the angels; those names we use represent their missions and define their personalities. Gabriel reveals himself by this name because it is the one by which he was commonly known to the Jews.

He, therefore, is not an unknown, startling apparition, but a recognizable person who makes himself comprehensible by his calling, purpose, and mission.

To leave no doubt whatever as to the reality of his presence, Gabriel strikes Zachariah dumb until after the birth of his son John who, in the spirit and power of Elijah, was to reconcile fathers and children and bring back the disobedient to the wisdom of the just: to make a people fully ready for their Lord.

Acccording to the ritual, when the officiating priest had burned the incense, he was expected, upon issuing from the sanctuary, to pronounce the blessing. Zachariah was only able to make the appropriate gestures, but no word issued from him. The impatient congregation that had wondered at his prolonged tarrying in the sanctuary, rightly concluded that he had had a vision. Although visions were by no manner or means everyday occurrences, the people were not so skeptical in those times, as to discredit them entirely. Thus, the stage was set, the long expected message had come: *The Lord is drawing nigh!*

> An angel stands before God, come in greatly rejoicing to the honored father Zachariah, while he was serving in the Temple, and brought great glad tidings of Thee Who art equal of the Angels: how Thou, O all-blessed, was to become the Forerunner and the friend of the Lord (*Canon of the Synaxis of St. John the Baptist*).[1]

Six months later, the message was carried to the very heart of the human race. In spite of its magnitude, it was heard that day only by an innocent and sinless girl. Insignificant in the eyes of the great world, living quietly in the village of Nazareth in the Galilean hills, Mary was the chosen of God. He who sees into the very heart and soul of man, found in her what no other human had been able to proffer, a pure and sinless selfhood. Mary's innocence was one of choice, not of ignorance; her will was to will God's will. Herein lies Mary's greatness, in her utter obedience which fashioned her into the perfect link to join God and man. She alone, of all the generations of womankind, was found worthy to give manhood to God. The thought is staggering to us as indeed it was to her.

St. Luke's lovely account of the Annunciation is drawn with a measured economy of words. He has left it to our imagination to paint in the details. The scene has been dear to painters down the ages. But what pen or brush could ever do it justice? It is only with the inner eye of the spirit that we can realize what that moment must have been when the angel came in to her and said: "Hail, thou that art highly favoured, the Lord is with thee: blessed art thou among women!" (Lk. 1:28). "Blessed," Gabriel called her. He gave Mary that title and it was to remain beloved to all generations.

Wonderful beyond compare must that hour have been when the young girl, alone in her tiny whitewashed room, became aware that she was in the presence of an angel of God. She felt the great wings spread over her, she looked upon the perfect face and steadfastly met the gaze of heavenly eyes that held both promise and understanding. Mary was not afraid of the angel, only troubled because she could not fathom the meaning of his greeting, and bewildered, sought for an explanation.

"O Angel, help me to understand the meaning of thy words. How shall what thou sayest come to pass? Tell me clearly, how shall I conceive, who am a virgin maid? and how shall I become the Mother of my Maker."[2]

"I stand before thee in fear, as a servant before his mistress, and in awe I am afraid to look at thee now, O Maid. In His good pleasure shall the Word of God descend upon Thee, as dew upon the fleece" (*Canon of the Annunciation*).[3]

It was an absolute and perfect moment of meeting between two beings, one heavenly, the other human, at one because both their wills fulfilled God's will. Obedience was to both the law of their being, only their knowledge as yet was not equal. In the lovely words of the *Akathistos*:

The holy one, seeing herself in chastity, said greatly daring unto Gabriel: "Thy dark saying seems hard to my mind; what birth of a seedless begetting dost thou name?" The Virgin, yearning to know the knowledge unknowable, made clamor to the servitor, "from a maiden womb how may a child be born? Tell me." To her he said, fearing yet crying out: "Hail, keeper of things kept silent. Hail, of Christ's wondrous begetting . . . . Hail, much sung marvel of angels."[4]

Mary did not protest her unworthiness, her incapacity to fulfill this task; with characteristic wholeness of personality, she remained the same. Obedient and serene, she bent her head and said: "Behold the handmaid of the Lord; be it unto me according to thy word" (Lk. 1:38). Was ever greatness so humbly accepted!

Gabriel, the man of God, the great heavenly messenger, knelt down before a mere slip of a girl, crossed his hands upon his breast, and bowed before one greater than himself. So did the holy Fra Angelico envision the wonderful scene of that blessed day. That man of God had met the perfect human being, and surely his angelic nature did rejoice. More freely and gloriously than at any time since the fall of Lucifer could he now adore, praise, and thank his Creator: soon the fallen human brothers would be recalled to their pristine place, and would enter the new life! At last, through one perfect human being God would come amid his people and redeem them!

A prince of the angels was sent from heaven to say to the Theotokos, "Hail!" And seeing Thee, O Lord, take bodily form at the sound of his bodiless voice, he was filled with amazement and stood still, crying to her thus:
Hail, thou through whom joy will shine forth:
Hail, thou through whom the curse will cease.
Hail, thou restoration of Fallen Adam:
Hail, thou redemption of the tears of Eve . . . .
Hail, thou Depth hard to perceive even for the
        eyes of angels . . . .
Hail, thou Star who dost make the Sun appear: . . . .
Hail, thou through whom the Creator becomes a newborn child.
Hail, thou Bride unwedded![5]

According to the Gospel of St. Matthew (Mt. 1:18-25), the angel of the Lord appeared in a dream to Joseph, Mary's espoused. Joseph was, as the chronicle tells us, "a just man"—one who observed the Jewish Law in every detail. Because he was so deeply law-abiding, Joseph was not only saddened, but troubled, when he heard that his bride, whom he had not yet taken into his home, was with child. Betrothal was almost equivalent to marriage and could not be broken off without a formal divorce. A Jewish husband could divorce his wife if she did not please him, but the legal penalty for Mary's supposed fault was stoning. We can understand Joseph's spiritual conflict, torn as he was between his love for Mary and his anxiety to do the right thing.

In his great bewilderment, Joseph earnestly sought God's will. Because his love for Mary (and we can believe in his fundamental kindliness) was at odds with the prescriptions of the Law, his prayers for guidance were all the more intense, and even while he slept the problem did not leave him.

Dreams belong to the imponderable, to the mysterious time of sleep in which the body rests but the soul and mind have an activity of which we have little knowledge. The Gospel does not say that Joseph dreamed of an angel, but that the angel *appeared* to him in his dream. His spirit had remained at the level to which his prayers had lifted him while awake. Through the purity of his petition he stood at the threshold of heaven where he had laid his very human problem.

Joseph was sensitive to the divine visitation and quick to comprehend the luminous moment.

> Looking on Thee, O Unwedded One, and dreading a hidden wedlock, O Sinless One, the chaste Joseph was riven in mind with storms and doubts; but having learned that the begetting was of the Holy Ghost, he said, "Alleluia!"[6]

The guardian angel is very close to all men when they sleep. Only we, unlike Joseph, are seldom predisposed by prayer, simple devotion and singleness of desire, and thus cannot hear or see him. We cannot at will see the heavenly host nor should we ask for such a vision, but at the same time, we must not build up impenetrable walls of disbelief and earthbound pre-occupations so that the angels cannot penetrate our consciousness to protect and guide us.

The angels, although bodiless, are no less real in dreams than in our waking hours. In sleep our prejudices and disbeliefs are less active than when we are in possession of our argumentative faculties. In any case, it is the humble, worshipful frame of mind and receptive spirit that are essential, as is a clear conscience. The guardian angel watches over our spirit as well when we sleep; the purer our thoughts, the closer he comes. Not in vain has our Mother the Church taught us evening prayers in which we confess our faults so that we may rest peacefully in body and mind:

> From all ill dreams defend our eyes,
> from nightly fears and fantasies,
> Tread under foot our ghostly foe
> that no pollution we may know(From the Benedictine *Breviarium Monasticum*).

The interpretation of dreams has worried the ancient and the modern mind, but the pure in spirit have no such trouble: to them the meaning is clear. When indeed the angel illumines them, why all for them is then made plain.

Indeed, "Blessed are the pure in heart: for they shall see God" (Mt. 5:8).

¹*The Festal Menaion*, trans. by Mother Mary and Archimandrite Kallistos Ware, with introd. by Prof. Georges Florovsky. London: Faber and Faber, 1969, p. 394.

²*Ibid.*, p. 449.

³*Ibid.*, p. 551.

⁴*Kontakion and Ikos 2*, trans. from Greek by Fr. Vincent McNabb, O.P. Oxford: Blackfriars Publications.

⁵*Festal Menaion*, p. 454.

⁶*Akathistos*, hymn to the Birthgiver of God, Kontakion IV.

# II

## The Angels at Bethlehem

*1. The Shepherds* (Lk. 2:8-14)

The choir of the shepherds abiding in the fields was overwhelmed by the strange sight they were counted worthy to behold: For they looked upon the all-blessed Offspring of an all-pure Bride; and they also saw the ranks of the bodiless angels who sang—in praise of Christ the King, incarnate without seed (*Canon of the Nativity*, Canticle III).

In the stillness of a starry night a group of shepherds guarding their flocks, had one of the most lovely visions ever known to man. So dear has this event ever been to countless generations, so many hymns praise it, so many painters have depicted it, that the real meaning tends to get lost. The account has become to many but a charming legend, while others have tried to rationalize it.

One of the symbolic meanings given the appearance of the angels to the shepherds outside Bethlehem is that Christ's message was for those of poor and lowly estate. But surely, Christ's message is addressed to *all* men, high and low, without exception, though those lowly and humble of spirit would naturally accept it most gladly, whatever their social standing. Pride of intellect is not the exclusive property of those who sit on thrones, but it is to be found in cottage as well as palace. Pride is less present, however, among those who live close to nature, who sleep under God's open sky, as shepherds do. They come closer to the wonders of heaven. It is as if the roofs of houses become more than a protection from the inclemency of nature and turn into spiritual blankets cutting off the soul from the purity of free communication with God.

Which of us, who have wandered out into a lonely spot on a still, starry night, has not been moved by a feeling of wonder, has not sensed things that are out and beyond our reach? Shepherds spend long periods of time in this atmosphere where communion with nature is as natural as breathing. They read the signs of the heavenly bodies with ease; with them it is second nature, not superstition. They are aware of their own smallness; contemplation comes to them in the great loneliness, right there where they live, and as a matter of course.

If we read St. Luke carefully, we shall see that the description is a sober one: it follows up with no flowery detail, it sets forth the event in simple words and without introduction. The angel of the Lord appears suddenly in the shepherds' midst so that they were fear-struck. The angel of the Lord repeats once again the well-known words: "Fear not." Always this quieting of fear, as if conveying to man the interrelation with the world of the spirit as one good and normal, nothing to be afraid of. The angels come to those who basically can accept them without questioning the evidence of their own senses. Thus, the glorious message was given first to those who, living close to God, could see and understand with a talent what sophisticated minds would not. The message is to all men, but not all will comprehend it.

The story of the angelic appearance to the shepherds is no legend or allegory; indeed, what point would such a legend have? St. Luke was writing to an intellectual Roman: the Most Excellent Theophilus, for whose instruction (as well as that of other Romans) he had gathered and recorded the facts concerning Jesus. One of these facts was the visit of the shepherds to the stable of Bethlehem. There they found a newborn child wrapped in swaddling clothes, lying in a manger, strange enough even in all conscience, which was proof to these simple, trusting men that their senses had not played them false. The child proved that what they had heard and seen was true, and what they had heard and seen convinced them that here was the Savior, born as the sacrificial lambs were being tended, born just where the sacrificial lambs they tended were born: in one of nature's caves! Here was the true "Gospel," the "Good News" from God who himself had taken the initiative in making it known to men.

To read more into this event than the words say is to rob it of its beauty and, especially of its true sum and substance: the Birth of Christ. The Incarnation in itself was so stunning an event that it needs no allegories nor legends to enhance it. Why should the sight of the heavenly host need explaining when the Incarnation cannot be explained any more than creation can be explained. The further science delves, the more unknown it uncovers. No amount of talk or writing has changed the fact of Jesus in history. It is curious, though, that those who believe in him will yet seek to belittle the apparition of the angels, an event in itself so much smaller than the Incarnation. They would deny man any participation in the joy of the angels and through them in that of all creation. Would we limit that joy to our own small world, now in an age discovering the immensity of the cosmos? Surely, we are being very small if we think that the Incarnation has importance for us alone.

If we want to read explanations into the vision of the heavenly hosts, would we not come closer to reality by seeing in St. Luke's description a brief moment of insight; an intuition of a *plenum* existing far outside and beyond our knowledge. Was it not a flash of recognizing a world only now bordering upon our ken? The angels link us with those other worlds to which we always belonged, although we did not know it scientifically.

To explain away the experience of the shepherds is like shutting the window and drawing the blinds to shut off a magnificent view. It is to deny the glory of space and the power of man to know and acknowledge the world of the spirit. We are much closer to the truth in humbly accepting the account as it stands than in finding interpretations for it.

Yes, "Glory to God in the highest and on earth peace, good will towards men" (Lk. 2:14). The beauty of this song of praise and pure joy rang out in the heavens at Bethlehem, a joy so great that it has gone on echoing down the ages in the hearts of all true believers. A joy that obliterates distances between man and man, man and God. A happiness intensely personal, yet belonging to all men and all creation. A joy at the birth of a Savior, a joy superbly in our midst for all time.

> He who rules the heights of heaven, in His compassion has become as we are, born of a Maiden who has not known man (*Canon of the Nativity*, Canticle III).
>
> The humble Virgin, gives her breast to the Child, and in the background, suggested by these angels, the aeons manifest themselves, the heavens with their cosmic dimensions, a vast shadow losing itself in the Milky Way; the Virgin with her diadem of stars feeds with celestial milk the Savior of the aeons . . . .[1]
>
> Thus the archangels are associated with all the mysteries in the life of Jesus. Gabriel presides over the Annunciation, over all Annunciations, over Mary, over Zachariah, over Joseph, over the shepherds, over the procession in which he is the supreme figure. Raphael presides over divine acts, miracles, healings; he is the angel of Bethseda, who troubles the waters of healing, and he is also the comforter, the protector. It is the angels who minister to Jesus in the wilderness at the Temptation and comfort him at the Agony.[2]

## 2. The Three Wise Men (Mt. 2:1-12)

The belief that all the stars are under the dominion of the angels has corroboration in the star that guided the three wise men of the East to worship the Christ Child in Bethlehem.

The Magi, or wise men, of those days believed the stars could be the angel of a great man, the *fravashi*, or counterpart. This word, *fravashi*, should not disturb us because the angel in a sense is the spiritual counterpart of our virtues forming a natural complement to the man over whom he watches, just as the devil can be the wicked counterpart of our bad instincts. The Magi were men of science, astrologers; therefore, they would, in their patient watching of the heavens, best understand an angel that revealed himself as a comet rather than any other semblance. Where to the simple shepherd the appearance of the angel of the Lord in human shape was credible, to the astrologer a new unexpected movement of an astral body was plausible.

Let the people that once sat in darkness see the light shine forth that knows no evening (*Canon of the Nativity*, Canticle V).

The humble and uneducated man and the man of science, both in their own way, saw and understood the sign, and in obedience to it went to worship the young child. Herein lies the great lesson of both these stories. Knowledge and simplicity, wealth and poverty, were laid at the feet of Jesus. In the Magi science paid homage to religion; in the shepherds, the ordinary man revered God. Alongside each, the angel was the guiding spirit and the joyful participant in the worship.

Thus it is today, too, where every creature follows his true destiny, which is to love and worship God. But we often refute this destiny, which is to love and worship God. Like Satan, we prefer, in selfish egocentrism to follow the path of our own aggrandisement and like him we fall, in strife and sorrow, further and further from God, our one and only true goal.

Not so, the wise men. As Ruskin so beautifully puts it: "These men, for their part, come—I beg you very earnestly to note this—not to see, nor talk—but to do reverence. They are neither curious nor talkative, but submissive."[3]

This submissiveness allowed the Magi to be warned in a dream not to proclaim the successful attainment of their quest. They did not go to show off before Herod. They moved on, humbly rejoicing, knowing that in God's good time all would be revealed.

Daily fidelity gives man a quicker awareness of Truth. The life-example of the shepherds and the wise men, patiently faithful to their jobs, close to God in their understanding is such as we should gladly follow. Even if we cannot outwardly see, we may within our hearts hear the heavenly hosts, and with them praise the newborn King.

Christ in strange wise comes to His own. Let us make ourselves strangers to sin, and let us receive Him who dwells in the souls of the meek (*Canon of the Nativity*, Canticle IV).

### 3. The Flight (Mt. 2:12-20)

"Arise and flee . . . ." While the Holy Family was still in Bethlehem, while the songs of praise were still singing in their ears, and while the visit of the Magi was vivid in their mind's eye, there came the unexpected call to flee! Once more we hear no protests from Joseph, nor from Mary. Obedient to the angel's bidding, they with the young child take the bitter road of exile.

Here we stand before one of the hardest of life's riddles: When is it right to stand and meet disaster and when is it right to flee? For, in which way is God's purpose best served? The angel's command to Joseph was to "Arise . . .and flee." This was no running away, no abandoning of a cause and people, but the fulfilling of a call. It was not out of fear but out of obedience that Joseph took the young Child and his Mother from the false security of a known environment into the apparent insecurity of the unknown.

The Evangelist leaves it to our imagination to follow those three lonely figures undertaking the perilous journey through the desert. Egypt was inevitably connected, in the minds of the Israelites, with serfdom and exile, although at the time of Jesus there was a prosperous and cultured Jewish colony living there. What stands out in Matthew's simple unadorned tale is the confidence with which, trusting the angel's word, Joseph unquestioningly took the perilous trip, exposing the Mother and Child to the hazards of a journey into foreign parts. This too, is a picture dearly loved by artists who have each depicted it according to his particular conception. But one feature in common to all pictures and verbal descriptions, is the protecting light that enfolds the Holy Family. There is a subordination of all danger in face of the spiritual strength of those three lone figures, apparently unprotected in a hostile world. Not all artists have painted the power they felt there, namely, that of the guardian angel, but there is no picture in which he is not somehow felt, even when not apparent.

The flight into Egypt should be a comfort and a sustenance to many who today wander far from home and country. For they, too, have left all for the sake of preserving something more precious than all else in the world, namely, freedom of worship.

> Beholding the Child in exile, let us too become exiles from the world and carry our thoughts to Heaven. For this reason God the most High appeared on earth as a lowly man to draw on high those who cry to Him: Alleluia! (*Akathis Hymn to the Theotokos*, Kontakion VIII).

"Arise . . .and flee." Joseph did not go alone, but he took with him the Mother and Child, as it is also always our privilege to do. The Christian can always have God with him in his heart. "Lo, I am always with you, even unto the end of the world" (Mt. 28:20).

It is that which man carries within his heart that matters, "let it be the hidden man of the heart" (1 Pt. 3:4), as St. Peter puts it. If we flee, this alone should be the motive of our flight. Then it may be given us to hear the voice of the angel calling us as he called Joseph to return not to where his desire led him, but to where he was sent, the insignificant Nazareth. Here, too, lies a lesson for the exiled: the way and destination of our return may not be of our own choosing, but we shall have to return to the place and the task which God has prepared for us.

Let the prayer to the angel guarding our wandering be that we, who carry Christ in our hearts, may unfailingly follow the path of righteousness. It may well be that we shall find the right way by the doors that are closed rather than by those that are open. Not to many is given the clear sight that was Joseph's, but his quiet confidence and implicit faith may easily be ours. Thus, the angel's guiding hand upon our shoulder may be felt by any of us, and the Psalmist's words ring true: "For he shall give his angels charge over thee, to keep thee in all thy ways. They shall bear thee up in their hands, lest thou dash thy foot against a stone" (Ps. 90:11-12).

The so intensely human experiences of the Incarnate Word lived by Jesus illustrate in many instances his attitude concerning angels. Deeply inter-woven, his life and teachings should always be the model by which to guide our own lives. "He that believeth in me, the works that I do, shall he do also" (Jn. 14:12). We shall see that Jesus' teaching about angels and his personal contacts with them are an integral part of his mission. To ignore this is sheer foolishness

As the late Jean Danielou, who has written so convincingly about the angels and their mission, says:

> We witness the appearance of the archangels who, with Gabriel, are henceforth to surround the Manhood of Jesus, to hover in the back-ground, but always to be present, and not so much to praise as to be themselves that Glory in the highest heavens which already surrounds the Child conceived in the Virgin's womb. Here is the very mystery of the Man-God, whom the angels worship, and who annihilates Himself in the flesh; here, side by side with the earthly appearances, is the celestial, hypercosmic event of the Incarnation.
>
> Henceforth we shall find Jesus everywhere surrounded by this twofold presence. There is the procession of angels that everywhere accompanies the Word, of which they are the radiance, the fringe of the intellectual realm; there is also the nakedness of the Cradle. We shall find the same contrast in the Agony, where twelve legions of angels are present at the very moment of the kiss of Judas . . . .[4]

The Christian who leaves the angels out of his concept of God's world is like a man who thinks he holds in his hands a faultless crystal goblet filled with the elixir of life; yet all the time the goblet has a leak and part of the precious liquid escapes him. The life of the New Testament is to accept all of it, not to select and reject arbitrarily, according to some sort of criterion established by ourselves on the foundation of our limited understanding.

Only when we accept and live the entire teaching of Jesus Christ, when we drink the whole cup, are we going to be whole and integral ourselves and attain the deification—Godlikeness of which the Fathers of the Church spoke with such assurance and which so few of us fully grasp.

All the angelic kind marveled at Thy great work of Incarnation seeing the inaccessible God become accessible to all as man, dwelling with us and hearing all cry: Alleluia! (*Akathis Hymn*, Kontakion IX).

[1]Jean Danielou, *The Presence of God* (trans. of *Le Signe du Temple*, by Walter Roberts). London: A.R. Mowbray and Co., Ltd., pp. 21-22.
[2]*Ibid.*, p. 22.
[3]Letter XII, December 23, 1871.
[4]Danielou, p. 21.

# III

## The Angels of the Temptation

And Jesus being full of the Holy Spirit returned from Jordan, and was led by the Spirit into the wilderness . . . (Lk. 4:1).

Jesus had gone down to the Jordan to be baptized, not because he needed to be cleansed from sin, but rather as a visible sign by which, in all humility, he put himself on the level of all sinners. He is the Lamb of God who thus takes upon himself the sins of the world. Jesus never manifested himself in isolation, but with complete sympathy he shared the needs of all people.

Baptism was for Jesus an hour of concentrated dedication and consecration to his Father's will. The heavens had opened to him and the voice of the Father spoke to him.

From the start of his history, fallen man, whom the devil had vanquished, could nonetheless look forward to the promise of that day when he would overcome his adversary. The victory of man over Satan is the very goal of Christ's mission. He came that " . . .he might destroy him that had the power of death, that is the Devil" (Heb. 2:14). In St. John's words: "For this purpose the Son of God was manifested, that he might destroy the works of the Devil" (1 Jn. 3:8). The battle starts for Jesus immediately upon his baptism in the Temptations he himself described to his apostles. It was for the first time since his fall from Paradise that man—in the Son of Man—finds himself face to face with Satan. The Temptations that beset Jesus during the forty days of fasting and prayer were the quintessence of all the problems that would dog his footsteps all the way to the Cross, and mankind's forever after.

We can grasp the entire meaning best if we keep in mind that Jesus fought Satan on Satan's own level; as "the Son of Man" he took upon himself the entire life-wrecking sinfulness and weakness of mankind and overcame the Adversary precisely there where he had originally pulled man down.

The sequences of the Temptations is given in different order by St.

Matthew and St. Luke. We shall follow St. Matthew's account as it seems the most logical sequence, though actually it is the content alone that is important. St. Mark devotes only two verses to the incident, important to our study because of the reference to the ministration of the angels.

During his ministry the need of food and rest was going to represent a very real problem to Jesus. His journeys were to be long, and he would expend much energy when preaching and healing. He would also have to ask for the same hardiness from his followers as he did from himself. "The foxes have holes, and the birds of the air have nests; but the Son of man hath not where to lay his head" (Mt. 8:20). Frequently he would have to forget his bodily hunger and thirst so as to minister to the spiritual demands of others, and "...His disciples prayed him, saying, Master, eat. But he said unto them, I have meat to eat that ye know not of" (Jn. 4:31-32). Being every inch a true man and a hard working one at that, hunger and the sheer bodily desire for repose must often have been much greater than we usually make allowance for. "For there were many coming and going, and they had no leisure so much as to eat" (Mk. 6:31). But Jesus never gave in to these needs, if it were at the expense of others. We hear only of his resting in prayer.

Yet in the wilderness it was just this that he was doing: *praying*. And it was just this time which Satan chose for his attack.

With the Incarnation of the Word, the advent of the Christ in our midst, right and wrong became clearly defined. It ceased to be a matter of opinion. As God manifested himself evil lost its nebulous character and Satan showed himself in his true colors, a real personality, believing that he was strong enough to tempt the Son of Man.

Until the coming of our Lord, Satan had it pretty much as he had liked. The world was at his mercy, and he had but scant mercy. But now through the Incarnation his rule was in imminent danger. He could no longer trust to equivocal confusion, but had to muster his forces, pit himself personally against the only One who could destroy him. Thus Satan attacked Jesus at the very outset of his mission. Because true prayer is the sharpest weapon against him, Satan always tries to blunt its blade. We have frequent examples of this in the lives of the saints, especially the Desert Fathers.

The desert encounter, therefore, is no fanciful story, but positive history. Everything that Jesus taught he also intensely experienced. He faced evil. He had no illusions about it. He knew its reality and the need to fight it positively and radically. Thus Jesus told the disciples the story of his own dramatic encounter with the forces which opposed him.

Jesus' first trial was to withstand during his long fast the perfectly natural craving for food. Jesus is, then, at the same time, the man who needs nourishment and himself the Word of God by which man is fed.

The Devil himself wished to know whom he was truly facing. Who was this

Being who did not hear him? He felt that he faced one of a mightier normal strength than any of the great patriarchs and prophets who had gone before. Satan sensed, but did not know before whom he stood.

The angels did recognize the Son of God, but we cannot know if they were permitted to know the entire implication of the Incarnation. They were in the background, ever ready to serve him, knowing that alone they could not save man from the grasp of Satan, and they rejoiced that the Son of God himself had personally descended to lead them in their mission. So many of the Fathers interpret the angelic role following the Incarnation as surrounding Christ at all times except upon his descent into hell.

Thus, the Devil, desiring to know whom he was facing, put him to the test. Had he, or had he not, the power to turn stones into bread? But Jesus answers Satan in words based on Scripture and the past experience of Israel, "Man shall not live by bread alone, but by every word that proceedeth out of the mouth of God" (Dt. 8:3).

How clearly Jesus readjusts the balance! Temptation ever lurks in our legitimate needs. There is nothing wrong in our being subject to material necessities. It is our trust in them *alone* that is ill-placed. The Fathers of the Church teach that by Baptism Satan is expelled from our inner selves and can therefore approach us only from without, primarily through the needs of the flesh. The flesh itself is no enemy, but the means by which we succumb.

Next Satan placed Jesus on the pinnacle of the Temple and said: "If thou be the Son of God, cast thyself down, for it is written, He shall give his angels charge concerning thee . . . ." Once again Satan wants to make sure of who exactly his adversary is. The Temptation for Jesus was to accede to the desire of giving this proof. Satan sought to prompt Jesus to take the short cuts, shun pain, disillusionment and death. Later on the words would be: "If thou be Christ, save thyself and us" (Lk. 23:39). But Jesus says: "It is written again, Thou shalt not tempt the Lord thy God." St. Luke has his reason for making this temptation the climax of his narrative, for there is subtlety and danger in it to a highly spiritual nature.

As for ourselves, there is always the danger of abusing God's gracious patience. One can become so sure of his forgiveness and of the sustaining presence of his angels as to become careless of sin and willfully do wrong, counting beforehand on his mercy. It is when we so "tempt God" that we shall find no angel's hands bearing us up, but rather the devil's derision dragging us down.

That Jesus was tempted, we have his own word. This gives startling realism to our own temptations. It takes them out of the realm of theoretical conjecture and places them plumb into everyday, concrete reality. At the same time, we must realize that Christ's temptations were spiritual and highly theological. Jesus' graphic narrative also tells us that in such moments of trial the angels stand aside and wait as they waited for him! Did their great and faithful hearts tremble in that hour when their Lord abased himself out of love for man, permitting himself to be tempted just as his disobedient creatures are? They must have longed to rush to his side, but no, they had to stand aside; the battle was not yet over!

Satan then showed Jesus all the kingdoms of the world, and the glory of them, saying that all could be his to reform at will would Jesus but bow down to him, Satan, accepting his might and power of worldly achievement! The full prospect was conjured up before his eyes of what it would mean to use his absolute power to oblige the world into accepting his teachings, to enforce our salvation. But the desire of personal power, on whatever level, is to disregard God, to usurp his province, to try and wrest from him what is his alone. "Get thee hence, Satan: for it is written Thou shalt worship the Lord thy God, and him only shalt thou serve." It is, indeed, the all-conclusive reply. Satan is beaten, but not yet conquered. This was to be only after the Crucifixion and the Resurrection of our Lord. For this reason, man is still engaged in the battle with Satan for the ultimate result is always the "age to come," for no individual in this world is as yet completed, except in Christ alone.

We have to bear in mind that

> Language descriptive of human heroism is entirely foreign to the New Testament. The events of the life and death of Jesus were not thought of as a human act, but as an act of God wrought in human flesh and blood, which is a very different matter.[1]

and "then the devil left him (for a while) and behold the angels came and ministered to him."

After the trials of the desert, the heavenly host surrounded to minister to their Lord with love and care; more completely was he their Lord at that moment than ever before: "Ye call me Master and Lord; and ye say well; for so I am" (Jn 13:13). Yes, Master, first of himself as man. This is his demand of us as well, to master ourselves and all temptation. Then, indeed, our angels are on hand to succor us. And this, too, is no fiction, but spiritual fact.

There is a subtle difference between us and the angels in the matter of temptation. Angels are not tempted as we are. Satan invented sin of his own volition and then tempted man. To man sin brought death, to the angels it brought degradation. Sin is not inherent to the angelic immortal nature as it is to our mortal one. This is Satan's and his angels' terrible damnation; they did what was not in their nature to do. Satan in his angry agony seeks to bring us under his sway and once we are in his power, we cannot of ourselves break it.

It is through Christ that we are set free from the power of sin. We never *have* to sin, although it is in our fallen nature to do so.

All wickedness, then, all impure passion are the work of their [the devils'] mind. But while at liberty to attack man . . .they have not the strength to overmaster anyone: for we have it in our power to receive or not to receive the attack.[2]

The Temptations of Jesus in the wilderness were not the end by a longshot, but only the beginning of the conflict for the redemption of man. The stage, however, was set; the forces of good and evil stood facing each other over the question of ultimate human destiny. Christ was not battling for the supremacy of God—never let us make that mistake—but for the salvation of man. Alone man cannot overcome the Prince of the world, for as St. Paul says:

Finally, my brethren, be strong in the Lord, and in the power of his might. Put on the whole armour of God, that ye may be able to stand against the wiles of the devil. For we wrestle not against flesh and blood, but against principalities, against powers, against the rulers of the darkness of this world, against spiritual wickedness in high places (Eph. 6:10-12).

We cannot win against the Devil, but Christ already has; we have but to take up our cross and to follow him. God became Man to set man free from the power that held him enthralled. Here is the great mystery, the wonder and the glory, a glory the angels participate in, but cannot bring about. The price of this triumph was the Cross, the transfiguring love of an all-merciful God.

To no true seeker after God is the flaming road through the wilderness spared. Yet, if he walk it—because Christ goes before him—he shall find the angels there to attend him, even as Jesus did.

Servant of God and my transcendent guardian, who are at all times by me a sinner, redeeming me from all the evil doings of demons, ever putting me onto the heavenly pathways, and urging me towards life uncorrupted, pray for me" (*Kontakion of the Canon of the Guardian Angel*).

---

[1]Gregory Dix, *The Shape of the Liturgy*. London: Dacred Press, 1945, p. 74.
[2]St. John of Damascus, *Exposition of the Orthodox Faith*, Book II, ch. IV, p. 20, in *Nicene and Post-Nicene Fathers*, Vol. IX. Grand Rapids, Michigan: Wm. B. Eerdmans Publishing Co., 1955.

# The Angels in the Ministry and Teaching of Our Lord

## 1. The Guardian Angel

Following the forty arduous days in the arid mountain wilderness overlooking Jordan, Jesus returned among men to teach, heal, and redeem. There is such great power, so much depth to his every word, that the commentaries written on them have filled numberless volumes from the time of the Apostles down to our own day. There is such wealth of meaning, such timelessness in his sayings that always and again a new and suitable sense comes to light in them, answering the needs of each consecutive age. His divine comprehensiveness and the depth of his human understanding render the teachings of Jesus unshakable, imperturbable.

One of the dearest and also very often misunderstood statements is the very one upon which we chiefly found our belief in the guardian angel. Pointing to a child, Jesus said:

> Take heed that ye despise not one of these little ones; for I say unto you,
> That in heaven their angels do always behold the face of my Father which
> is in heaven (Mt. 18:10).

This has given rise to the thought that children are angelic in nature and that when they die young they automatically become angels. This heresy in some instances has gone so far as to give birth to the idea that human beings generally, if very good, can become angels. There is no Scriptural authority for this outlandish belief, neither is this notion to be found in the New Testament Apocrypha, nor in the writings of the Fathers. Jesus quite clearly stated, when speaking of man's life after death that "...they are *equal* unto angels: and are the children of God, being the children of the resurrection" (Lk. 20:36). Equal, yes, but not transformed into. The angels are of a different race from men, they are spirits and were created angels, as we were created man, and not any other kind of animal or plant. There is a powerful and profound order in God's creation that cannot be upset. It is the desire to reverse this sta.e that is a sin, therefore we need a return to, not a change from, the God-made Law and Order.

Jesus showed us man transfigured and in his true light. There is subtle difference between the transfiguration and the transformation of man. The first of a spiritualization of substance; the second seems to indicate its remodelling. For men to become angels would be for God to upset his own order of creation in which each thing, life, and time have their appointed post. Man may become the equal of an angel, by virtue of the resurrection and through Christ—as we shall note more fully later—ascend even above them, but man never *becomes* an angel. Such a belief would fall within the heathen concept of re-incarnation or the transmigration of souls.

The quotation about the children's angel, taken in itself, would lead to the assumption that children have a guardian angel, but if we read it in the context of Matthew 18, we shall see that Jesus was concerned in defining the qualifications demanded of us for heaven. To be humble-hearted, or humble-minded, is the best passport to paradise.

> And Jesus called a little child unto him and set him in the midst of them, and said, Verily I say unto you, Except ye be converted, and become as little children, ye shall not enter into the Kingdom of Heaven (Mt. 18:2-4).

This was in answer to the question "Who is the greatest in the kingdom of heaven?" Jesus pointed out childlike qualities as the ideal to be striven for. He was not speaking of childishness, but of childlikeness. An inquiring mind, perseverance, innocence and trust are peculiar characteristics of children. A child knows no false pride nor false humility. Jesus was known to address his followers as "little flock." "Fear not, little flock" (Lk. 12:32). And, does he not again and again reassure us of being God's children? It is just under this qualification of his children that a guardian angel is given to us.

Jesus' words actually pinpoint the old proven belief in a guardian angel. This, according to Daniel (10:13), given especially to the nations, as the angel promised to Moses and seen by the people as a column of fire by night and a cloud by day. "My presence shall go with thee, and I will give thee rest" (Ex. 33:14). Isaiah, too, speaks of this angel: "In all their afflictions he was afflicted and the angel of his presence saved them" (Is. 63:9). David was more personal and saw the angel protecting all the truly faithful. "The angel of the Lord encampeth round about them that fear him" (Ps. 33:8). It remained for Jesus to make it clear that we each have our own angel. The Jews saw salvation through the community of Israel and as such a collective or communal angel, so to speak, sufficed. But Jesus taught that the community was redeemed through each individual, thus each of us as God's own particular child has a personal angel to enhance our human dignity.

> O Holy Angel, that keepest guard over my despondent soul and passionate life, leave me not a sinner nor depart from me . . . (Prayer to the Guardian Angel, *Orthodox Prayer Book*).

## 2. The Angels of Death and Justice

Also in the hour of death the angels are with us accompanying us over the threshold. Jesus tells us this in the beautiful parable of the rich man and Lazarus the beggar at his gate (Lk. 16:19-31). From this saying we may infer that our guardian angel is not of the same heavenly company which at the end of the world will sever the wicked from the good and whom we call the Angels of Justice.

Our guardian angel has accompanied us a long way, during the faltering steps of babyhood, through the escapades of childhood, and got us out of many a tight corner. (Which of us has not held his breath over some child's foolhardy prank and has not agreed that children *must* have a guardian angel!) The angel who has watched us through the years of our earthly life with all its ups and downs, now carrying us to the very threshold of the New Beginning, passes us over into other angelic hands—or so it would seem. In any case, we do not go out upon that last journey alone. An angel, or even several angels, are with us even then. This should be a true consolation to us when watching those we love go, or when preparing to do so ourselves. Not very different from taking a journey into a faraway country, is it? Therefore, the Church has prayers for the dying in which she invokes the presence of an angel of light to accompany the departing soul.

Enoch, whose descriptions of Sheol our Lord uses in the Lazarus parable, has a beautiful verse concerning the prayerful activity of the angels in our behalf: "And they petitioned and interceded and prayed for the children of men, and righteousness flowed before them as water."[1]

Jesus also spoke of the angels in their roles as the executors of God's justice. When explaining the parable of the tares among the wheat to his apostles (Mt. 13:24-41), Jesus points out that evil thoughts and impulses— the tares—are planted by the enemy, that is, Satan, in the midst of the good seeds. The tares, or the children of the Evil One will be gathered together at harvest time, and burned. Jesus goes on to say that "the reapers are the angels." This story's imagery of the angels accompanying the Son of Man is borrowed from that used by Enoch in describing God's majesty as he dispenses judgment. Our Lord makes an equivalent attestation following the parable of the dragnet cast into the sea: "...at the end of the world: the angels shall come forth and sever the wicked from among the just" (Mt. 13:49).

For, speaking of his Second Coming, Jesus once more depicts the angels as his heralds of fearful justice and retribution: "And he [the Son of Man] shall send his angels with a great sound of a trumpet and they shall gather together his elect from the four winds, from one end of heaven to the other" (Mt. 24:31; cf. Mk. 13:27).

The angels of themselves have no foreknowledge of events, they are only bent eternally upon the execution of God's will, the fulfillment of their deaconship, their stewardship. When describing the events of those last days, Jesus says: "But of that day and hour knoweth no man, no, not the angels of heaven, but my Father only" (Mt. 24:36).

At *the hour* it is Jesus himself who shall be our interpreter before the courts of heaven. He promises us his witness if we are true to his word. "Also I say to you; whoever shall confess me before men, him shall the Son of Man also confess before the angels of God" (Lk. 12:8). Evidently the angels await to see our attitude towards Christ. They expect us to be true to our Lord before they will show friendship. If we are disloyal we can expect nothing but pained disdain from them because of the uncompromising nature of their entire being. Disloyalty even Jesus will not defend. "But he that denieth me before men shall be denied before the angels of God" (Lk. 12:9). Terrifying the thought! St. Mark uses the word "ashamed" (Mk. 8:38), in place of "deny." In our day perhaps "freeze" is more appropriate because for people who live behind the Iron Curtain, fear of ridicule rather than fear of persecution makes *many* faithless. Our fickleness and instability may also be one of the reasons why our angels do not always see the face of God . . . .

### 3. The Devil and His Angels

Any discussion of angels in our Lord's ministry would be incomplete unless we spoke of the fallen angels also. The belief in demonic possession was a general one in Christ's day, a conception which many today consider unenlightened, obscurantist, and superstitious. To many, in those centuries, it was a popular interpretation applied to things that were not immediately explicable otherwise, or even understandable. Today, we use other words, but know almost as little about, say, the mentally disturbed, as people did when they believed generally in demonic possession and even indiscriminately categorized in this regard. Now, of course, we use electric shocks to "exorcise," still knowing very little of what is occurring. But Jesus "cast out devils" fully aware of what occurs. He fought evil in all its forms wherever he encountered it.

But it is not with the question of exorcisms that we are concerned here, so much as with Jesus' general teaching and attitude about the powers of evil. Jesus employed the language of his times. But we would be far off the mark if we thought that Jesus himself believed in myths. Rather, in all these accounts, we must see primarily the continuation of Jesus' battle with Satan which began in the wilderness. Jesus taught of the reality which is evil, and, that illness as such is the result of the world's collective sin, rather than any particular sin or any individual's sin. It is, simply, the direct outcome of Satan's power over the world. Some people Christ would pardon of their share in sin because of their spiritual qualities, and thus make them whole: "For which is easier, to say, Thy sins be forgiven thee; or to say, Arise and walk?" (Mt. 9:5). He spoke of the woman who had an infirmity for eighteen years, as being bound by Satan (Lk. 13:16), claiming she had as much right to be freed from him, as any ox or ass had to be loosened from the stall and led to watering. Thus Jesus considered his healing a freeing from evil, and only God's forgiveness could accomplish this. "It is not easy to forgive. Forgiveness is much more than laying aside claim to requital or revenge; it is love bearing pain and shame with strong will to redeem."[2] This indeed Jesus did to the full.

Jesus freed people not by denying the existence of evil, but by recognizing the validity of the existence of sin and the identity of its author whom he called "a liar, and the father of it," (Jn. 8:44), in other words, a real personality to be dealt against, overthrown and vanquished. When the Pharisees accused Jesus of casting out devils by Beelzebub, he said, ". . .if Satan is cast out by Satan he is divided against himself: how shall then his Kingdom stand? . . ." and further he says, "how can one enter into a strong man's house, and spoil his goods except he first bind the strong man?"; thus Jesus plainly means that either we bind Satan or he will bind us, and for this we need him, Jesus Christ, for: "He that is not with me is against me: and he that gathereth not with me scattereth abroad" (Mt. 12:24-30). It would be good if we would recall these words often.

There is another simile upon the habits of devils, one which we often must have experienced, but not always recognized. On occasion we feel very self-assured and good because we have just been purified by some spiritual exercise and find that we are terribly nonplussed that a perfectly trivial incident can completely upset our applecart. Jesus knew this only too well.

When the evil spirit comes out of a man, it wanders through waterless places looking for a rest, and when it fails to find any it says "I will go back to my house where I came from!" When it arrives it finds it clean and all in order. Then it goes and collects seven other spirits more evil than itself to keep it company and they all go in and make themselves at home. The last state of that man is worse than the first (Lk. 11:24-26).

Indeed we have always to be on guard against our archenemy and not rest upon our laurels, for not in vain did Peter call him "A roaring lion . . .seeking whom he may devour" (1 Pt. 5:8). We must keep our house actively filled with the spirit of God. There is no danger so great as spiritual complacency.

For in the parable of the tares and the wheat Jesus plainly says that the bad seed is planted by Satan or, in that of the sower, that he snatches the good seed from out of our hearts. Nor does he mince words as to the fate of the devils and their dupes: "Then shall he say also unto them on the left hand,

Depart from me, ye cursed, into everlasting fire, prepared for the devil and his angels" (Mt. 25:41).

One of our Christian characteristics, one of the signs that distinguishes us, sets us apart, is that we need not fear Satan: "And these signs shall follow them that believe; In my name shall they cast out devils . . ." (Mk. 16:17). The narrative in Mark (5:1-13) concerning the legion of devils which Jesus exorcised from a demented man, and which entered a herd of swine that rushed down the hill into the sea and was drowned, is of special interest. It is a scene which at first sight may be hard to understand; but, actually, it is quite clear. It is no allegory, the demons quite really are there. Jesus is confronted by an evil which calls itself legion "because we are many." They are well aware of the power they are facing and cry for mercy, for permission to go somewhere else. Jesus allows them to enter the herd of swine nearby. It promptly rushed down to the sea to death, not because Jesus willed it, but because evil is self-destructive. Evil destroys whatever it touches and, finally, itself. Materialistic despotic systems end in disaster, bringing hunger to great wheat-growing countries over which it rules, not because it desires famine, but because the seed of corruption is in the evil system itself. Those whom the devil enters he finally drives into the sea of despair, until he himself has nowhere to go, except deeper into the pit of his own wretchedness.

Jesus Christ knows the ultimate end of Satan, because he knew him from the first, and saw him fall from grace. "I beheld Satan as lightning fall from heaven" (Lk. 10:18). This is a reference to Isaiah's vision: "How art thou fallen from heaven, O Lucifer, son of the morning . . ." (Is. 14:12-17). Some commentators have seen in the above saying a cry of triumph on the part of Jesus when his disciples returned from a successful mission in which they had exorcised evil spirits. But a cry of triumph for Jesus would be out of character. It is much more a firm statement of fact, which for us is a proof not of superstitious belief but of true knowledge.

## 4. The Joy of the Angels

After telling the two exquisite stories of the one lost sheep and that of the mislaid silver-piece (Lk. 15:1-10), Jesus draws this analogy: "Likewise I say unto you, there is joy in the presence of the angels of God over one sinner that repenteth." The angels rejoice and receive each one of us who repents. What a lovely assurance of welcome, so much more generous, all-embracing and cleansing than any human re-acceptance and reconciliation. Another interpretation to these two parables is that the ninety-nine sheep or nine pieces of silver are the angels of those worlds which did not fall and are in no need of redemption. But the lost sheep is our world for which Christ left all the others to come in search of, the misplaced penny he gave his life to redeem.

To believe in the holy angels and to trust our guardian is unquestionably part of Christ's teaching. His words authorize our confidence in them and justify our humble prayer:

> Angel of the Lord, my holy guardian, who art given me of God to shield me: I earnestly pray thee enlighten me this day and from all harm protect me; in all good things advise me; and on the path of redemption guide me. Amen. (From an *Orthodox Prayer Book*).

[1]R.H. Charles, *The Book of Enoch*. London: Society for Promoting Christian Knowledge, p. 58.
[2]George A. Buttrick, "Exposition on St. Matthew," in *The Interpreter's Bible*, Vol. 7. New York: Abingdon Press, p. 35.

# V

## The End and the New Beginning

*1. Gethsemane*

As Jesus' ministry drew to its close, he was faced once again and more intensely than ever before, by the first temptations he had overcome in the wilderness. We must not forget the cryptic words closing that episode: "And when the devil had ended all the temptation he departed from him *for a season*" (Lk. 4:13). Satan continued his attacks in various ways; the possibility of power had often been thrust upon Jesus, at one time all but forcibly imposed upon him. "When Jesus therefore perceived that they would come and take him by force, to make him a king, he departed again into a mountain himself alone" (Jn. 6:15).

We know that Jesus warred unceasingly against evil in every form, but now at the end all the powers of evil conspired in one grand effort toward a final destruction. But this time, unlike the time of his birth, there was no angel appearing so as to tell him to flee. This time he had to face the issue alone, for now it was through his death that he would redeem his people and win the crown of glory. He could have called the angels to his aid, but he cast the thought aside. "Thinkest thou that I cannot now pray to my Father, and he shall presently give me more than twelve legions of angels?" (Mt. 26:53). His earthly friends were to fail him, his heavenly friends he was not to call! Well can we understand his heart-rending words: "Now is my soul troubled: and what shall I say? Father save me from this hour: but for this cause came I unto this hour" (Jn. 12:27). For this had he been born, been saved from the hands of Herod, been brought back out of Egypt, increased in wisdom and stature, been baptized, had taught, ministered and healed; all for the salvation of man and to break the power of Satan. "Now is the judgment of this world; now shall the prince of this world be cast out, and I, if I be lifted up from the earth, will draw all men unto me" (Jn. 12:31-32).

Here in a few words we have it all summed up: the eradication of all evil through the ultimate sacrifice. This oblation was not offered vainly to destroy something that did not exist! So busy are we to follow the teachings of Jesus that we tend to gloss over the end without which his teachings would have been like the teachings of so many other engrossing, interesting, enlightened men before and since, wonderful, assuredly, but not life-giving. The very casting out of the prince of this world was the reason for his Incarnation; it was also the reason for his death in the form in which it came:

> . . .if His body had fallen sick and the Word had left it in that condition, how unfitting it would have been! Should He Who healed the bodies of others neglect to keep His own health? How would His miracles of healing be believed, if this were so?
>
> Then, again, suppose without any illness He had just concealed His body somewhere, and then suddenly reappeared and said that He had risen from the dead. He would have been regarded merely as a teller of tales, and because there was no witness of His death, nobody would believe His resurrection . . . .
>
> Or how could the end of death and the victory over it have been declared, had not the Lord thus challenged it before the sight of all, and by the incorruption of His body proved that henceforward it was annulled and voided . . . .
>
> Death came to His body, therefore, not from Himself but from enemy action, in order that the Savior might utterly abolish death in whatever form they offered it to Him . . . . How could He have called us if He had not been crucified, for it is only on the cross that a man dies with arms outstretched? . . . Again, the air is the sphere of the devil, the enemy of our race who, having fallen from heaven, endeavors with the other evil spirits who shared in his disobedience both to keep souls from the truth and to hinder the progress of those who are trying to follow it . . . . But the Lord came to overthrow the devil and to purify the air and to make "a way" for us up to heaven . . . .[1]

If Jesus' example was to save and serve us in our own individual bout with evil and death, it had to be pertinent to each one of us. For his example to be real, he had to subject his divine power to human struggle and limitation, and to subordinate his human will to his divine will. It is only as we begin to comprehend this mystery's depth that we realize the immense loneliness of the Passion and the hours in Gethsemane. No wonder his sweat was like drops of blood. Jesus' mortal body did not want to die; his loving human heart could not endure the betrayal of his friends. As God he had full knowledge of the world's sin for which he was to die. All the grief of man up to his day and beyond was his own at that hour. He prayed the cup might pass him by in that last terrible struggle with an immeasurable sorrow only God could know as he comprehended the appalling sinfulness of which man was capable. He begged his nearest and dearest friends to watch with him, not to leave him alone. But they were tired, nor could they then have plumbed the depth of Jesus' grief and his longing for reprieve, not for himself, but for man. Twice he went back to his companions, as if seeking reassurance, an avenue of exit, but they slept!

There was no response but one: "O my Father, if this cup may not pass away from me, *except I drink it*, thy will be done" (Mt. 26:42). Except I drink it! Here lay the solution. No grief is overcome, no pain cured, no disaster made good unless the cup of sorrow is drained to its very dregs.

Once more, and for the last time, the angels stood by in agony of suspense; at that hour the entire destiny of man hung in the balance. Would Jesus accept the cup? There was still time to refuse. Judas had not yet given him the betraying kiss. Comprehending with an all-seeing clarity the whole immensity of his responsibility, the intolerable burden of the world's pain, Jesus bowed his head: "not my will, but thine, be done" (Lk. 22:42).

As he prayed in agony "there appeared an angel unto him from heaven, strengthening him" (Lk. 22:43). Now that the struggle was over and temptation defeated, the angels could gather round him to comfort and strengthen him to go unfalteringly through with the terrible course he had chosen. The triumphant march had started—the royal way was open. No one at that moment recognized in the man "despised and rejected of men: a man of sorrows and acquainted with grief," (Is. 53:3)—the King of Glory! But the angels *did!*

Only in reverence and silent, wordless, ineffable meditation can we rightly comment upon the angels' presence at that hour of supreme trial. In the Garden of Eden Adam had betrayed the human race; in the Garden of Gethsemane Jesus redeemed it.

### 2. Golgotha

Although we read nothing of either the good or the bad angels at the site of the crucifixion, in the light of what has gone before, we can hardly doubt that they were present. In a final effort to win an already lost battle, Satan sought to reach Jesus through the taunts of the sensation-loving crowds milling about the Cross.

"Let Christ the King of Israel descend now from the cross, that we may see and believe" (Mk. 15:32). With devilish perspicacity Satan entered one of Jesus' fellow sufferers: "If thou be Christ, save thyself and us" (Lk. 23:39). This is but a repetition of that first trial in the wilderness. "If thou be the Son of God, cast thyself down . . ." (Mt. 4:6). Jesus only answered by calling upon his Father, and submitted to the law of the flesh he had taken on himself.

Christian art through the ages has depicted angels as hovering above the Cross, and we may suppose that in truth they were present and accompanied their Lord even as he descended into hell to free those imprisoned there.

There is a belief that the Cross stood where once the Tree of Knowledge had grown. May we not carry this thought further and think that the Cross was of the same wood as that Tree? "In much wisdom is much grief: and he that increaseth knowledge increaseth sorrow" (Eccl. 1:18), said the prophet, and did not Jesus tell us to take up our cross and follow him? Indeed all the worldly knowledge we have accumulated has hardly made us happier or turned this earth into paradise. But now it is only by shouldering the weight of our knowledge that we can return whence we started and find that joy which no man can take from us and, thus, indeed, be equal to the angels. The full circle has been made. "For as in Adam all die, even so in Christ shall all be made alive" (1 Cor. 15:22).

The angels who once excluded Adam and Eve from Paradise now open the door for their return.

### 3. The Stone

Who removed the stone? That is the question which unbelievers cannot satisfactorily answer. All arguments to disprove the Resurrection get tripped over the stone that sealed Jesus' tomb. In an effort to belittle the great event of the Resurrection, a great deal is made of the slight differences in the four Gospels. But to no avail, for the essential facts are the same in all four Gospels. The stone was removed, and no human agent who could have rolled it away was ever found; neither then nor after two thousand years of probing, arguing and research.

All four Gospels tell us how, as dawn was breaking over Jerusalem, the women who had served the Lord in his ministry, hurried to the grave to perform the last embalming rites which had been curtailed on Friday evening because of the approaching Sabbath day: "And they said among themselves, who shall roll away the stone from the door of the sepulchre?" (Mk. 16:3). It is not surprising that they were filled with fear and that they promptly jumped to the conclusion that some enemy had stolen the beloved body of the Lord.

The Pharisees had had the same idea from a different viewpoint. They feared that the friends of Jesus would remove the body and claim that he had risen from the dead; in fact, they begged Pilate to set a guard at the grave to prevent such an eventuality. These guards were the ones who, as Matthew tells us, saw the angel roll away the stone.

> . . .There was a great earthquake: for the angel of the Lord descended from heaven, and came and rolled back the stone from the door, and sat upon it. His countenance was like lightning and his raiment white as snow: And for fear of him the keepers did shake, and become as dead men (Mt. 28:2-4).

The angel of the Resurrection was a messenger of power: an earthquake shook the earth, and angel hands easily rolled away the massive stone. The angel was a messenger of purity: he was like lightning in revealing light and like snow in his judgment on the darkness of men's deeds. He struck fear into men's hearts and held them in speechless awe . . . .[2]

The watchmen were bribed to hold their tongues or spread the word that the Apostles had stolen the body of Jesus.

But the Apostles themselves sat grieving and had no such thought. They had not even accompanied the women to the grave. One can then well imagine how bewildered the women were and how greatly alarmed. Once more the angel used the words that come as an eternal refrain all the way through the Holy Scripture: "Fear not!" Words full of tenderness and understanding that ever and again the angels use to calm the fears of man. How much more comforting were these words when the women, gripped by utter fear, looked into the empty tomb, for so it seemed to them until they saw the angels—"the one at the head, and the other at the feet, where the body of Jesus had lain" (Jn. 20:12). According to St. Matthew there was one, according to St. Luke and St. John, there were two. "Why seek ye the living among the dead?" (Lk. 24:5). Thus the angels questioned, in words that have rung down the centuries as one of the greatest questions ever put to man. In the tremendous impact of the moment we must not be surprised that the women did not all see exactly the same thing, nor relate it in exactly the same way! Besides, the event was committed to writing much later. However, what does emerge with altogether startling clarity is the emptiness of the tomb, and the presence of the angels.

Angels announce the Resurrection even as the news of the birth of Christ was heard in their heralding: "...behold I bring you tidings of great joy...." (Lk. 2:10); now of course the message is of still greater joy and meaning: "He is risen...go quickly and tell his disciples!" (Mt. 28:6-7).

At all times the angels surrounded our Lord on earth, even if their presence was not always manifest, but at the Great Hours they showed themselves to those who were worthy of seeing them.

The holy angels are part of Jesus' glory as is his halo. In our anxiety to simplify things, to have him come down to our level, and utterly dwelling upon his humanity, we tend to forget that he never ceased to be God, and, as such, he is never parted from his angels. Jesus is ever with us, as he promised: "Lo, I am with you always, even unto the end of the world" (Mt. 28:20). As we stand in his presence the angels are there too. As they removed the stone that closed his grave, so they remove from us the impediments that shut us away from the truth.

Gathered silently together on every Easter night, we leave the darkened church behind us, walking around in procession with our lighted candles as we solemnly chant, "The Angels in Heaven O Christ our Savior, sing Thy resurrection, enabling us on earth, to glorify Thee with a pure heart." We are retracing the steps as we have through the centuries of the faithful women, who on that first Easter morn wound their way, with fear in their hearts, through the garden searching for the beloved grave. Like them we stand before closed doors waiting. Involuntarily the heart bounds, as after the reading of the Holy Gospel the words burst forth in a shout of joy, "Christ is Risen!" The priest knocks on the door, "Open ye the gates for the King of Glory . . . ." The door swings open, the burning tapers turn the empty church into a sea of light, rose-scented incense mounts upward, the tomb is empty, but the glory of God is there. "Christ is Risen! Truly he is Risen!" resounds from every throat as the faithful flow back into the church to shout for joy and sing their song of praise; we on earth and the angels on high, in one great chorus of faith and unassailable knowledge, "Christ is Risen, risen from the dead!"

### 4. The Ascension and the Second Coming

For forty days after the Resurrection, Jesus walked among his friends, was seen by them, talked to them, supped with them, journeyed with them, taught them many mysteries regarding the Kingdom of God, broke bread with them, and entrusted to them their missionary task and their apostolic commission. Even then the Apostles hoped for another miracle restoring the dominion of Israel then and there. Patiently Jesus once more told them that times and seasons were in God's hands alone, enough for them that the Holy Spirit was to be among them.

> When he had said this, they saw him lifted up, and a cloud caught him away from their sight. And as they strained their eyes toward heaven, to watch his journey, all at once two men in white garments were standing at their side. Men of Galilee, they said, why do you stand here looking heavenwards? He who was, has been taken from you into heaven, this same Jesus, will come back in the same fashion just as you have watched him going into heaven (Acts 1:9-11).

There is a lovely Russian icon of this scene in which the two white figures mingle with the crowd of disciples. It expresses as no words can the intimacy of that moment. It is a joyful and reverent picture which should often come to our minds, for thus always are the angels with us as we look upward and adore Jesus the Christ!

The Mother of God, the Apostles and the two angels gaze upwards to the heavens where Jesus is already now seated upon the throne, presaging the second coming. The angels carry him aloft in an arch of light as seen by Isaiah and Ezekiel in their vision of God. Jesus the beloved is powerfully Christ the King, the Pantocrator, the fearful judge, yet ever blessing his people and assuring them of his unbounded love and mercy.

The angels accompanied our Lord to heaven in a cloud of glory: "God is gone up with a shout, the Lord with the sound of a trumpet" (Ps. 46:5). At the gates of heaven they shouted:

Lift up your heads, O ye gates; and be ye lifted up ye everlasting doors: and the King of glory shall come in. Who is the King of glory? The Lord strong and mighty, the Lord mighty in battle. Lift up your heads, O ye everlasting doors: and the King of glory shall come in. Who is the King of glory? The Lord of hosts, he is the King of glory (Ps. 23:7-10).

Thus the Son of Man enters that he may sit at the right hand of God: "Which he [God] wrought in Christ, when he raised him from the dead, and set him at his own right hand in the heavenly places" (Eph. 1:20).

Let us not be confused by the beauty of symbolic language, but seek rightly to understand it.

For how could He that is uncircumscribed have a right hand limited to place? Right and left hand belong to what is circumscribed. But we understand the right hand of the Father to be the glory and honour of the Godhead in which the Son of God existed as God before all ages and is of like essence to the Father and in the end became flesh, has a seat in the body, His flesh sharing in the glory. For He alone with His flesh is adored with one adoration by all creation.[3]

By the fact of our Lord's Ascension and his redeeming power, "man" is lifted up also with and through him and can be set even among the angels themselves. Above all, the all-pure Virgin Mary, the Mother of God, is higher than the cherubim and seraphim, and is rightly called Queen of Heaven.

The final role of the holy angels in the destiny of men shall be at the *Parousia* or Second Coming. For this particular belief we find several clear and authoritative references in the New Testament.

Jesus thus describes his Second Coming:

. . .they shall see the Son of man coming in the clouds of heaven, with power and great glory. And he shall send his angels with a great sound of a trumpet, and they shall gather together his elect from the four winds, from one end of heaven to the other (Mt. 24:30-31).

Following upon his parable of the ten virgins and upon that of the talents, Jesus again gives a portrayal of his Second Coming:

When the Son of man shall come in his glory, and all the holy angels with him, then shall he sit upon the throne of his glory (Mt. 25:31).

St. Paul found great comfort in the thought of Jesus Christ's triumphant return in which all the Christian faithful will be caught up in the same cloud to meet the Lord at the call of the archangel:

For the Lord himself shall descend from heaven with a shout, with the voice of the archangel, and with the trumpet of God: and the dead in Christ shall rise first: then we which are alive and remain shall be caught up together with them in the clouds, to meet the Lord in the air: and so shall we ever be with the Lord (1 Thes. 4:16-17).

At the crucifixion all wept, but as Jesus had promised, "your sorrow shall be turned into joy" (Jn. 16:20), so it was that at the final earthly parting, his Ascension, the apostles rejoiced.

The *Parousia* is in the future when we shall see the full glory of God and of his heavenly hosts. Meanwhile, the angels and archangels are right here with us, for they are our elder brethren, guarding us, teaching us, rejoicing and sorrowing with us, but above all swelling the chorus of our worship:

Therefore with angels and archangels, and with all the company of heaven we laud and magnify thy glorious Name; ever more praising thee, and saying, Holy, Holy, Holy, Lord God of hosts, Heaven and earth are full of thy glory: Glory be to thee O Lord Most High. Amen (*Book of Common Prayer*).

[1]St. Athanasius, *The Incarnation of the Word of God*, trans. by a Religious of C.S.M.V. New York: The Macmillan Company, 1951.

[2]George A. Buttrick, "Exposition on the Resurrection" in *The Interpreter's Bible*, Vol. VII. p. 616.

[3]St. John of Damascus, *Exposition of the Orthodox Faith*, Book IV, ch. 2, p. 74 in *Nicene and Post-Nicene Fathers* (Series Two), Vol. IX. Grand Rapids, Michigan: Wm. B. Eerdmans Publishing Co., 1955.

# VI

# Angels in the Young Church

## 1. St. Peter and St. John

St. Luke, the trustworthy historian, begins his account of the Acts of the Apostles with the story of the infant Christian Church in action: with the forty days of Jesus' appearances to his friends between his Resurrection and Ascension. During those forty days our Lord taught his followers many things pertaining to the Kingdom of God, thus instructing them in many matters that were not written down, but which have lived in the heart of the Church, and have been handed down from generation to generation in Holy Tradition.

The Ascension made no radical break in the relationship that Jesus had with his Apostles; "visibly he ascended to Heaven, and to their minds he was everywhere present."[1] At the moment when Jesus was taken from their sight, the Apostles were aware of the holy angels in their midst, and they remained aware of them throughout their missionary lives. The angels tread in and out of the activities of the saints from those early beginnings even unto this day. Today we take the appearances of angels with a pinch of salt, or in total unbelief. Nonetheless, there are occurrences in the Acts of the Apostles for which there are no so-called rational explanations. The events were real, unquestionably so, and unless we are prepared to disbelieve St. Luke, we shall follow and trust his report.

Obeying Jesus' last command on the Mount of Olives, and greatly heartened by the angels' words, the Apostles returned in joy to Jerusalem. There they would await the descent of the Holy Spirit upon them. The little band of once so badly frightened men now became a living and unconquerable force. Following Pentecost they boldly, fearlessly stood up and preached Jesus Christ, the resurrected Lord, to an astonished, disbelieving and increasingly hostile world. Notwithstanding disapproval in high places, they made converts among the people because of the many signs and wonders they wrought.

Long before the official pagan world took notice, the Jewish High Priesthood and Sadducean party, hoping to frighten the followers of Jesus into silence, had Peter and John arrested. The Sanhedrin forbade them to preach, an injunction which the Apostles disregarded and were consequently once more apprehended and thrown in the well-guarded common jail. Later, when the senate of the people of Israel sent to the prison for the Apostles to be brought before them for judgment, the prison, to everyone's astonishment, was found to be empty! The captain of the Temple guard and the Chief Priest were utterly mystified by the disciples' disappearance and quite nonplussed to discover them standing quietly in the Temple, openly teaching the people.

What had taken place? St. Luke narrates it briefly:

> . . .in the night, an angel of the Lord came and opened the prison doors, and led them out; go, he said, and take your stand in the temple; preach fully to the people the message of true life (Acts 5:19-20).

No further explanation is given; the Apostles themselves hardly seem to have regarded this intervention as miraculous, or even as an escape, but rather the opportune removal of an impediment which stood in the way of God's plan. The angel freed them from prison but not from danger; on the contrary, he sent them out to face danger by preaching openly. They taught the True Life as the living principle, not merely as a "way of life" but the transcendent supernatural life implanted in us by Christian Baptism which endows us, as we believe, with a heavenly guardian. The Baptismal prayer requests for the neophyte: "Yoke unto his (or her) life a radiant angel."

The Apostles unquestioningly accepted the angel's intervention and unhesitatingly obeyed his bidding. There is a joyous courage about this story, a touch of nonchalant audacity that all but makes one chuckle. It is as if Peter and John were sharing a huge joke with the angel over the self-righteous authorities by returning to preach in the very spot whence they had been forcibly ejected the previous day! Yes, the Apostles rejoiced when they were accounted worthy to suffer shame for Jesus Christ's sake. God's power over all things was so clear to them; and, further, death presented so few terrors that they could afford to laugh in the face of any personal peril.

## 2. St. Peter's Escape (Acts 12:3-17)

During a renewed and much more intense and violent persecution of those who at that time began to be known as *Christians*, Peter, once again, found himself behind bars. King Herod had just had James, John's brother, executed; then Peter was thrown into prison, this time securely confined so as not to escape. Meanwhile, the faithful prayed earnestly on Peter's behalf.

> On the very night before Herod intended to bring him out, Peter was asleep between two soldiers, chained with double chains, while guards maintained a strict watch in the doorway of the prison. Suddenly an angel of the Lord appeared, and light shone in the cell. He tapped Peter on the

side and woke him up, saying "Get up quickly." His chains fell away from his hands and the angel said to him, "Fasten your belt and put on your sandals." And he did so. Then the angel continued, "Wrap your cloak around you and follow me." So Peter followed him out, not quite clear as to the angel's realness: indeed he felt he must be taking part in a vision. Thus they passed right through the first gate that led out into the city. This opened for them of its own accord, and they went out, and when they had passed down the street the angel suddenly vanished from Peter's sight. Then Peter came to himself and cried out, "Now I know for certain that the Lord has sent his angel to rescue me from the power of Herod and from all that the Jewish people are expecting." As the truth broke upon him he went to the house of Mary, the mother of John surnamed Mark, where many were gathered together in prayer. As he knocked at the door a young maid called Rhoda came to answer it, but on recognizing Peter's voice failed to open the door from sheer joy. Instead she ran inside and reported that Peter was standing on the doorstep. At this they said to her, "You must be mad!" But she insisted that it was true. They then said, "Then it is his angel." But Peter continued to stand there knocking on the door, and when they opened it and recognized him they were simply amazed. Peter, however, made a gesture to them to stop talking while he explained to them how the Lord had brought him out of prison. Then he said, "Go and tell James and the other brothers what has happened." After this he left them and went on to another place.[2]

As we read this account, especially in its modern translation, it rings so true that we cannot doubt its genuineness. The remark "Then it is his angel," probably indicates that the brethren shared the current belief that the guardian angel was his charge's spiritual counterpart, thus making a visible distinction between the guardian angel and the Angel of the Lord.

Peter was rescued by God's messenger, not by his personal guardian. His escape was engineered by the Lord's direct intervention. The guardian angel assists man in his good endeavors, responds to man's will for right, while the Angel of the Lord acts outside of man's free choice through man's obedience to God's call. Peter, though very heavy with weariness and sleep, as to believe that he was taking part in a vision, unhesitatingly obeyed.

Always we come back to this fundamental law of life: obedience to God's will. Is it perchance because our modern ears are so little attuned to hearing God's ordinance that our eyes so seldom see his messengers?

### 3. St. Stephen (Acts 6:14—7:53)

St. Stephen the deacon was the first Christian martyr. He was an outstanding personality with great organizational talent. He was also a cosmopolitan scholar, well versed in the Scriptures, full of courage and conviction. Stephen's practical wisdom and spiritual force soon brought him into conflict with certain of the Jews who marched him off before the Sanhedrin, arraigning false witnesses against him.

When Stephen stood before his accusers, his defense was clear and bold, taking the Scriptures for a witness. When read with care, this speech is indeed remarkable, but we shall deal with it only as it concerns the angels in his tragic resume of Israel's age-long repudiation of her prophets and saints even unto the Messiah. When speaking of Moses in clear reference to Exodus (3:2), Stephen averred:

> . . .a vision came to him in the wilderness of Mount Sinai; a bush had caught fire; and an angel was standing among the flames . . . . It was this same Moses, the man whom they disowned . . .that God sent to be their ruler and their deliverer, helped by the angel he saw there in the bush . . . . He it was who took part with the angel . . .with our fathers, at the meeting in the desert. There he received the words of life to hand on to us: you are forever resisting the Holy Spirit, just as your fathers did . . .it was death to foretell the coming of that just man, who you in these times have betrayed and murdered; you who received the law by angels and did not keep it (Acts 7:30-53, Knox trans.).

Among those present who heard Stephen and gave silent consent to his execution was a young man by the name of Saul, who many years later, himself well upon the way to martyrdom, was to use the same words: "Its [the law's] terms were dictated by angels, acting through a spokesman" (Gal. 3:19), and again, "The old law which only had angels for its spokesman" (Heb. 2:2). These are two of the very few verbal echoes we have between the Acts of the Apostles and the Epistles of St. Paul.

The angels of the Old Testament ordained the law, but once the Lord had himself taken the redress of the world upon his own shoulders, the angels became the friends of man. By the new dispensation of grace and truth, the relationship of Christian and angel to each other becomes so close that at certain times, at particular supreme moments, a singular resemblance becomes apparent between them.

St. Stephen, whose superior spirituality enabled him, while yet on this earth to see the heavens open for him and Jesus standing on the threshold to receive him, was so transfigured that those beholding him at his trial, " . . .fastened their eyes upon him, saw his face looking like the face of an angel" (Acts 6:15). Through the great purity which his nature had attained Stephen bore the marks of the heavenly prototype, and we may presume he transcended his angel as he walked through martyrdom into the open arms of his Lord.

### 4. Cornelius (Acts 10:1-23)

In those first years of Christianity, the chasm between Jew and non-Jew was immensely great, almost impossible to bridge; even Jesus seldom bridged it, although most certainly in his teaching intended to include all people for his love was truly universal. Nonetheless, to his disciples, contact with Gentiles was not only deeply distasteful, but utterly irreconcilable with their rabbinical upbringing. It required a direct heavenly intervention to make Peter break through the racial and religious law of his people. One noon, as he prayed upon the housetop of a tanner in Joppa, Peter had a vision in which the Lord's voice bade him eat non-kosher food. Close upon this singular experience, Peter was informed that a Gentile delegation waited upon him outside, calling him to the house of a certain Cornelius, a Roman centurion in Caesarea.

> Ye know, said Peter, how it is an unlawful thing for a man that is a Jew to keep company or come unto one of another nation; but God hath showed me that I should not call any man common or unclean (Acts 10:28).

The centurion's request also was quite unusual; it was hardly customary for a Roman to request a favor from someone of a conquered nation. But Cornelius, though most likely a Gentile adherent of the synagogue, close to God in heart and mind, was granted this vision. The angel of the Lord appeared to him and said, "Cornelius . . .thy prayers and thine alms are come up for a memorial before God" (Acts 10:4). Was this perhaps the angel Raphael who carries our prayers to God? St. Luke does not identify him. The angel instructed Cornelius to send for Peter, and this injunction the centurion unhesitatingly obeyed. Peter came, preached the word of God and baptized Cornelius and his household. The conversion of Cornelius is an important milestone in the Church's early history, and St. Luke devoted much space to it, purposefully repeating the story of the angel twice in order to underscore the portent of this first uncircumcised convert's entrance into the Church.

It would seem that the angels were particularly detailed to help the new Christians in their difficult and novel task of conquering the world for God, not by the sword or physical force, but by the might of their overwhelming love for Jesus, a love so powerful and transcendent that it united man and angel in common cause and in a common sense.

### 5. Philip (Acts 8:5-13; 26-27)

After the death of Stephen, the still unconverted Saul with persecuting zeal created havoc in the church at Jerusalem, scattering the brethren abroad. Philip, one of the seven deacons chosen at the same time as St. Stephen, preached in Samaria with remarkable success; there his preaching was accompanied by signs as foretold in Isaiah (35:6), chiefly in the casting out of demons. An angel appeared to him saying: "Arise and go towards the south unto the way that goeth down from Jerusalem unto Gaza which is desert. And he arose and went" (Acts 8:26-27).

Philip obeyed promptly, left off the work he was engaged in, did not quibble, asked not the why or the wherefore, nor even what was expected of him when he would reach his destination. What a wonderful sense of submission to the heavenly decree. What quiet and unquestionable confidence in the angelic message. We would well emulate Philip's calm acceptance. As Philip journeyed, he came up with an Ethiopian eunuch, a man of great authority under Candace, the Queen of Ethiopia. This man was searching for an interpretation of a passage in Isaiah. Philip immediately knew that here was the reason for which he had been sent on this trip. He enlightened the eunuch, converted and baptized him. Eunuchs were outside the community of Israel (Dt. 23:1), thus his baptism is an extension of the Christian mission to all categories of people.

How often are we ourselves sent upon seemingly goal-less, purposeless, "endless" journeys to find that God has something for us to do just there, at precisely that very time. We seldom hear the voice clearly because, unlike Philip, we are not possessed by the joyful impulse to share the good news of Jesus with all men, at whatever cost to ourselves. Were we indeed so concerned with our Father's business instead of our own, our lives would be purposeful and joyous, and angels as natural to us as they were to the men and women of the early Church.

## 6. St. Paul

Paul, once he had seen the true light, gave his life and power unstintingly to Christ. He was a Pharisee, and well versed in the Scriptures. His theology was sound: he firmly believed that Jesus fulfilled all of the Law. The Resurrection was to him clear proof and, too, he had no doubts about angels.

It was inevitable that Paul should himself soon be brought up before the Sanhedrin. He sowed dissension among his accusers by putting it up to them to decide whether he was right or wrong in believing in the resurrection from the dead. Now the Sadducees denied these things, but the Pharisees believed in them; but both denied Jesus Christ. Paul's question set the two factions at loggerheads. Feelings ran so high that the soldiers had to remove Paul for fear he would be torn to pieces. This, in spite of the warning given by one of the scribes of the party of the Pharisees: "We find no evil in this man. What if a spirit or an angel spoke to him?" (Acts 23:9).

It is clear that Paul believed in the existence of angels to whom he refers convincingly and explicitly in several of his letters.

St. Luke recounts one of Paul's most striking experiences on the island of Malta. Here is no hearsay. Luke was himself on the boat with Paul and witnessed all that had happened. As the storm reached its peak, and all hope for the small vessel's survival was abandoned, Paul stood up and said:

There stood by me this night the angel of God, whose I am, and whom I serve, saying, Fear not Paul; thou must be brought before Caesar: and lo, God hath given thee them that sail with thee" (Acts 27:23-24).

This message gave Paul new courage and such strength that he not only convinced the soldier not to kill the prisoners, but the sailors took heart and finally all landed safely and unscathed on the island.

How often in the storms of life does our angel stand by us and say: Fear not. But we hear him not, for the noise of the winds and the waves, and the echo of our own terror and distress which deafens our ears and blinds our eyes.

In the Acts of the Apostles we see what we have seen all along the road of man's religious history. The angels intervene and make themselves clearly visible to those found worthy of seeing them. As in all the other books of the Bible, the men in the Acts who saw angels were men of action and creative vision, not vain dreamers. Peter, Paul, John, Philip, Cornelius saw them, and Stephen at his trial reminded men of an angel.

There is no question but that the infant Church abounded with spiritual power and joyfulness, that signs and wonders followed the disciples wherever they went: that people were healed, the dead raised, that their actions and words convinced and converted others. The modern Church seems in places to have lost these distinctive signs of its Godliness. Happily, consciousness of these gifts is returning. May we hope a worthiness to see the holy angels may be regained so the ancient prayer rings true once more:

> An angel of peace, a faithful guide, guardian of our souls and bodies, let us ask of the Lord.

Let this lovely petition of the Liturgy be no vain repetition; may our response carry conviction: "Grant this, O Lord!"

---

[1]St. Gregory of Nyssa, *Oratio Catechetica*, 32, as cited in Robert Payne, *The Holy Fire*. New York: Harper and Brothers, 1957, p. 149.
[2]J.B. Phillips, *The Young Church in Action*.

# VII

## The Angels in the Epistles

The great majority of the Epistles are accredited to St. Paul and it is therefore chiefly with his thoughts that we have to deal. It is not our purpose to discuss here the question concerning the authorship of some of the Epistles. Our study will follow the age-old tradition of the Church and abide by the titles as given in all the authorized versions of the New Testament.

St. Paul is generally accepted as an organizer, theologian, traveller and letter-writer, and we are inclined to forget he was a very great mystic as well. He is, in fact, a remarkable combination of the two. He proves that a mystic is not necessarily a recluse, living far from the world and reality; and also that actual, factual life in no way prohibits or excludes spiritual experiences. Above all, that this latter life in the midst of the world, surely does not preclude contemplation of the Godhead. We know that Paul was called to his apostleship on the road to Damascus by Jesus himself. From his writings we may gather that Paul several times experienced heavenly visions and, as an example, in his Second Epistle to the Corinthians he describes one such vision in illuminating words. When exactly and where it took place, we do not know. He mentions it almost as if to excuse himself, after enumerating his many sufferings and countless humiliations endured in the service of the Church; this was written sometime around 55-57 A.D.:

> If we are to boast (although boasting is out of place), I will go on to the visions and revelations the Lord has granted me. There is a man I know who was carried out of himself in Christ, fourteen years since; was his spirit in his body? I cannot tell. Was it apart from his body? I cannot tell. God knows. This man at least, was carried up into the third heaven. I can only tell you that this man, with his spirit in his body, or with his spirit apart from his body, God knows which, not I, was carried up into Paradise, and heard the mysteries which man is not allowed to utter (2 Cor. 12:1-4).

Paul, in fact, is saying that he cannot explain whether he saw with his spiritual or his physical eyes; all he knows is that his experience was real beyond doubt, but that what he saw he could not put into words. His use of the term "third heaven" reminds us of Enoch—Paul had a vision of what some privileged few saw before him and which other saints have since, on rare occasions, also seen. With what kind of eyes do men see into the world of the spirit? It may not be with mortal eyes, yet what they see their memory holds as something their physical eyes comprehend.

There are many references to the angelic hosts in Paul's letters. He refers to them naturally and in no way theoretically. Being both Jew and Christian, he plainly distinguishes now between the role of the angels in the Old and in the New Covenants.

No question of it, it is a great mystery we worship. Revelation made in human nature; justification won in the realm of the spirit; a vision seen by angels, a mystery preached to the Gentiles; Christ in this world, accepted by faith, Christ on high, taken up into glory (1 Tm. 3:16).

"A vision seen by angels," yes, the angels saw and knew all things from the first, before we accepted by faith; they alone witnessed the moment itself of the Resurrection and made it known to the visitors at the sepulcher on Easter morn, before Jesus showed himself to his friends.

Paul is always intensely aware also of the powers of evil. Immediately following the above words, he warns that if inspiration of good comes to us through the angels of light, those of darkness lead us astray:

. . .There will be some who abandon the faith to false inspirations, and doctrines taught by the devils (1 Tm. 4:1).

He is exhorting us to strengthen ourselves for the battle; he fully recognizes the tremendous powers of evil with which we have to contend:

You must wear all the weapons of God's armoury, if you would find strength to resist the cunning of the devil. It is not against flesh and blood that we enter the lists; we have to do with princedoms and powers, with those who have mastery of the world in these dark days, with malign influence in an order higher than ours (Eph. 6:10-12).

Paul cautions us never to give our wily adversary any opening by which he could inveigle us into wrongdoing: "Do not let resentment lead you into sin; the sunset must not find you still angry—Do not give the devil his opportunity" (Eph. 4:27-28). Paul has no illusions; he fears that Satan should take advantage over us, for we know well enough how resourceful he is (2 Cor. 2:11). "Satan himself can pass for an angel of light, and his servants have no difficulty in passing for servants of holiness" (2 Cor. 11:15).

St. John sustains St. Paul's contention that we are tempted to evil by a force outside ourselves:

The man who lives sinfully takes his character from the devil; the devil was a sinner from the first. If the Son of God was revealed to us, it was so that he might undo what the devil had done ... (1 Jn. 3:8).

Let those who doubt the real power of evil think upon these words and upon Jesus Christ's sacrifice for us!

St. Peter likened the devil to a roaring lion:

> Be sober, and watch well. The devil, who is your enemy, goes about roaring like a lion, to find his prey, but you grounded in the faith, must face him boldly; you know well enough the brotherhood you belong to, pays all the world over, the same tribute to suffering (1 Pt. 5:8-9).

In the nearly two thousand years that have passed since these words were written, they have remained unalterably true. The tribute to suffering is still being paid! The "Brotherhood of Pain," as Schweitzer calls it, is more violently apparent today perhaps than ever before. As we do not seem to know how to avail ourselves of unity in love and joy, we are bound together by suffering. How the angels must weep over us!

From the Old Testament times the accepted belief was that the angels were so close to God "as almost to be God," the means through which he often communicated with man. Paul makes the new situation created by Christ quite clear. He makes the point that whereas in the old days the Law had only angels for its spokesmen, we have Jesus Christ.

> In the old days, God spoke to our fathers in many ways and by many means ... now, at least, in these times he has spoken to us with a Son ... a Son, who is the radiance of his being .... Now ... he has taken his place on high, at the right hand of God's majesty, superior to the angels in that measure in which the name he has inherited is more excellent than theirs (Heb. 1:1-4).

Paul reminds us that as we have the Son of God as our guide, we must never risk drifting away from the truth, that the world's salvation has been given into the hands of man, because God became man to redeem the world.[1] In this sense through Christ man is raised above the angels:

> ... to whom has God entrusted the ordering of the world? Not to the angels .... What is man, that thou shouldst remember him ... man whom thou has crowned with glory and honor, setting him in authority over the works of thy hand .... Observe he has subjected all things to him ... we can see one who was made a little lower than the angels, I mean Jesus, crowned, now with glory and honor because of the death he underwent .... The Son who sanctifies and the sons who are sanctified have a common origin, all of them; he is not ashamed then to own them as his brethren (Heb. 2:5-11).

For the brotherhood of man through Christ is the redemption of the world.

The task is ours, and not one of us can be outlawed, not the least nor the worst of us.

Angels can be misunderstood at all times, and in the pagan days in which St. Paul lived, they could easily be confused with winged goddesses and the like; therefore St. Paul gives stern warning:

> You must not allow anyone to cheat you by insisting upon false humility addressing its worship to angels. Such a man takes his stand upon false visions; his ill-founded confidence that comes of human speculation (Col. 2:18).

These words are as meaningful today as they were in 63 A.D. Many are the fanciful speculations and errors of the modern mind about angels and their role in creation. Many assertions wander from the sober truth into heresy. The tradition of the undivided Church teaches as St. Paul taught in recognizing the full reality of both the physical and spiritual worlds, that all honor and glory is due to Jesus Christ, the Incarnate Word of God. In the worship offered him, all creatures join and support each other in prayer. To dismiss this subject by saying, I need no intermediary between me and my God is to put the accent in the wrong place and summarily to dispense with one of our great blessings: the power of united prayer—"When a just man prays fervently, there is great virtue in his prayer" (Jas. 5:16). Jesus insisted upon the need of collective, communal prayer, and his apostles did the same. The very essence of the angels' nature is worship, therefore to call upon them in prayer is only natural and right.

We have no conception of how God, who is undefinable, receives our prayers, or by what channel he answers them. We only know that we are fully justified in seeing under the image of our guardian angel the manifestation of his love for us. In Tobit we are told that the Archangel Raphael carries our prayers before the throne of God. If this be so, then it in no way makes our contact with the Lord less direct. A mundane simile is the television; we receive the picture directly from the sending station, but it comes by a certain wavelength, and we do not consider it any less direct for that reason. Moreover, it is not the channel we fix our eyes upon, but the picture. So, too, in our worship, we concentrate upon God and use the channels happily given to us.

Nothing except our own sin can come between us and God, as St. Paul says.

> Of this I am fully persuaded; neither death nor life, no angels or principalities or powers, neither what is present nor what is to come, no form whatever, neither the height above us nor the depth beneath us, nor any other created thing, will be able to separate us from the love of God, which came to us in Christ Jesus our Lord (Rom. 8:38-39).

St. Paul is not denying the reality of the things enumerated above, on the contrary, he underscores both their reality and our own nearness to God by showing that great as they may be they cannot and do not separate us from God.

That St. Paul in every respect believed in angels is unquestionable. He had personal experience and visions of them, as he himself related both in Acts and in his Letters. In fact, he warns that we could meet them at any time: " . . .do not forget to show hospitality, in doing this, men have before now entertained angels unaware" (Heb. 13:2).

It is chiefly from St. Paul's writings that the angelic choirs have been named. It will be useful to indicate the principal Scriptural passages whence these come.

| FIRST CHOIR | SECOND CHOIR | THIRD CHOIR |
|---|---|---|
| *Seraphim (Is. 6:2-6)* | *Dominions (Eph. 1:21)* | *Principalities (Rom. 8:38; Eph. 1:21)* |
| *Cherubim (Ezek. 1:10)* | *Virtues (Authorities) (1 Cor. 15:26)* | *Archangels (1 Thes. 4:16; Jude 9)* |
| *Thrones (Col. 1:16)* | *Powers (Eph. 1:21)* | *Angels (passim)* |

Actually, it was a great anonymous mystic of the fifth century who arranged the choirs in this manner. He is known to us under the name of Dionysius the Areopagite. It may be that he wrote under this assumed name which belonged to one of St. Paul's disciples, because it was from St. Paul's enumeration that he initially conceived his magnificent theme on the Celestial Hierarchy. This will be viewed in the chapter on Dionysius.

It has been said that St. Paul thought angels to be essentially inimical to man, but this is, surely, a misconstruing of the fact. Paul was very aware, as we have seen, of the occult power of evil and, therefore, he often calls attention to the angels of darkness. He saw their evil works in the wickedness of the heathen world in which he moved. He has also been considered harsh to women but he only urged them toward dignified modesty for their own protection in keeping their heads covered in church: "The woman ought to have authority over her head for the angel's sake" (1 Cor. 11:10).

St. Paul saw the angels above all in their attributes of worshippers and executors of the divine will, who of their own volition acted neither for nor against men. The angels of light, obedient to God, the source of all good, could themselves only be good. It was in the self-willed, fallen Satan and his angels that Paul saw man's adversaries prompting him to evil. For one brief moment Paul seems to draw aside the curtain of mystery and permits us a glimpse of the glory of heaven as it had been revealed to him:

The scene of your approach now is Mount Sion, it is the heavenly Jerusalem, city of the living God; here are gathered thousands upon thousands of angels, here is the assembly of those first born sons whose names are written in heaven, here is God sitting in judgment on all men, here are the spirits of just men, now made perfect; here is Jesus, the spokesman of the new covenant.... The kingdom we have inherited is one which cannot be shaken; in gratitude for this, let us worship God as he would have us worship him, in awe and reverence ... (Heb. 12:22-29).

In the above we have the summing up of Paul's belief and mystical insight into the final gathering before the throne of God, of all God's creatures, praising and glorifying their Lord, and which we echo in the ancient Ambrosian anthem:

We praise thee, O God; we acknowledge thee to be the Lord.
All the earth doth worship thee, the Father everlasting.
To thee all Angels cry aloud; the Heavens and all the powers therein;
To thee Cherubim and Seraphim continually do cry,
Holy, Holy, Holy, Lord God of Sabaoth;
Heaven and earth are full of the Majesty of thy glory
(*Te Deum Laudamus*).

¹Cf. Book II, pp. 132-134.

# VIII

## The Angels in the Book of Revelation

The Holy Scriptures end with the Book of Revelation of St. John the Divine, the Beloved Disciple and Evangelist. A book so full of metaphor that it is not easily comprehended and is open to many interpretations, but how singularly fitted to conclude God's own Book! The Book of Revelation pictures the Church emerging triumphant out of all tribulation. For St. John the only true Jews were Christians. He saw, as indeed we do, that the Christian Church is continuous with the community of God's Chosen People. The Bible reveals, as we progress through it, the perpetuity of the Church on earth. It is into this "Church" that Jesus was born, and whereof St. John had his revelation.

John wrote out of the fullness of his vision; time and place are but figures of speech. He visualized the "War of Heaven" (12:7), which in heaven was fought out *before* time as still present in our struggles here on earth today. He also saw the end of all travail in the new heaven and the new earth (21:1) as a sure fact laying *beyond* time and eternity. *Between the beginning of time and eternity*, he saw the unremitting stress and strain between good and evil in which all created beings are involved *until* "the first heaven and the first earth" are passed away. The unquestionable triumph of light over darkness was perfectly clear to the Son of Zebedee. The price was the Blood of the Lamb and that of his saints and martyrs.

The Book of Revelation is composed in the traditional style of the Old Testament apocalypses and is full of references and illusions to the books of the Bible, thus in a remarkable way linking them together and writing "Amen" to what has now become "One Book."

It is generally agreed that the Book of Revelation was written around 95 A.D. during the reign of Domitian who, like Nero, persecuted the Christians. This date argues for the authorship of St. John while the difference in style between it and the Gospel argues against it. But the Gospel is a theological recounting of Jesus' life and could hardly have been written in the same manner as the jotting down of what was seen as a vision by the sacred writer. J.B. Phillips, for example, believes that John actually wrote "during his

visions."[1] Church tradition also leans heavily towards the Joannine authorship. The writer himself at once states that he is John, living on the island of
Patmos (1:9), a penal colony used by the Romans, and lying just off the coast
of Asia Minor.

What John saw there was the undeserved suffering which may well have
given expression to his clear illustration and descriptions of the woes, while
his knowledge of God was a kind of "Open Sesame" to his visions of heaven.

It is not our purpose here to draw up a commentary on this prophetic
work. Our concern here is for the angels. Nonetheless, there are certain
points it would be useful and helpful to clarify, at least briefly. This would
seem necessary if we are even to begin to comprehend this extraordinary
work and the predominant part the angels have to play in it. One might best
read and study this chapter of our reflections with a New Testament at hand,
so as to more easily and clearly discern what is being written about the
various scattered quotations being cited.

A most important fact is that John tells us quite plainly that his revelation,
imparted and deciphered to him by an angel, comes directly from none
other than Jesus Christ himself.

"This is a revelation from Jesus Christ which God has allowed him to make
known to his servants of things which must soon find their due accomplish-
ment. And he [Jesus] has sent his angel to disclose the pattern of it to his
servant John" (Rev. 1:1).[2] "The words point to the unfolding of God's
providence now in the fullness of time, a providence that both punishes and
rewards."[3] John, very clearly, is not writing of his own volition, but is
impelled to do so. Consequently, this is no commonplace apocalypse,
although the phraseology is reminiscent of the Old Testament.

The symbolic language is one which was easily understood by John's own
contemporaries, though it may remain somewhat baffling to the modern
mind.

> There are three traditional interpretations of the book, the Praeterist, the
> Continuous, or Historical, and the Futurist. The Praeterists consider that
> the prophecies refer to events now passed and especially the overthrow of
> Jerusalem and of the heathen Rome. The second school interprets the
> book as a series of prophecies which are being continuously fulfilled of the
> whole series of prophecies bound up with the second coming of Christ.[4]

For myself, I think there is good reason for all three opinions and that the
truth is to be found in an amalgamation of the three theories.

John was, of course, addressing the harassed Christians of his own time in
a language they would more readily comprehend. He spoke words of sublime encouragement and strength to the faithful, and of dire warning to the
weak and sinful. But, still, what fitted those days of trouble surely fits our
own times of turmoil quite as adequately.

People have seen, in various historical characters of their day, from Nero to Brezhnev, the embodiment of John's prophecies of evil. Very likely there will be other historical figures in the future who will not fail to correspond to this role, for the Revolution, in fact, is timeless.

But the most pertinent to all times of trouble is John's firm knowledge that those who are faithful even unto death, shall ultimately stand before the throne and behold the face of God. Here is more than a record of punishment and reward: it is, indeed, a vision of a state for which there are no human expressions—for how is one to describe the utter joy of those who live in the love and knowledge of God, and the unutterable misery of sinners who live in the outer darkness of their own denial? Yet, this is exactly what John attempted to do!

The whole of the Book of Revelation is a series of pictures, alternating between dire calamities that befall the world of men, and the untold beatitude of heaven that awaits, nay already is, the reward of the blessed martyrs and saints. These scenes are often shown to be concomitant, for all through this colossal book we are made aware that God is triumphant at all times, and that good has *already* vanquished evil. The Lord of hosts is the arbiter of our fate, and it is his will which will ever be supreme.

In these pictures the divine seer depicts the angels superbly as the executors of the will of God. They are God's messengers, sent to illumine our faulty and limited understanding. They hold back or let loose, as the case may be, the elements in their charge, and they herald great tidings, while they interpret, punish, and reward.

St. John shows them to us in nineteen different functions which for the sake of interest and instruction it is useful to enumerate here:

1. *The Interpreting Angel* who speaks the words of Jesus to John and is his mentor for all he sees.
2. *The Seven Angels of the Seven Churches of Asia* (1:20—3:4).
3. *The Heralding Angel* (5:2).
4. *The Four Angels of the Four Winds* (7:1).
5. *The Angel of the Seal of the Living God* (7:2).
6. *The Seven Angels of the Seven Trumpets* (8:2-10).
7. *The Angel of the Incense* (8:3).
8. *The Seven Angels of the Seven Thunders* (10:1-4).
9. *The Angel of the Great Oath* (10:5-7).
10. *The Angel of the Little Book of Life* (10:8-11).
11. *The Angel of Good Tidings* (14:6).
12. *The Angel of Judgment* (14:7).
13. *The Angel of Fire* (14:18).
14. *The Angel of the Sharp Sickle* (14:17-20).
15. *The Seven Angels of the Last Seven Plagues* (15:1).

16. *The Seven Angels of the Seven Bowls of Judgment* (15:5-8).
17. *The Angel of the Waters* (16:5).
18. *The Angel of Prophetic Doom* (18:1-3).
19. *The Angel Having the Key of the Bottomless Pit* (20:1).

Throughout the stupendous events of this marvelous apocalypse, we see these splendid and majestic spirits hold, by the Lord's permission and command, the reins of events in their masterful hands. In all things they are present to fulfill the will of God.

Chapter one of the Book of Revelation is an introduction to what is to ensue. It sets us in the presence of the Living God and we hear his commission to John.

Chapters two and three comprise the messages sent to the angels of the seven churches of Asia. This is a heavenly judgment and so the churches' spiritual selfness, that is, their angels, are invoked. Through them the churches are encouraged when being persecuted, praised for valiantly seizing their opportunities, or admonished for being loveless, over-tolerant, or ready to compromise. We hear of every human failing, but also of human courage and endurance. So many fine passages are just so many excellent messages and strike a familiar note for our day.

In chapter four John brings us, with the first of his lightning changes of which we shall meet so many in this apocalypse, back into the presence of the Maker and Ruler of the world. The central point in this heavenly vision is the Throne, an unchanging symbol right through the Book of Revelation, the focus of eternal stability and steadfastness. Here, indeed, there is no chaos, but authority in justice and unchanging loveliness whence all authority flows.

John will carry us ever and again back to the central vision of beauty and godliness where the angels are, so to speak, "at home." At the same time, he will not hesitate to show us the staggering brutality and rottenness of sin.

Chapter five shows us the Book of the Reign of God; in the hands of the Maker, it is sealed with seven seals which none can open, save the One who had already redeemed what lies bound within it.

Chapter six describes the point of the opening of the first six seals. As the initial four are consecutively broken, the Four Riders of the Apocalypse charge across the scene. This brings back to mind the visions of Zechariah (1:8f and 6:2f). These riders, if we connect them to Zechariah's vision, are charged with carrying out judgment, using the very results of man's revolt against God, to forge the means for executing God's moral sentence. The first rider, mounted on a white charger is bent upon conquest and epitomizes the aggressive subjugating tendencies of nations.

The second, war, rides a red horse, and is the inevitable result of the former's rapaciousness.

The third, famine, seated upon a black horse, is the unavoidable consequence of the first two, to be followed just as surely by the fourth rider, death, seated upon a horse of sickly green. Here are plainly displayed the consequences of sin. If not love, then at least the fear of the disastrous results will open men's eyes. The breaking of the fifth seal shows the souls of those who have died in loyalty to the Word of God, crying for retribution.

The sixth seal lets loose a terrible cataclysm upon the universe before which all, great and low, seek to take cover in abject terror.

At this moment of seeming chaos, the four angels of the four winds stay the cataclysm and all is quiet. The servants of the Lord are reassured and receive from a mighty angel the stamp of the Living God upon their foreheads; thus acknowledged, they can go through any kind of tribulation. All who have a steady faith, even today, may feel this touch of the Lord's angel upon their foreheads, and can face the worst days of testing without surrendering. God's chosen are not insignificant, their number is vast.

Following closely upon vivid descriptions of the awful anger of God, John carries us into the exquisite beauty of the heavenly scene in which we witness the beatitude of the vast assembly of the redeemed who, clad in white robes, sing their praises, joining their happy voices to the chorus of angels, and with them fall down in adoration before the throne of God. It is as if we were finally given a fleeting view of the new men in the very secret citadel of worship, swelling the rolling tide of prayer. Here is heavenly security in which tears are the memories of things gone by. This brings to mind, very specifically, the prophecy of Isaiah: "And the Lord shall wipe away the tears from all faces" (25:8; 49:10).

The splendor of this heavenly felicity is what we must keep in mind as we proceed to the next set of woes that are heralded by the seven angels of the seven trumpets in chapter eight.

But just before we plunge from one extreme into the other as the seventh seal is opened, there is a breathless pause, "a silence in heaven, about the space of half an hour" (8:1). Time and quietude and reflection have their place in heaven as well as on earth. Both rest and action are part of God's Kingdom, even as the rhythmic beat of the heart includes its period of rest. When we take time off for the interval of retreat, far from going out of the flow of life, we are but coming more closely into contact with its inner rhythm.

> And another angel came and stood at the altar, having a golden censer; and there was given unto him much incense, that he should offer it with prayers of all the saints . . . (8:3).

Here again we are given an insight into the great merit that the prayers of all the saints have, their petitions made acceptable to God by the censing of the angel, through which they are rendered part of the Kingdom's ritual forever. In the everlasting sphere worship is what we would expect to find. By being true to their own nature which God has given them, his creatures show forth his glory.

The angels who do not share man's fallen, but redeemable nature, still join them in the grand worship of the Lamb. Thus it is in Vespers that we sing: "Let my prayer be set forth before as incense" (Ps. 140:2).

In the Jewish tradition, which we have to a great extent and in no small measure inherited, the archangels are often the intercessors for men with God, and convey petitions to him. We are reminded of Raphael who is one of the seven holy angels who ever present the prayers of the saints to God (Tb. 12:15), of Michael, offering the prayer of the Jews (Dn. 12:1), and in 1 Enoch of Michael, Uriel, Raphael and Gabriel carrying the cries of the martyrs to God. John stresses this prayerful union of man and angel and it remains for all of us a most lovely and consoling thought.

All true prayer mounts heavenward mingling the prayers of the faithful people with those of the holy angelic spirits even as an aroma of all the incense spices blend into one grand and common fragrance. Lest we be carried away by the sensual loveliness of these figures of speech, let us hearken to the words of Dionysius the Areopagite:

> And this I take to signify that the divinest and highest things seen by the eyes or contemplated by the mind, are but the symbolical expression of those that are immediately beneath Him who is above all.[5]

But John himself passes from the beauty of the incensing imagery to the next tragic scenery in a sequence of events. The angel hurls the burning coals from the altar fast upon earth and there ensues thundering and lightning and earthquake. In this cataclysm, following abruptly upon the breathless silence, the first angel sounds his trumpet!

The seven seals represent divine decision; the seven trumpets symbolize divine action. In the perusal of the following terrible woes we who are studying angels must give more heed to them than to the actual message conveyed in the passages (8:7—11:15). We must also keep in mind that in no book of the Bible are we ever really being told the story of the angels, but only allowed glimpses of their activities, from which, of course, we can draw our own conclusions.

Above all, the Book of Revelation has the angels appearing as the executors of God's holy will, the personification of his detailed power, by which ultimately, even the forces of evil are placed under the divine control. Therefore, the tormenting afflictions which befall those who choose a way that is not God's, can do no permanent harm to the faithful who are under

God's own guardianship, and who need fear no evil, for their guardian angel is powerful to protect them.

Evil is self-destructive; the sounding of the seven great trumpets heralds deathly, fearful retribution both through the agency of so-called natural forces, as that of the malignant spiritual powers. But none of these disastrous events is senseless, for their determinative goal is to induce repentance.

Just as we are about prostrated from hearing of so much misfortune, there ensues a pause similar to that which introduced the breaking of the seventh seal, keeping in mind the even just before the sounding of the seventh trumpet. The interruption this time (10:1—11:14) is created by a mighty angel clothed with a cloud, and a rainbow upon his head, and his face, as if it were the light of the sun, and his feet as a pillar of fire! (10:1). This angel stands with one foot upon the land, one foot upon the sea, while in his hand he holds a little book. He speaks with a voice like seven thunders, the echo of which reverberates down the ages. "The voice of the Lord is upon the waters, the God of glory thundereth—the voice of the Lord shaketh the wilderness" (Ps. 28:3-9). When Jesus and his disciples heard the voice of God, the people said it thundered (Jn. 12:28-29). The mighty angel lifts his right hand and with a sweeping gesture he makes a mighty oath to and by him who created all and from whom all things spring. As he bestrides land and sea he calls for attention; there is no more time for the tentative; the ultimate realities are indeed at hand! (10:5-6). Time has no more reality than transient things; now is really only a part of eternity, for without eternity the present would in an instant be nothing but the past.

In the little book that the angel holds the past and future meet. It is sweet to taste, but bitter to digest, because although the glad tidings of companionship with God are like honey to the tongue, to do the business of God demands austere discipline and many a bitter abnegation. To digest the little book of knowledge calls for a deeper understanding in our judgment of events. We must study history with Christian discernment, having the mental penetration of the anointed and the sealed. We must acquire the insight which will permit us to single out the clues that will bring all knowledge and the history of recorded incidents into correlation and under the authority of the Word. The great angel of Christian understanding stands astride land and sea, mastering every element, physical and abstract. This same great angel stands astride our lives, claiming our attention, bidding us call all men to God before it is too late, for the seventh trumpet is about to sound!

This trumpet heralds in the final afflictions that shall scourge all wickedness and all malefactors. At the same time those *sans peur et sans reproche*— that is, without fear or reproach—are assured of full reward and glory.

The scenes of this apocalypse are so vivid, so strangely arresting, so kindling to the imagination, so dialectic in possible interpretations, that it is a great temptation to linger to comment upon all of them, but it is the activity of the angels that we follow. Hence, we go on yet to chapter twelve, and the war in heaven.

> And there was a war in heaven, Michael and his angels fought against the dragon, and the dragon fought and his angels and prevailed not, neither was their place found any more in heaven. And the great dragon was cast out, that old serpent, called the Devil, and Satan, which deceiveth the whole world, he was cast out with him. Now is come salvation and strength and the kingdom of our God, and the power of his Christ. And they overcame him by the blood of the Lamb, and they that loved not their lives unto death. Therefore rejoice ye heavens! Woe to the inhabitants of the earth, for the devils come down unto you, having great wrath because he knoweth that he hath but a short time (12:7-12).

In this vision a tremendous "now-ness' is symbolized, the past and the present are wrought into a kaleidoscopic presentation of the terrible and tremendous fight between good and evil. It shows us the powers of evil as in revolt against God, but never equal to him, for they fight only with his angels who are under the leadership of Michael, the interpretation of whose name, "Who is like God?" is here most particularly apt.

This is a point well worth our deeper reflection. God's attributes are not only the property of the angels but are reflected also by our own virtues which make us only a "little lower than the angels" (Ps. 8:5).

It is against these very qualities that evil carries on its titanic war in our hearts and in the world at large. We are assaulted by Satan because of our indivisible unity with God by grace. "His glory," says Philaret of Moscow, "is manifest in the celestial glories, is reflected in man, and puts on the splendor of the visible world."[6] Therefore, Satan is conquered not alone by the blood of the Lamb (5:11), but also by the testimony of the martyrs of all times who "loved not their lives even unto death" (12:11).

John gives no description of the war in heaven, he states, though, that it is an accomplished fact. Evil has long since been cast out of heaven, and we are reminded of Jesus' testimony: "I beheld Satan as lightning fell from heaven" (Lk. 10:18).

The war is on earth, but here, too, evil is doomed to defeat. The mark of self-destruction is upon it, as it is upon all malefactors. As we fight let us strengthen our souls with the knowledge that we are on the side that has already won. Our struggles are part of a pattern that belongs to heaven as well as to earth. The appalling cruelties of our time are the result of human iniquity and gives us opportunity to share in the redemption of the Cross. The Incarnation and Golgotha make us co-heirs to heavenly victory with Christ. We have eternity on our side. Meanwhile evil is desperate because its time is short. "Heaven has already fought and won the very conflict in which we are now contending. On the vast fields of eternity the victory has been won for which we are not contending in time."[7] What the exile of Patmos is telling us is that the true witnesses are abiding by the very character of God himself who humbled himself and became man, and they share in his very nature when they are humble and selfless. Humility, then, is our greatest safeguard. We are then truly in Christ, enthroned with the Lamb in heaven, when we sacrifice ourselves. This war in which we contend with evil is no illusion; our sufferings are real, but they also are not in vain, for they, too, are part of God. "The Cross is the expression in time of that which God is in eternity."[8]

Courageous suffering, radiant with love and faith, is stronger than any thermonuclear power. It was upon the rock of Christian martyrdom that the pagan Roman Empire did break, and it is upon this same very unspectacular endurance that Communism is slowly to flounder and upon which all enslaving powers will ever perish. The fearless are always indestructible. Therefore, John sees them close to the throne of God as they contribute their share to the celestial melodies, united with the angels in gladsome worship.

The seer of Patmos shows us the fearsome pictures of the reign of the beast. Then, another interlude occurs and we sight the Lamb and his triumphant host. The Angel of Good Tidings (14:6-7), appears flying in mid-heaven, calling all mankind to give God the glory in love and fear for the hour of judgment is at hand, and to be proclaimed by the Angel of Judgment. We are shown the contrast now between the rewards that shall be dealt out to the righteous and that which will go to the transgressors. Those who bear the mark of the Lamb sing a new song that they alone can learn. Their joy and glory stands out radiantly against the utter destruction of those who are marked with the stamp of the beast. These are felled by an angel who with a sharp sickle cuts down all evil growth which is thrown into the great wine press of the wrath of God (14:19).

This angel is called to his work by the angel of fire (14:18).

So that we may not forget that the frightening events on earth have a heavenly source, we are shown the Seven Angels of the Seven Last Plagues. Always and again, the Book of Revelation passes back and forth from the eternal to the transient, as we witness the process and the ultimate result. These pictures are intermixed to make us more strongly aware that at all times, be they peaceful or turbulent, the mercy of God is a steadfast and immutable fact. The frightful scenes of doom are relieved by the glorious visions of perfect joy.

We are never permitted to forget that judgment must precede recompense. Thus the seven angels who come out of the temple which is filled with the smoke of God's glory and power must fulfill the judgment before man can enter the sanctuary. They are clothed in pure white linen and have their breasts girded with golden girdles (15:6-8), as they advance swathed in stainless purity in an aura of florid beauty and glory, pouring out God's last great retribution upon evil (16:1-2). The punishment is just, because evil reaps its own reward, for even the pure water of rivers and fountains turns to blood for those who have shed blood. The Angel of Water praises God for his just judgment (16:5).

The Book of Revelation is filled with tremendous action: its lesson is often repetitious, as indeed life itself is repetitious, for evil must be rooted out before we can sit back and enjoy the fruits of virtue; in fact, most of all, it is virtue which *must* be active. All action is in the hand of the Eternal whose righteous indignation is released against evil.

The Angel of Interpretation (17:1-13), now carries John into the wilderness and explains many strange symbols to him. The explanation is confusing because its language is unfamiliar to us, though its deeper meaning is clear. The figures of speech were veiled illusion to the power of the Roman Empire. But they stand today equally well for the embattled imperial forces of wickedness in any modern state, destined in its turn as was Rome, to be overcome by the armies of the Lamb. Whatever the opposition, the One who is Lord of Lords and King of Kings wins the final victory. Let us pray that we too may have the grace of an interpreting angel at our side as John had, so that we may see all the formidable events that encompass us in their true light, with God always in command of events and of us.

Our next angel (18:1-3) is the Angel of Prophetic Doom who calls us to project our minds into a time when the actual evil we are surrounded by and are acutely aware of, has already been destroyed. Another angel throws a great stone into the sea (18:21-24), exemplifying the swift destruction that shall be the end of pagan Rome and all powers like her, whatever the guise even of law and justice, under which iniquity may be perpetrated. The destroying angel is close at hand and at the appointed hour shall bring retribution.

However imposing and unassailable evil should appear, its doom is nonetheless certain, its dirge already sung.

Meanwhile in heaven another chorus is heard full of triumph ascribing all honor and glory to God on high. All creation bows before the throne of God. A great *Alleluia* swells up from every side as the voice of many waters and mighty thunderings. The Lamb is wedded to his Church whose white raiment is the righteousness of the saints.

John, overcome by all that he sees, falls down to worship the angel who has shown him all these things. One can well understand his doing this, for we are all inclined to admire, even worship a worthy teacher; how much more so

John after all that has been made known to him! But the angel catches him up short with a loving reprimand: "See thou do it not: I am thy fellow servant, and of thy brethren that have the testimony of Jesus: worship God." God alone is to be worshipped, all honor, all devotion, all praise, all longing, must tend towards and concentrate upon him. We must never confuse the means with the goal. There can so easily be an idolatry of good. This is a very subtle sort of temptation to which we fall in all good faith. "See thou do it not!" says the angel, and he points to the conquering Christ riding towards us followed by his white army of angels.

The last great war is waged and the battle is won; hell is forever divorced from heaven. There is no compromise between good and evil. Evil is bound hand and foot and cast into the deep pit. "And I saw," says John, "an angel come down from Heaven, having the key of the bottomless pit and a great chain in his hand. And he laid hold on the dragon, that old serpent, which is the Devil and Satan, and bound him a thousand years, and cast him into the bottomless pit, and shut him up, and set a seal upon him, that he should deceive the nations no more . . ." (20:1-3).

Not only the impersonal evils of earthquakes, plagues, and wars are over, but the personal wickedness that dwells in the hearts of men.

The devil is hopelessly bound by our certitude that God is infinitely stronger than the mightiest forces of evil. We are no longer devilishly deceived, therefore when after one thousand years of bliss the devil is loosed again, it is but a short while in which, after vainly assaulting the beloved city of the saints, that he forever disappears together with all his false prophecy, lying and deceit. Evil drops back into its original nothingness, forever failing, falling down the burning, bottomless pit.

Both heaven and earth as we know them pass away, alone the throne of God remains, as from all time it stood. Before the throne the living and the dead now stand in judgment. Character is shown to be destiny, men are judged on the merit of their own words and deeds. All those whose names are not in the Book of Life, are cast out with Death and Hell into the lake of fire. This is the second death from which there is no resurrection. But over the blessed this death has no power.

A new heaven and a new earth appear. In them is found and gathered the true meaning of all things from start to finish, for all things begin and end in God. "I am Alpha and Omega, the beginning and the end." In the City of Happiness, the New Jerusalem, the measure of man and angel is the same. They have the same standard (21:7). There, Angel and Man have found perfect equality, not in substance, but in essence. They dwell together in the Holy City, the pearly gates of which are forever open, for there are no more enemies. They find that they drink together of the pure rivers of the water of life, their souls aglow with the light of God himself.

Lost in wonder at the beauty of what the angel shows him, John once more so forgets himself as to fall down at the very feet of his heavenly mentor. The angel once again points to the Truth as the only Worshipful One, the Living God, and bids him listen to Christ's own words:

> Behold, I come quickly and my reward is with me. I am Alpha and Omega, the beginning and the end, the first and the last. I, Jesus, have sent mine angels to testify unto you. I am the root and offspring of David, the bright and morning star. And the spirit and the bride say, Come. And let him that heareth say, Come. And let him that is athirst come. And whosoever will, let him take the water of life freely.... Surely I come quickly. Amen. (Rev. 22:12-20).

Could we but project our thoughts into that Holy City and see what John saw! Even if we cannot do this we can, humbly kneeling here on earth, join in that great overwhelming chorus of angels, saints, and martyrs, crying with them out of the well of our longing and our love: *Even so, come Lord Jesus!* (22:21).

*        *        *

Thus, with the culminating cry to our Lord, we end our study of the angels as they appear revealed to us in the Holy Scriptures.

We see them slowly advance towards us through the overcast mist of distant spiritual history, as great, mighty beings full of light, strength and beauty. They are Bearers of the Word of God, executors of his Will. They call us, they coerce us to love and to obedience. They lead, teach, advise, punish, and reward. They guard and protect us; they become our companions so that ultimately we poor humans, redeemed by Christ, may find ourselves mingling in their bright company when, at last, we have found our home in our native land with them in the perpetual presence of God!

[1]J.B. Phillips, *The Book of Revelation, A New Translation of the Apocalypse*. New York: Macmillan Publishing Co., 1951. p. xii.

[2]Knox translation.

[3]W.A. Heidt, O.S.B., *The Book of the Apocalypse*. Collegeville, Minnesota: Liturgical Press, p. 12.

[4]*The Bible Reader's Encyclopedia and Concordance*, ed. Rev. W.M. Collins, p. 327.

[5]Dionysius the Areopagite, *Mystical Theology and the Celestial Hierarchies*. Surrey: The Shrine of Wisdom, p. 11.

[6]Vladimir Lossky, *The Mystical Theology of the Eastern Church*. London: James Clarke and Co., Ltd. 1957.

[7]Lynn Harold, "Exposition on Revelation," *The Interpreter's Bible*, Vol. 12., p. 586.

[8]*Ibid*

# Book III

**The Angels in the Christian Church**

# I

# Introduction

## 1. Prefatory Comment

Having devoted ourselves to the study of the truly lovely role played by the angelic beings through the pages of the Scripture, we may now turn our attention to their role and position in the life of the Church.

In one volume it is not possible to cover two thousand years of the life of the Church, nor its many facets and branches, each in its own way, often having an individual and canonized approach to the angels. Here we limit ourselves to the manifestation of the angels and the literature about them until the time of the Great Schism which split East and West asunder. The Church Fathers' ascendancy was recognized by the Church at large. Though today their import is often forgotten, it remains a fact that the great influence of their lives and writings had much to do with authentic doctrinal development, as begun in the Patristic period, when, of all times, the teaching of the Apostles was most reverently preserved. Many of the Fathers, all highly educated men of action and organization, had much to say of the angels and gave them a very distinct place in the order of worship they established. And, to this day, many of these prayers are in wide use.

From a very early date the title of Father was applied to bishops and witnesses of the Christian tradition. From the end of the fourth century on, the term began to have a more restricted and clarified sense, defining a group of ecclesiastical authors whose authority on doctrinal matters came to carry especial weight. The group known as the Apostolic Fathers, for example, belongs to the age immediately succeeding the New Testament period, whose works have, in whole or in part, survived. The next group, often referred to as the Church Fathers, are those theologians whose proved orthodoxy was in keeping and agreement with the Scriptures and the texts of the earlier Fathers. The Fathers as a whole are characterized by orthodoxy of doctrine, holiness of life, the approval of the universal Church, and marked by relationship with antiquity. Their authority is held to be infallible when they teach a doctrine unanimously, but the individual teachings of the Fathers are not infallible, though to be regarded with utmost respect. In some instances, we may find that they do, in fact, contradict each other. But more remarkable, however, is the consistency of their overall teaching, and the many certitudes they held in common; especially notable is their distinct fidelity through success and tribulation, to the orthodoxy of the Church.

We divide this study of Patristic times into two main parts, with certain subdivisions:

First, the holy angels in the primitive Church, that is, the Apostolic Fathers. This period would cover, roughly, the years from the Apostolic Era to the Council of Nicea, that is, from about 100 to 325 A.D. Second, the holy angels in the age of Orthodox Theology: This was the time when the "Catholic" (that is, universal) Church's supreme and concentrated aim was to keep the faith "Orthodox" (that is, of true belief, in keeping with the revelation of Sacred Scripture and Holy Tradition). This part covers the years from Nicea to the Great Schism, that is, approximately from 325 to 1054 A.D.

We will also aim as comprehensively as possible to deepen our knowledge of the holy angels in liturgies and prayers. In this we should try to understand the true significance of the words, and the light they throw upon the participation we assume the angels to have in our worship.

There are certain concomitant writings with those of the Apostolic Fathers which, though not requiring a chapter to themselves, still need to be sketched so as to give a more complete picture of those distant times, and so more fully appreciate the writings of the Church Fathers in general.

First, mention should be made of the New Testament Apocrypha, though without any real authoritative status, still representing a certain trend of thought among some of the early Christians. A naive and uninstructive way, doubtless, but which played a very real part in the development of the imagination of future generations, especially in the Middle Ages. Much of the quaint imagery that may often puzzle us, with devils and spirits and yawning jaws of hell abounding, has origin in the apocryphal books.

## 2. The Apocryphal New Testament

The word "apocryphal" here has a different connotation from that of the Old Testament Apocrypha. Really, the words mean "hidden writings." When applied to the New Testament it has acquired the meaning "of doubtful authenticity." It is possible that some of the apocryphal "Gospels" embody certain trustworthy oral traditions. The stories ought to be regarded as legends that grew up in the early Church about real persons and events. Their point was to underscore ideas and beliefs, for which we have far better evidence than these stories to support them. Angels and devils abound in these books and they are surrounded by much fancy and magic.

The angels hurl surly sinners into hell and chivvy the righteous into heaven. Hell is an open-mouthed dragon, with jaws like precipices, while the devils are hairy, black-winged and with mouths that spew sulphur and flames. The angels, on the other hand, are white-robed and too numerous to have much individuality. The descriptions are more quaint than interesting.

One of the most typical is the Gospel of Bartholomew which gives a good illustration. This Gospel was known to St. Jerome in the fourth and fifth centuries, and it has decidedly Gnostic tendencies. The Gnostics believed, to put it briefly and inadequately, in a Creator God, or *Demiurge*, entirely distinct from the supreme, unknowable Divine Being; this basic tenet had many and varied interpretations. Bartholomew's Gospel deals with what Christ is to have revealed to his apostles after the Resurrection. It tells of Jesus' descent into hell, the showing of the bottomless pit to the apostles, the account of the devil and his doings, and a report on the Annunciation, supposedly given by the Virgin Mary herself.

Bartholomew alleged to have seen the angels come down and worship Jesus as he hung on the Cross, from which in the darkness he disappeared. Jesus explains that "when I vanished away from the Cross then I went down into Hades that I might bring up Adam and all them that were with him, at the supplication of Michael the Archangel."[1] Many Orthodox icons of the Resurrection symbolically represent Christ wrenching Adam and Eve out of their sepulchres.

In another section, Bartholomew asked Jesus to show the adversary to the apostles so that they might see and know his works and whence he comes. Jesus complied and took them to the Mount of Olives where he ordered Michael to sound the trumpet and summon Beliar. The sight was fearful indeed and the apostles fell down in fear, but Jesus told them to rise and commanded Bartholomew to place his foot upon Beliar's neck and ask him whence he came, to which the beast is reported to have replied:

> . . .at first I was called Satanael, which is interpreted a messenger of God, but when I rejected the image of God my name was called Satanas, that is, an angel that keepeth Hell. . . . For indeed I was formed the first angel: for when God made the heavens, he took a handful of fire and formed me first, Michael second . . .(when he thought to create all things, his son spake a word) so that we also were created by the will of the Son and the consent of the Father. He formed, I say me, next Michael, the chief captain of the hosts that are above, Gabriel third, Uriel fourth, Raphael fifth, Nathanael sixth, and the other angels of whom I cannot tell the names. For they are the rod-bearers (lictors) of God, and they smite me with their rods and pursue me seven times in the night and seven times in the day.[2]

Satan then describes the myriads of angels and declares the name of the
angel of the north which is Oertha, and the angel of the south Kerkoutha,
and tells of an angel who makes the snow fall and another who makes the sea
rough. To Bartholomew's question as to how he ensnares men from the
paths of God and how he leads them by "arts, that are slippery and dark,"
Beliar replied and "smote his teeth together, gnashing them, and there came
up out of the bottomless pit a wheel having a sword of flashing fire, and in the
sword were pipes." There follows a strange description of all the instruments
of hell. Explains Beliar:

> "We have other ministers we command, and we furnish them with a hook
> of many points and send them forth to hunt, and they catch for us the
> souls of men, enticing them with sweetness of divers baits, that is by
> drunkenness and laughter, fornications, by backbiting, hypocrisy, plea-
> sures, and the rest of the trifles that come out of their Treasures." Satan
> also declares that when man was created in the image of God Michael
> requested of him to worship man because he was made in God's image,
> but Satan cried: "I am fire of fire, I was the first angel formed, and shall I
> worship clay and matter? . . . God will not be wroth with me; but I will set
> my throne over against his throne, and I will be as he is!"[3]

There follow most unappetizing descriptions of how from the sweat of his
breast and from below his arms he made a vial with which he bewitched the
waters whence Eve drank, and so was able to deceive her.

We can see the fertile imagination of those early days let loose in a riot of
legend, but it is not devoid also of touching and true piety in Bartholomew's
prayer:

> Thou that didst wear a crown of thorns that thou mightest prepare for us
> that repent the precious crown of heaven; . . . My God and Father, the
> greatest, my King: save Lord, the sinners, and Jesus answered: "My
> Father did name me Christ, that I might come down upon earth and
> anoint every man that cometh unto me with the oil of life: and he did call
> me Jesus that I might heal every sin of them that know not . . . and give
> unto men the truth of God."[4]

The Virgin's account of the Annunciation is very fanciful and adds
nothing to a deeper knowledge of the angels, not even to imagery.

### 3. The Dead Sea Scrolls

The Dead Sea Scrolls belong to this period, the first century after Christ,
and to the period directly preceding it. They are of great intrinsic merit and
should be mentioned here. The Qumran writings contain striking equiva-
lents to Christianity, but they also have equally striking differences. The
greatest dissimilarity lies in the fact that the Essenes were exclusively Jewish

and that they held the belief that the coming of the Messiah would coincide with the end of the world.

In angelology we find some of the greatest similarities. The Qumran writings give a preponderant place to angels, surpassing that given them in the New Testament. This is bound up with the fundamental teachings of the sect that believed in the existence of two spirits and of two ways. But this principle of the two paths, one of righteousness, and one of evil, is more of a moral concept, than a belief in two different beings or entities. Nonetheless, those who choose either of the ways become respectively the "sons of light" and the "sons of darkness," coming under the dominion of either the Prince of Light (Angel of Truth) or the Angel of Darkness (Belial, or Mastema). St. Michael is the protector of the "sons of light" as also the leader of Moses and Aaron. The sectarians looked forward to praising the Lord in the company of his "marvelous assembly" of angels as we ourselves do.

Belial, or the Angel of Hostility or of Darkness, rules over the "sons of iniquity"; the same end is foreseen for those as we find in the New Testament and many of the apocryphal writings. In fact much of the language and symbolism has a great resemblance. This is not astounding, nor should it be given too much importance. We must not forget that the Christians and the Essenes spoke a common language and had a common heritage, the Old Testament. They lived in the same land, and a very narrow strip of land at that, so that inevitably similar expressions and metaphors are employed. The interpretation though is quite different. In the Scrolls it is an angel who is the "Prince of Light," while for Christians it is Christ himself. Also the Essenes' Angel of Darkness is equal in power to the Prince of Light and they live in a sort of peaceful co-existence, despite certain wars and total divergence of ways. In the New Testament the Angel of Darkness attacks Jesus directly and is overcome by him. Through this "overcoming" Jesus subjugates sin and death and by this grace leads the believers in the way of light. On the other hand, in the Scrolls the children of light have to find their "way of truth" unaided. The two Qumran spirit leaders are from the outset created "angels" of light and of darkness, without any previous free choice.

In fact, the Scrolls, interesting and valuable as they are, are definitely not Christian, and therefore do not belong to our study. Nor do they throw much light on angelology, but prove that the same currents of thought, based upon some of the Old Testament books, were active in Qumran, and prevalent among the early Christians as well. Further, the last word on the Scrolls has not been said, despite over four hundred books already published on the subject. We will not carve our way through that labyrinthine maze of literature.

The Gospel according to Thomas, as far as it has to date been made available to the general public, has only one reference to the angels: "Jesus said: 'The angels and the prophets will come to you and they will give you what is yours.' "[5] This seems rather a lovely promise for the pure in heart, and a rather fearsome one for the impure. The angels always and again appear as the executors of recompense.

### 4. The Desert Fathers

We must pass a fleeting glance upon the Desert Fathers; though they themselves left no written record, yet by the great piety of their lives, lived out in the solitude of the desert, they had a powerful influence upon the Christian Church at that time.

The Desert Fathers are a category all their own. They are the athletes of God. Men who left the world behind them to find in God their solace, in the midst of the deep silence of the great open spaces and there, too, to face Satan and combat him. Men of true sanctity, they all were unsparingly harsh with themselves, practicing austerities which may seem to us strange and even terrible. But to their fellow man they were invariably gentle, kind, forgiving and thoughtful, and of heartrending humility. They were the first Christian monks, men who searched for the true peace of an inner life. They wrote nothing for they possessed nothing but what they stood up in; they earned the bare necessities of life by humble jobs they performed, such as plaiting reed mats and baskets for sale. The most we know of them is what other people related about them; the most famous report is the life of St. Anthony, attributed to St. Athanasius. This book was partly responsible for the conversion of St. Augustine, so it should not be overlooked. It tells us of Anthony's call to the desert life through obedience to Christ's words, "Sell all thou hast and follow me." It tells of his teachings, trials, and miracles. The temptations and fights the holy man had with the evil spirits are vividly portrayed. Later history and legend made much of these incidents, leaving out the sublime simplicity and devoutness of Anthony and the deep wisdom of his teaching. Here, for instance, is what he said concerning visions and how to distinguish the good from the evil ones:

> The vision of the holy ones is not fraught with distraction: "For they will not strive nor cry nor shall anyone hear their voice" (Mt. 12:19). But it comes so quietly and gently that immediately joy, gladness and courage arise in the soul. For the Lord who is our joy is with them, and the power of God the Father. And the thoughts of the soul remain unruffled and undisturbed, so that it, enlightened as it were with rays beholds by itself those who appear.[6]

The quiet beauty of these words have in them the ring of true spiritual insight divested of any superstitious or ignorant hallucination. It is clear that it is neither the imagination nor the mortal eye that sees, but by the grace of God the soul itself.

The hermits who spent long years in absolute solitude could not at all times master their imaginations nor the desires that conjured up for them visions of the world they left behind. Peace was not easily won. They felt themselves attacked by Satan even as Jesus was in the wilderness, but with less power to defend themselves. Their mind's eye saw many strange pictures which at some time they must have related in graphic words which, when chronicled, were doubtless further enhanced. So we have inherited strange tales of even bodily attack by the demons. But there are also stories of angels and blessed visions that brought solace to the striving souls that had chosen so arduous a way of living for God. They chose solitude for as one hermit said: "A thousand and a thousand thousand of the angelic powers have one will and men have many."

One holy man, Peter by name, who dwelled in Petra was harassed by lusts he could not overcome and so he went for help to the Abbot Isidor who told him to return to his cell and pray, but Peter protested that he could not, so Isidor told him to look at the sunset, and there he perceived a great assembly of devils preparing to do battle and then Isidor said:

> "Look to the East," and he looked and saw an innumerable multitude of angels in glory. Whereupon the Abbot Isidor said: "Behold, these are they that are sent to our aid. Those that are climbing up in the west are they that fight against us; and they that are with us are more than they that be against us."[7]

And who can gainsay that these men *saw* clearly what we at times only *feel*? We so easily disclaim experience we have not ourselves ever known. If we go right back into the Old Testament we have a very similar statement made by the prophet Elisha when the armies of the King of Syria surrounded the city of Dothan. "...Fear not; for they that be with us are more than they that be with them...and Elisha prayed...and behold the mountain was full of horses and chariots of fire round about Elisha" (2 Kgs. 6:16-17; 2 Chr. 32:7). We have the testimony of saints and holy people right up to our own times who have seen both the flames of hell and the light of heaven. Eyes that are long closed in prayer are apt when open to be clear-sighted. Such eyes have a clearer vision than ours, which mostly look upon the material world, or when closed are directed usually to sleep. Our sight becomes blurred, not by the dazzle of light, but by the murk of our daily rounds.

From here we shall move on now to the writings of the Fathers of the Church in which there is neither hesitation, nor doubt, nor hearsay, but the solid world of the teachings of the great Doctors of the Faith.

¹*The Apocryphal Gospel of Bartholomew*. Trans. by M.R. James. Oxford: Clarendon Press, 1957, p. 167.

²*Ibid.*, pp. 175-176.

³*Ibid.*, p. 178.

⁴*Ibid.*, p. 179.

⁵*The Gospel According to Thomas*, trans. A. Guillaumont, H. C. Puech, G. Quispel, W. Till, and Yassah 'Abd Al Masih. New York: Harper and Brothers, 1959, p. 47.

⁶*Life of St. Anthony*, in *Nicene and Post-Nicene Fathers*, Series Two, Vol. IV., p. 205.

⁷Helen Waddell, *The Desert Fathers*. New York: Sheed & Ward, p. 171-172.

# II

## The Angels and the Early Christian Fathers
### (100-325 A.D.)

The Early Christian Fathers cover a span of approximately two hundred and twenty-five years. They fall into two categories, the Apostolic Fathers and the Apologists.

The Apostolic Fathers are those Fathers who immediately followed the Apostles, and faced the first six anti-Christian persecutions. Therefore, for them, missionary action and heroic sacrifice took priority over theology. The Apologists were those who, coming slightly later into the arena, found they had to turn to the pen to defend their faith, as well as face physical persecution. It was the period when Christianity, having made converts among the intellectual pagans, demanded a fair hearing, and it became, as well, imperative to reply to certain popular slanders and misconceptions.

The Apostolic Fathers had direct contact with the Twelve themselves. It is to them that we owe the preservation of Holy Tradition in word and in fact; they picked up the thread where the Apostles' deaths had let it fall, twining it into an ever stronger cord that even when divided has never snapped.

We have comparatively few written records of this period, because in those troubled days they had little time for writing, and besides, documents were compromising to possess and difficult to hide and find again. We have seen in the Dead Sea Scrolls how such documents could lie hidden for hundreds of years. Those who had hidden them vanished while faithfully guarding the precious secret. This was a time of heroes rather than of writers, of soldiers and martyrs, rather than of theologians and dogmatic specialists.

These witnesses to the faith were the first members of the fledgling Church. They were converts of many nations and from all walks of life, simple men, most of them, but full of that childlike faith which was to prove stronger than all the wisdom of this world: "God hath chosen the foolish things of this world to confound the wise" (1 Cor. 1:27). These are the men who preserved the Gospels and Epistles for us, and in whose ranks the continued presence of the Lord on earth was made possible in their acts of faith. To them we look with gratitude and reverence for to them we owe the survival of the Christian Church.

References to the angels are few and far between, but those that are present show the uninterrupted belief and consciousness of the Church's attitude. Here are a few passages pertinent to the study we are making.

### 1. St. Ignatius of Antioch (c. 35-107 A.D.)

St. Ignatius may well be considered the first of the Apostolic Fathers. He was bishop of Antioch, and it is believed that he was, before his conversion, an oppressor of the Christians. Little is known of his life beyond his journey as a prisoner from Antioch to Rome where he was to be martyred. Enroute he stopped in Smyrna where he was treated with great honor by St. Polycarp, the leading Christian figure in Roman Asia, who had received his bishopric from St. John the Evangelist. It was during this journey that Ignatius wrote the letters from which we quote. He was a man deeply convinced of Christ, thirsting to suffer martyrdom for his sake.

There is also a charming story which claims that Ignatius was the child placed by Jesus in the midst of the apostles (Mt. 18:2-3). The probable date of his birth does put this story in the realm of the possible; it certainly makes the assertion that he was a fellow disciple under St. John quite credible. As the immediate disciple of St. John, Ignatius' references to the angels should then take on special significance.

> ...might I not write you things more full of mystery? But I fear to do so, lest I should inflict injury on you who are but babes (in Christ). Pardon me in this respect, lest, as not being able to receive their weighty import, ye should be strangled by them. For even I, though I am bound (for Christ), and am able to understand heavenly things, the angelic orders, and the different sorts of angels and hosts, the distinctions between powers and dominions, and the diversities between the thrones and authorities, the mightiness of Aeons, and the pre-eminence of the Cherubim and Seraphim, the sublimity of the spirit, the Kingdom of the Lord, and above all, the incomparable majesty of the Almighty God—though I am acquainted with these things, yet am I not therefore by any means perfect....[1]

It is of interest to note, and to refer to later, that the belief in the angelic hierarchy was no invention of later centuries. For instance, Dionysius the Areopagite, of whom a chapter later, based all he wrote on a knowledge passed down from the very inception of the Church. Ignatius, moreover, held the view that all creation must accept Christ if it would live:

> Let no man deceive himself: both the things which are in heaven, and the glorious angels and rulers, both visible and invisible, if they believe not in the blood of Christ, shall in all consequence incur condemnation.[2]

Another quotation comes from the unauthenticated letters of Ignatius. These, if he did not write them, are of unknown authorship, and were referred to in the sixth century and unquestioned until the end of the fifteenth century when they became subject of a long dispute concerning the episcopate, though this in no way impairs their angelological value. Here he turns to the problem of evil:

> ...The prince of this world rejoiceth when anyone denies the confession of the cross, since he knows that the confession of the cross is his own destruction. For that is the trophy which has been raised up against his power, which when he sees he shudders, and when he hears of, is afraid....
> ...before the cross was erected he was eager that it should be so; and he "wrought (for this end) in the children of disobedience" [Eph. 2:2]. He wrought in Judas, in the Pharisees, in the Sadducees.... But when it was just about to be erected, he was troubled and infused repentance into the traitor, and pointed him to a rope to hang himself with.... And he who had tried by every means to have the cross prepared now endeavored to put a stop to the erection; not because he was influenced by repentance...of his crime but because he perceived his own destruction to be at hand.[3]

When referring to Satan himself, Ignatius describes him as ignorant and "wont to walk with slanting and uncertain steps." Yes, ignorant of all the great wonders of the Incarnation, of the lowliness of the Child for whom there was no room, of the miracles of the Baptism and teachings and sacrifice of the Lamb. Ignatius speaks straight at the devil and says:

> Seeing these things thou wast in utter perplexity...that it was a Virgin that should bring forth; the angel's song of praise struck thee with astonishment.[4]

Had Satan remembered the prediction of the Scriptures of the one of whom it is said, "Thou shalt tread upon the lion and the adder: the young lion and the dragon shalt thou trample under thy feet" (Ps. 90:13), there would not have been any need to remind him that "man does not live by bread alone."

The knowledge of the triumph of Christ over evil not only sustained, but also made Ignatius eager for martyrdom, and gave him the courage to face the claws of the lions with joy instead of fear.

### 2. St. Clement of Rome (c. 96 A.D.)

St. Clement of Rome is held to have been the third bishop in succession to St. Peter. He was a young contemporary of St. Ignatius and it is just possible that he was a fellow laborer of St. Paul, one of his "fellow workers whose names are in the book of life" (Phil. 4:3).

St. Clement was a moralist, a sober person concerned with the organization of the Christian community, its ministry and liturgy. Therefore his mention of the angels takes on particular importance because it shows how from the very start it was believed that the holy angels were participants in our corporate worship, of which the following is clearly a liturgical reference:

> Let us think of the whole host of angels, how they stand by and serve his will. For the Scriptures say: "Ten thousand times ten thousand were doing service to him, and they cried out: Holy, holy, holy, Lord Sabaoth; the whole of creation is full of his glory." Then let us gather together in awareness of our concord, as with one mouth we shout earnestly to him that we may become sharers in his great and glorious promises.[5]

There are many legends about St. Clement, but this one has particular appeal. It relates that St. Clement was banished to the Crimea during the reign of Trajan where he did forced labor in the mines (history repeats itself!)—but this far from deterring the saint only offered him new openings for preaching the Gospel. He was so successful in his mission that the authorities felt that only by throwing him into the Black Sea tied to an anchor could they effectually silence him. But, the legend adds, the angels built him a tomb in the depths which was shown once a year to the coast dwellers by the miraculous ebbing of the tideless sea.

By way of a fragment, we interpose here a rather illuminating quotation from a letter written by an Alexandrian Jew who lived at the time of the Emperors Trajan and Hadrian:

> There are two ways of doctrine and authority, the one of light, and the other of darkness. But there is a great difference between these two ways. For over one are stationed the light, bringing angels of God, but over the other, angels of Satan. And indeed He [that is, God], is Lord for ever and ever but he [that is, Satan], is the prince of the time of iniquity.[6]

Thus we see the enigma of evil, its origin and personality in the tempter, becoming of increasing concern to the Fathers. The many temptations and trials that afflicted the Christians had to be dealt with and explained. Good was self-evident and needed less explication, while evil, tortuous as is its nature to be, was a real problem; hence more reference to the devils, than to the angels.

### 3. Justin Martyr (c. 100-165 A.D.)

Justin, saint and martyr, was probably pagan-born of Roman descent in Flavia Neapolis, the ancient Schem of Samaria, today known as Nablous. His conversion was due to his admiration of the way in which Christians faced horrible forms of death, when a simple recantation could have saved them. At first he had studied pagan philosophy, but later lived as a Christian teacher in Rome in the reign of Antoninus Pius and suffered martyrdom under Marcus Aurelius. He was the first and greatest Apologist. He is chiefly known for the First and Second Apologies and the *Dialogue with Trypho.*

Based on Genesis 6:2, Justin believed the "sons of God" to have been angels, and advanced the opinion that God when he created the earth committed it both to men and angels, and that these last were captivated by the beauty of women and transgressed and begot children who were demons or gods. These gods had names, while the one and only-unbegotten God has no name. In spite of this rather strained and strange interpretation, not prevalent for long in the Church, his teaching on free will is quite orthodox. He held that both men and angels shared it equally, and through it he seeks to answer the question, "Why does God permit evil?"

> Could not God have cut off in the beginning the serpent so that he exist not, rather than have said "And I will put enmity between his seed and her seed." Could He not have once created both angels and men free to do that which He knew it would be good for them to have the exercise of free will and because He likewise knew it would be good, He made general and particular judgments; each one's freedom of will power however being guarded.[7]

Justin here is in line with all Christian teachers in saying that evil has to be willed before it becomes reality. He has a rather lovely passage of praise which includes so much:

> ...the God who is without a trace of evil—Him we worship and adore, and His Son . . .and the hosts of the other good angels who attend on God and are of godlike nature and the spirit of prophecy.[8]

Justin died for his faith, having been scourged and beheaded, with the same courage which, in his youth, he had so admired in others and which has characterized the true Christian throughout the ages.

### 4. St. Irenaeus (c. 130-202 A.D.)

St. Irenaeus was bishop of Lyons, though probably was born in Smyrna. He is a true link between East and West. He was sent to the western outpost of Christianity by St. Polycarp, the famous bishop of Smyrna. In those early days the missionaries were Greek; Latin Christianity, oddly enough, began in Africa.

St. Irenaeus was the first great theologian of the universal Church. He was a diligent searcher of the doctrines of the Fathers who went before him. By the depth of his arguments and his forebearing example, he at one point saved the Church from a controversy that threatened Christian unity. In the end he received the crown of martyrdom, together with countless other members of his flock in the massacre of 202 A.D., instigated by the cruel Emperor Severus.

In Irenaeus' writings angels are mentioned in order to refute heretical notions about them, rather than to describe them. For instance, one of the concepts he refutes is that the world was created by the angels.

### 5. Tertullian (c. 160-220 A.D.)

Tertullian was of the African Church, a native of Carthage. He had a through and through pagan education and was a lawyer in Rome when converted to Christianity. Later he sided with the Montanists. He is not, therefore, considered an altogether orthodox theologian, and though he must be taken into serious account for his brilliance, he nonetheless cannot be properly numbered among the Fathers. He was a great scholar and many of his views are acceptable in his numerous theological, apologetical, ascetical and controversial writings.

Among the many ideas that cropped up in the first centuries, sustained by the Gnostics in particular, was that Jesus had assumed "angelic flesh," and therefore did not need to be born. Tertullian has an interesting passage on this and in it elucidates a point about the angels as well:

> No angel ever descended for the purpose of being crucified, of experiencing death, of being raised from the dead. If there was never such a cause for angels to be embodied, there you have the reason why they did not receive flesh through the process of birth. They did not come to die, and therefore they did not come to be born. But Christ was sent to die, and therefore he had of necessity to be born, that he might be able to die; for this is the rule that only that dies, which is born.[9]

This quotation unequivocally asserts the belief of the incorporeality of the angels, a belief that has remained firmly established in the Church.

### 6. St. Clement of Alexandria (c. 150-215 A.D.)

In the early centuries Alexandria was the great center of learning. It was the intellectual center of Christianity, as its heart was in Antioch. Greek was the universal language of the times. Justin and Irenaeus are considered the founders of Christian literature, aside of course from the New Testament which is Sacred Scripture and not exclusively literature. Titus Flavius Clemens was a worthy successor to them in the catechetical school of Alexandria. In his writings St. Clement laid forth the basic Christian philosophy and the faith with precision and clarity. With regard to angels, in opposition to the Gnostics, he wrote:

> . . .by angels whether seen or not, the divine power bestows good things. Such was the mode adopted in the advent of the Lord. And sometimes also the power "breathes" in men's thoughts and reasonings and "puts in" their hearts "strength" and a keener perception, and furnishes "prowess" and boldness of clarity.[10]

In another fragment of Clement's writings, we come upon a statement underlining the traditional concept of angels, another portion of that unbroken thread concerning their nature, in spite of occasional divergent speculation. He writes:

> ...these primitive and first created virtues are unchangeable in substance, and along with subordinate angels and archangels whose names they share, effect divine operations. Thus Moses names the virtue of the angel Michael, by an angel near to himself and of the lowest grade.... Moses heard him and spoke to him face to face. On the other prophets through the agency of angels an impression was made as of beings hearing and seeing.
>
> On this account also they alone heard, and they alone saw.... If the voice had been open and common, it would have been heard by all.... It was heard by him alone, in whom the impression made by the angels worked.[11]

Clement further states that:

> ...by an ancient and divine order the angels are distributed among the nations...[and] the best thing on earth is the most pious man; and the best thing in heaven, the nearer in place and purer, is an angel, the partaker of the eternal blessed life. But the nature of the Son...is the most perfect....[12]

### 7. Origen (c. 185-254 A.D.)

Origen was St. Clement's most brilliant and prolific pupil, and is said to have written six hundred books. He was essentially a biblical scholar, absorbing the Scripture in the depth of his soul, believing always in the absolute integrity of its inspiration. Controversy still rages over certain details of what is considered his departure from orthodoxy of doctrine. Some of his views, alas, led to heresy and to his condemnation. Whatever the mistakes he may have made, Origen remains the first and greatest biblical critic of Christian antiquity, and as such he is invaluable. Thus he comments on the different roles that God has assigned to his angels:

> ...we are [not] to suppose that it is the result of an accident that a particular office is assigned to a particular angel, as to Raphael, e.g. the work of curing and healing; to Gabriel, the conduct of war; to Michael, the duty of attending to the prayers and supplications of mortals. For we are not to imagine they obtained these offices otherwise than by their own merits, and by the zeal and excellent qualities which they surely displayed before this world was framed...so that to one angel the Church of the Ephesians was entrusted; to another that of the Smyrneans; one angel was to be Peter's, another Paul's; and so on through everyone of the little ones that are in the Church...and there also be some angel that encampeth

round about them that fear God . . .it is to be believed that they were conferred by God, the just and impartial Ruler . . . .[13]

It is interesting that Origen believed that even the angels had to strive for perfection:

I am of the opinion then . . .that it is neither from want of discrimination nor from accidental cause, either that the "principalities" hold their dominion, or the other orders of the spirit have obtained their respective offices; but that they have received the steps of their rank on account of their merits although it is not our privilege to know or inquire what these acts of theirs were, by which they earned a place in a particular order.[14]

This progression worked inversely for those angels who chose wickedness. The devils "have obtained these degrees in proportion of their conduct, and the progress which they made in wickedness."[15] Origen does not believe that Satan and his angels were damned once and for always, that is, forever, an opinion that some of the later Fathers held, but which is not the teaching of the Church.

For in our view, not even the devil himself was incapable of good; but although capable of admitting good he did not therefore also desire it, or make any effort after virtue.[16]

Therefore Origen argues:

When it is said that "the last enemy shall be destroyed," it is not to be understood as meaning that his substance, which is God's creation, perishes, but that his purpose and hostile will perishes; for this does not come from God but from himself. Therefore his destruction means not ceasing to exist but ceasing to be an enemy and ceasing to be death. Nothing is impossible to omnipotence; there is nothing that cannot be healed by the Maker; the Creator made all things in order that they might exist; and if things were made that they might exist they cannot become non-existent.[17]

Origen opposed the notion that any good angel would ever hurt anyone, not even those who offend him. The devils alone inflict evil and that of their own volition for, as he maintains, "they have received no office of that kind from God." He also reminds us that we are not obliged to suffer at the hands of the demons:

But the Christian, the true Christian who has submitted to God alone and to His Word, will suffer nothing from demons, for He is mightier than demons. And the Christian will suffer nothing for "the Angel of the Lord will encamp about them that fear Him and will deliver him and his 'angel' who 'always beholds the face of his Father in heaven' " offers up his prayers through the one High Priest to the God of all, and also joins his own prayer with those of the man who is committed to his keeping.[18]

These words need no commentary. Their beauty ought sink deeply into our hearts and become a conscious part of our thinking.

Although our last subject in this chapter will deal with the Pastor of Hermas, we might say, in a sense, that it ends really with Origen, before our entry upon the consideration of the great Fathers of the Church in the age of Orthodox Theology when the Christian Church emerged out of the shadows and became a religion recognized by the State and would have more subtle dangers to face than the lions of the Roman arenas. It was, however, clearly upon the foundations laid by the Early Fathers that the Church would grow, expand, and flourish.

## 8. The Pastor (Shepherd) of Hermas

Because of a certain spiritual beauty, clear and in a sense of granite quality, the discussion of this writer is left to the last, though he probably wrote during or shortly after the reign of Trajan though we know little of him. In the Pastor of Hermas we find the first distinct mention in Patristics of a guardian angel as well as of an attendant devil attached to each person:

> Now I will show you the powers of these that you may know what power each possess. For their powers are double and have relation alike to the righteous . . . . But walk in the straight and even way . . .the crooked path has no roads: but has many pathless places and stumbling blocks in it, and is rough and thorny. But they who walk in the straight road walk evenly . . . .
>
> There are two angels with one man—one of righteousness and the other of iniquity . . . . The angel of righteousness is meek and peaceful. When therefore he ascends into your heart, forthwith, he talks to you of righteousness, purity, chastity, contentment, and of every righteous deed and glorious virtue, when these ascend into your heart know that the angel of righteousness is with you . . . . Look now at the works of the angel of iniquity. First he is wrathful, and bitter, and foolish, and his works are evil and ruin the servants of God. When he ascends into your heart know him by his works. You may trust the works of the angel of righteousness and doing them you may live to God.[19]

There is a wondrous timelessness about our unknown Hermas whose Shepherd was the Angel of Penance who revealed himself to Hermas in a series of visions. Hermas stands out as one who heard, lived, suffered and died according to the voice of his good angel. Indeed, he "lived unto God."

[1]"Epistle of Ignatius to the Trullians," *The Ante-Nicene Fathers*, Vol. I. Grand Rapids, Michigan: Wm. B. Eerdmans Publishing Co., 1956, p. 68.

[2]"Epistle of Ignatius to the Smyrneans," *Ibid.*, p. 88.

[3]"Epistle of Ignatius to the Philippians," *Ibid.*, p. 117.

[4]*Ibid.*, p. 118.

[5]St. Clement of Rome, "Epistle to the Corinthians," XXXIV, *The Early Christian Fathers*, ed. and trans. by Henry Bettenson, Geoffrey Cumberledge. Oxford: Oxford University Press, 1956, p. 47.

[6]*The Epistle of Barnabas*, in *The Ante-Nicene Fathers*, Vol. I, p. 149.

[7]Justin Martyr, "Dialogue with Trypho," *The Ante-Nicene Fathers*, Vol. I, p. 250.

[8]*Apologia I*, VI, in *The Early Christian Fathers*, p. 81.

[9]*The Stromata of Miscellanies*, in *The Ante-Nicene Fathers*, Vol. II, p. 518.

[10]*Ibid.*

[11]Fragments from Cassiodorus, *Ibid.*, p. 575.

[12]*The Stromata*, p. 524.

[13]Origen, "De Principiis," *The Ante-Nicene Fathers*, Vol. IV. p. 266.

[14]*Ibid.*

[15]*Ibid.*

[16]*Ibid.*, p. 265.

[17]"De Principiis," III. VI, 5, *The Early Christian Fathers*, p. 355.

[18]*Against Celsus*, Book VIII, Vol. IV, p. 653.

[19]*The Pastor of Hermas*, in *The Ante-Nicene Fathers*, Vol. II, p. 24.

# III

## The Angels in the Age of Orthodox Theology

In 313 A.D., after Constantine the Great became sole Emperor of the Roman Empire, he gave full and official sanction to the Christian religion. Soon thereafter he removed the seat of imperial government from Rome to Constantinople. At this very moment the Church was being rent by various trends and heresies, the most serious of which was Arianism. To save the unity of the Church the Symbol of Faith, known also as the Nicene Creed, expressing the Christian faith, was evolved at the Council of Nicea (325 A.D.) and the Council of Constantinople (381 A.D.), and accepted by almost the entire Christian world. The Fathers of this time are therefore called the Nicene Fathers; our concern here, however, embraces equally those who followed upon them. Each of these great doctors of theology, in his own time and sphere maintained the Christian Faith in its orthodoxy and did so with magnificent courage and singleness of purpose.

### 1. St. Athanasius (c. 296-373 A.D.)

"I believe in One God, the Father Almighty, Maker of heaven and earth, and of all things visible and invisible."

Thus opens the great unifying Creed of Christendom. The official world of imperial Rome gave it sanction. Emperors came under the new banner of the Cross, but the road for the Church was far from smooth.

The Church Fathers, deeply in love with God and dedicated to his service, feared no one; they stood up to Emperors (and Empresses) and philosophers; neither the erudition of the wise, nor the might of the Empire could move them from their convictions.

As the great list of names rolls before our eyes, we would be pleased to hear each one speak. Unfortunately, not all the writings of the Fathers have been translated into modern languages and even from those that have, the choice of quotations is difficult. We can but choose what we can best understand, seeking to follow the golden thread of the angels through the maze of theological literature

Principally of course, the Fathers' firm belief in a spiritual world is stated in the first article of the Creed in the words, "all things visible and invisible."

By invisible things they meant the angels and the human soul.

One of the greatest architects of the Creed was St. Athanasius. He, too, was a pupil of the famous catechetical school of Alexandria and, when bishop, was exiled six times from this see, this because of his adamant adherence to orthodox theology. With great fortitude he surmounted all his personal misfortunes, but above all, it was his resolute character and unimpeachable theology which triumphed over all opposition to the benefit of the Church.

Athanasius undauntedly maintaining the Holy Tradition, evidently never questioned or even envisaged any doubt where angels are concerned but explained their appointed place:

> ...Without the Word was made not one thing. But as regards ministrations, there are, not only one, but many out of their whole number whomever the Lord will send. For there are many archangels, many thrones, and authorities, and dominions, thousands of thousands, and myriads of myriads standing before Him, ministering and ready to be sent.[1]

Athanasius further elucidates that the angel cannot of himself save, but does so at the will of God:

> It is proper then to an angel to minister at the command of God, and often does he go forth to cast out the Ammonite: and is sent to guard the people in the way: but these are not his doings, but of God who commanded and sent him, . . . But at any time when the angel was seen he who saw it heard God's voice.[2]

St. Athanasius had much to say about demons, especially in his biography of St. Anthony the Great. He saw a very positive personification of evil in the wicked spirits that plague us. He stresses at the same time that we should have no fear of them for Christ has destroyed their power. "Let us consider and lay to heart that while the Lord is with us, our foes can do us no hurt. For when they approach us in the form corresponding to the state in which they discover us, they adapt their delusions to the condition of mind in which they find us." St. Athanasius believes that if we are timid and confused the demons have a heyday, but if we are singleminded with our thoughts concentrated on the Lord, they vanish like smoke. He is a firm believer in the power of the Sign of the Cross to dispel the evil spirits. This is a fact many Christians have found to be true.

In the joy of Easter, Athanasius sees us all uniting with the angels in joyous praises. He speaks of the psalms and hymns, in all of which he sees men, not standing alone, but being part of the grand chorus of all created beings:

> The whole of creation keeps a fast, my brethren, and everything that hath breath praises the Lord . . .
> Who then will lead us to such a company of angels as this? Who, coming

with a desire for the heavenly feast and the angelic holiday . . .let us not celebrate the feast after earthly manner, but as keeping festival in heaven with the angels.[3]

Athanasius also interprets with profound theological meaning the allegory referred to in the chapter on the Ascension of the Lord, where the angels heralded Christ's arrival before the gates of heaven. This is also referred to by St. Ambrose. St. Athanasius believed that the angels accompanied Christ on his Ascension, and that they were not angels charged with things pertaining to earth, but had descended with him from heaven and accompanied him on earth, in seeing him mount announced him to the celestial virtues that they might open their gates.

> The powers are in a stupor at seeing Him in the flesh. For which reason they cry, stupefied at this astonishing economy: Who is this? The angels mounting with Christ answer them: the Lord of virtues, it is the King of Glory who teaches those who are in the heavens the great mystery, to know that he who has vanquished the spiritual enemies is King of Glory.[4]

Such the thoughts of Athanasius who passed on the holy flame of Christianity to us. It burns now more luminously than ever, offering to future generations the enlightenment of Christ in the Church.

### 2. St. Basil the Great (c. 330-379 A.D.)

As she lay dying, St. Macrina prayed for "an angel of light who will lead me to the quiet pastures and waters of peace and the bosom of the Holy Fathers."[5] Thus the sister of St. Basil the Great and of St. Gregory of Nyssa went to meet her Lord. This holy woman exercised a tremendous influence upon her famous brothers. She and their mother had led them into the path of Orthodox Christianity and monasticism.

St. Basil, rightly named the Great, gave his name to the monastic guidelines of the East. It is also attached to one of the Holy Liturgies. He is among the most outstanding and heroic figures of the Church. He was greatly learned, statesmanlike, of deep personal holiness, a magnificent organizer, and what we would today call an efficient social worker.

To St. Basil and to his spiritual forebears, the angels were an unquestionable fact. He says of their creation:

> It appears, indeed that even before this world an order of things existed of which our minds can form an idea . . . . The birth of the world was preceded by a condition of things suitable for the exercise of supernatural powers, outstripping the limits of time, eternal and infinite. The Creator and Demiurge [craftsman, from the Greek *demiourgos*] of the universe perfected his works in it, spiritual light for the happiness of all who love the Lord, intellectual and invisible natures, all in orderly arrangement of pure intelligences, who are beyond the reach of our mind and of whom we

cannot ever discover the names. They fill the essence of this invisible world, as Paul teaches us: "For by him were all things created that are in heaven, and that are in earth, visible and invisible, whether they be thrones or dominions or principalities or powers or virtues or hosts of Angels or the dignities of Archangels.[6]

In the *De Spiritu Sancto*, written to dispel any doubts there might be as to the true doctrine of the Holy Spirit, St. Basil speaks of the holy angels in relation to the Third Person of the Trinity:

> Moreover from the things created at the beginning may be learned the fellowship of the Spirit with the Father and the Son. The pure, intelligent, and supermundane powers are and are styled holy, because they have their holiness in the grace given by the Holy Spirit . . .thou, who hast power from the things that are seen to form an analogy of the unseen, glorify the Maker by whom all things were made, visible and invisible . . . the ministering spirits subsist by the will of the Father, are brought into being by the operation of the Son, and perfected by the presence of the Spirit . . . . Moreover, the perfection and continuance of it.[7]

St. Basil has little if anything to say of the devil. His attitude to evil is astoundingly modern and concerned with cause and effect. God, he says, is not the origin of evil, for the contrary cannot come from its very opposite.

> Life does not engender death: darkness is not the origin of light; sickness is not the maker of health . . .but in genesis each being proceeds from its like . . . . If then evil is neither uncreated nor created by God, from whence comes its nature? Certainly that evil exists, no one living in the world will deny . . . . Evil is not a living animated essence; it is the condition of the soul opposed to virtue . . . .

and he goes on to tell us that we must not seek beyond ourselves for evil, because we are ourselves the authors of our own vices. That our fall has no other origin than in our free will, is also true of the angels. St. Basil also seems to believe that devils were actively concerned in destruction and in gluttony, but he speaks of these things only in passing. For him, darkness and all it hides does not exist in essence; he seems incapable of looking for long upon the darkness. His soul strives upward toward light, for him, then, heaven is the only reality where

> The orders of the angels, the heavenly hosts, all intellectual natures, named or unnamed, all the ministering spirits, did not live in darkness, but enjoyed a condition fitted for them in the light of spiritual joy.[8]

Like Athanasius, Basil does not attribute to the heavenly host inborn virtues, but rather the capacity and will to attain them. Therefore, they, too, strive, or did strive in aeons past, to attain ever greater perfection.

The powers of the heavens are not holy by nature: were it so there would be in this respect no difference between them and the Holy Spirit.

Here is a very salient point. There are many to whom the differences between angelic guardianship and the inspiration of the Holy Spirit is not clear. In the first place, the Holy Spirit is the Third Person of the Holy Trinity, and inspired both men and angels. We could use the simile of a sentry set to protect some sovereign. The guardian and the guarded would ideally, in their several functions, be inspired by the ideal of a common goal, as a sovereign and a soldier both serve their country. Man and angel serve God; the angel protects man where he cannot guard himself, but the goal of both is God; the comprehension of this is given them by the Holy Spirit. St. Basil gives a noteworthy definition of the angels' nature and substance thus:

> It is in proportion to their relative excellence that they have their need of holiness from the Spirit. The branding iron is conceived of together with the fire: and yet the material and the fire are distinct. Thus too in the case of the heavenly powers: their substance is, peradventure, an aerial spirit, or an immaterial fire, as it is written "who maketh his angels spirits and his ministers a flame of fire": *wherefore they exist in space and become visible, and appear in their proper bodily form to them that are worthy.* But their sanctification, being external to their substance, superinduces their perfection through the communion of the Spirit. They keep their rank by their abiding in the good and true.[9]

We may infer from this last that those who do not abide in the good and true fall from grace or have already done so. It is the inspiration of the Holy Spirit that moves the heavenly beings to cry "Holy, Holy, Holy," to the God of hosts.

St. Basil sees the angels as an unquestionable reality; if he saw them we know not, but that he was convinced of their existence, we do know.

### 3. St. Gregory of Nyssa (c. 330-395 A.D.)

St. Gregory of Nyssa was a younger brother of St. Basil and St. Macrina, both of whom had a great influence upon him. He is one of the most lovable of the Fathers, a truly great theologian of remarkable insight, knowledge and originality. He was a powerful upholder of the Nicene dogma regarding the Trinity. Origen's influence in Gregory's writings is easily notable. They shared the opinion that ultimately both the souls in hell and the devil will return to God. In his work *On the Soul and Resurrection*, written after the death of St. Basil, he records a discussion with his beloved and remarkable sister. Here is a reply of St. Macrina's to one of his searching questions:

> I do not think...that the divine Apostle (Phil. 2:10-11) divided the intellectual world into localities. There are three states in which reasoning creatures can be: one from the very first received an immaterial life, and

we call it angelic: another is in union with the flesh and we call it human: a third released by death from fleshly entanglements, and is to be found in souls pure and simple. We certainly believe . . .that there exists another world of being besides, divested of such bodies as ours are, who are opposed to that which is good and are capable of hurting the lives of men, having by an act of will lapsed from the nobler view, and by their revolt from goodness personified in themselves the contrary principle: and this world is what . . .the Apostle adds to the number of the "things under the earth," signifying in that when evil shall have been some day annihilated in the long revolution of the ages, nothing shall be left outside the world of goodness, but that even from these evil spirits shall rise in harmony the confession of Christ's Lordship.[10]

Good and evil, are not for St. Gregory two positive existences opposed to each other, but Being against non-Being,

for the distinctive difference between virtue and vice is not to be contemplated as that between two actually subsisting phenomena: but as there is a logical opposition between that which is and that which is not . . .non-entity is logically opposed to entity.[11]

All that is created is subject to change according to St. Gregory. The Trinity alone is changeless, while creation owes its very being to change, by the very fact that it was called out of non-being into being. He believes this to include both angelic and human beings. Change initially began with their very beginnings and they must inevitably move toward something.

Freedom of will St. Gregory takes for granted to be our inalienable heritage, a part of our being created in the image of God:

. . .Free-will—this likeness to Him whose Will is over all . . .[man] was a free agent . . . . He became himself the discoverer of evil. So the first man on the earth, or rather he who generated evil in man had for choice the Good and the Beautiful . . .yet he wilfully cut out a new way for himself against this nature. For be it observed there is no such thing in the world as evil irrespective of a will . . . . But the habit of sinning entered . . .with fatal quickness into the life of man.[12]

Gregory is speaking both of angels and of men for he mentions the generator of evil; the action of that angelic being who turned his eyes away from Good to a lesser good, with the inevitable sequence that led to evil. St. Gregory notes:

Well, it is undeniable that the beginning of any matter is the cause of everything else that by consequence followed upon it . . . . As, then freedom from the agitation of the passions is the beginning and groundwork of a life in accordance with virtue, so the bias of vice generated by that envy is the constituted road to all evils. For when once he, who by apostasy from goodness had received this bias for evil, like a rock torn asunder from a mountain-ridge, which is driven headlong by its own weight . . .was he deliberately forced and borne away as by a kind of gravitation to the utmost limit of iniquity.[13]

St. Gregory maintained that all angels were created perfect, and also free. This in itself made them liable to change. Evil is not, he insisted, in matter, but in the soul's tendency toward matter. Of course those who look to material happiness rather than the spiritual, he says "[if] they had looked at the nature of existing things dispassionately, they would have understood that there is no evil other than wickedness. No evil of any kind lies outside and independent of will."[14]

Therefore matter is not to be annihilated; both soul and body and the fallen angels will be refined as gold in the fire. Upon the salvaging of the fallen angels the other Holy Fathers do *not* share St. Gregory's opinion.

> He who is at once just and good and wise once used his device for the salvation of him who had perished, and thus not only conferred benefit on the lost one, but on him too, who had wrought our ruin . . .for it is as when some worthless material has been mixed with gold, and the gold-refiners burn up the foreign refuse part in the consuming fire, and so restore the more precious substance of its natural lustre.[15]

In this salvaging work the great multitude of the heavenly hosts of which St. Gregory holds there are overwhelming numbers, play their plenary part.

> . . .These powers are ministers that do God's pleasure, effecting the "purging of sin" according to the will of Him who sent them: for this is the ministry of these spiritual beings, namely, to be sent forth for the salvation of those who are being saved.[16]

What more beautiful words could be found than these, of the gentle saint and theologian, Gregory of Nyssa, on the prime mission of the holy angels among us?

### 4. St. Gregory Nazianzen (c. 329-389 A.D.) and St. Cyril of Jerusalem (c. 315-389 A.D.)

St. Gregory Nazianzen, "the Theologian," was the best friend of St. Basil and St. Gregory of Nyssa. The three together are known as the Cappadocian Fathers, because they came from and lived out most of their lives in that part of Asia Minor. St. Gregory Nazianzen and St. Cyril of Jerusalem were contemporaries, upholders, too, of the Nicene Creed.

Generally speaking, St. Gregory went less extensively into the matter of the angels, nonetheless, it would be a pity to leave out a rather lovely quotation which puts things in their proper order; it has a particular quality of timelessness:

God always was and always is and always will be, or rather God always is . . .what time, measured by the course of the sun, is to us, that Eternity is to the Everlasting, namely, a sort of time-like movement interval co-extensive with their existence.

When St. Gregory speaks of God, he always means Father, Son and Holy Spirit, the perfect society of three in One. He interprets creation as the outpouring of this splendid unity:

But since this movement of self-contemplation (the Three Persons of Each Other) alone could not satisfy goodness, but good must be poured out and go forth beyond itself to multiply the objects of its beneficence, so for this essential to the highest goodness, the first conceived the Heavenly Angelic Powers and this conception was a work fulfilled by His Word, and perfected by His Spirit . . . . I should like to say that they were incapable of movement in the direction of evil and susceptible only of the movement of good . . .but I am obliged to stop short saying that—and to conceive and speak of them only as difficult to move—because of him who for his splendor was called Lucifer, but became and is called Darkness through his pride; and the apostate hosts who are subject to him, creators of evil by their revolt against good and our inciters.[17]

Once more we see that the Fathers, as a whole, agreed that sin itself is not being and, consequently, not a creature, has no real substance, but is the deterioration of substance, a falling away from being. Its only reality consists in its creation by the free will both of angels and of man. All the more frightful is its aspect. It is, to see it as a paradox, the incarnation of non-being. God made all perfect from perfect love and from the urge to expand love, to give and to receive it.

St. Cyril of Jerusalem, though not divergent in essentials, gives a slightly different slanting. To him, above all, the angels serve to expand and extend the glory of the Trinity. Lecturing to converts upon that article of the Creed which avers: "And in the Holy Ghost which spake by the Prophets," St. Cyril asserts:

Thou hast seen His power, which is in all the world; tarry now no longer upon earth, but ascend on high . . .in imagination . . .behold there are so many countless myriads of Angels. Mount up in thy thoughts, if thou canst, yet higher; consider, I pray thee, the Archangels, consider the Principalities, consider the Powers, consider the Thrones, consider the Dominions: of all these the comforter is the Ruler from God, and the Teacher and the Sanctifier . . .of Him Michael and Gabriel have need among the Angels . . .all their hosts assembled together have no equality with the Holy Ghost . . .and they indeed are sent forth to minister, but He searches even the deep things of God . . .[18]

Angels are part of the Trinity's glory; its messengers, but never to be thought of as equal or to be confounded with the attribute of the Holy Spirit, either within the Holy Trinity itself or in the souls of men. Cyril is profoundly moved and awed by the magnificence of God and his creation, and impatient with man for wanting, in his littleness, to comprehend the boundlessness of the Creator. He remarks:

> For my part I have ever wondered at the curiosity of bold men . . . . For though they know nothing of Thrones, and Dominions, and Principalities, and Powers, the workmanship of Christ, they attempt to scrutinize their Creator Himself. Tell me, first, O most daring man, wherein does Throne differ from Dominion . . . . Tell me what is Principality, and what a Power, and what a Virtue, and what an Angel: and then search out their Creator for "all things were made by Him."[19]

St. Cyril, in fact, says that we cannot comprehend those things which are created; that we cannot really understand precisely what the angels are and still less can we understand God. Nonetheless, it is through these creatures that we arrive at a certain knowledge of God. He placed emphasis upon this especially in view of the Creed's first article, namely "Maker . . .of all things visible and invisible." St. Cyril was lecturing to the catechumens of his day, not to theologians. He wanted to make his point clear in the minds of those who were about to be baptized, so he stressed the point repeatedly:

> Creator of Heaven and earth, the Maker of Angels and Archangels: of many the Creator, but of One only the Father before all ages . . .our Lord Jesus Christ, by whom he made *all things visible and invisible.*[20]

A strong upholder of the Nicene Creed, St. Cyril teaches nothing that is not in accord with it and the original precepts of its dogma. It is only recently that we have tended to forget that "invisible" refers to the angels. He also lays great stress upon the fact that the angels of whatever category, are primarily Christ's trustworthy servants under his lordship. An angel was charged with the message of his birth at Bethlehem; the angels ministered to him in the desert: "the Scripture saith not 'succoured' Him, but ministered unto him that is like a servant."[21]

Gabriel when he came to the Virgin Mary received his employ as a peculiar dignity. The angel who appeared to Joseph in his dream was obeying a command even as the angel who announced the Resurrection was faithfully discharging the supreme mission laid upon him.

St. Cyril does not circumvent the problem of sin either for ourselves or for the angels; he stresses that God's love is always greater than any other power, even that of sin for

> If a whole people sin, this surpasses not the loving kindness of God . . . . Men denied God, but God denied not Himself . . . . Only, O man, repent

...and grace is not forbidden thee...for God is truly loving unto man...
but how much He forgave the Angels we know not: for to them also He
forgives, since One alone is without sin, even Jesus who purgeth our sins.[22]

All created beings, both human and angelic, are capable of sin, for Christ
alone is perfect as the only-begotten of the Father. The royal road retains the
Word, following which in varied degrees of perfection, all creatures are
fellow servants of the Lord.

The angels are also witnesses to our life, for they are present at our
Baptism, a moment which should be approached with great heed: "Each one
of you is about to be presented to God before tens of thousands of the
Angelic Host,"[23] St. Cyril admonishes his catechumens. Similarly, the angels
will be present upon the Day of Judgment.

> Behold, O man, before what multitudes thou shalt come to judgment...
> reckon all from Adam to this day. Great indeed is the multitude; but yet it
> is little, for the Angels are many more. They are *the ninety and nine sheep*,
> but mankind is the single *one*...the whole earth is but as a point in the
> midst of the one heaven...and must not the heaven of heavens contain
> unimaginable numbers.[24]

How astoundingly modern these words sound! In the fourth century people
were not aware of the immensity and multiplicity of the cosmic worlds, as we
are today, but the saints through spiritual discernment recognized our
minuteness.

St. Cyril, like St. Athanasius, was a firm believer in the power of the Sign of
the Cross. His words are worthy of meditation:

> For when thou art going to dispute with unbelievers concerning the Cross
> of Christ, first make with thy hand the sign of Christ's Cross and the
> gainsayer will be silenced. Be not ashamed to confess the Cross; for the
> Angels glory in it, saying: *We know whom ye seek, Jesus the Crucified.* Mightest
> thou not say, O Angel, "I know whom ye seek, my Master"? But, "I," he
> says with boldness, "I know the Crucified" for the Cross is a crown not a
> dishonor.[25]

The angels know whom we seek: may they guide the hand that signs with the
Cross.

### 5. St. Ambrose (c. 339-397 A.D.)

St. Ambrose, bishop of Milan, is one of the four great Latin Doctors of the
Church, in the company of St. Jerome, St. Gregory the Great and St.
Augustine. He descended from a patrician family and began life by devoting
himself to legal studies. He became a judge, but was so merciful that most
people thought of him more as a father. He became bishop of Milan rather
unanticipatedly, and in an altogether unprecedented manner. While he was
present at the discussion for the choice of the new bishop, a child in th

crowd cried out: "Ambrose, bishop " and chosen he was, on the spot, in spite of the fact that he was not even baptized. The sacrament was promptly conferred and eight days later he was consecrated bishop.

He was a great Greek scholar, and had made a deep study of the Scriptures and of the earlier Fathers, especially of St. Basil. His teaching in angelology differs very little from that of the other Fathers, and it is, in fact, remarkable how these men agree in the main, though differing, at times, in detail. St. Ambrose is preoccupied with the question of their immortality, which he does not consider in an absolute sense. In fact, he says:

> In truth, even the soul may die: "The soul that sinneth, it shall die" [Ez. 18:4] and an angel is not absolutely immortal, his immortality depending on the will of the Creator.[26]

Immortality is not of the essential nature of an angel, as of God's nature. God cannot not exist, because his very essence is existence. On the other hand, the angels owe their existence to his will, and are immortal, of course, in the sense that there is no created force by which they might be destroyed. St. Ambrose gives mortality a very wide meaning to include every aspect of capacity for change or mutation. Immortality to his way of thinking is absolute changelessness.

Because of their capacity for change, angels, although not under the same "learning" discipline as ours, have the ability to sin:

> "For God shall bring all this work to judgment" (Eccl. 12:14). Every creature, then, has within it the possibility of corruption and death, even though it does not (at present) die or commit sin . . . . Immortality, then, that is a gift, is one thing: immortality without the possibility of change is another.[27]

In other words: the angels are immortal by the grace of God, while the immortality of the Son is *de jure*, therefore, absolute.

Like all the other Fathers, Ambrose stresses the angels' diaconate, or service to Christ.

> The Angels come in obedience, he comes in glory, they are his retainers, he sits upon his throne; they stand, he is seated; to borrow terms of the daily dealings of human life, he is the judge: they are the officers of the court.[28]

He believed that the angels progress from perfection to perfection and advance in knowledge.

> Howbeit, seeing that the angels (as well as ourselves) acquire their knowledge step by step, and are capable of advancement, they certainly must display differences of power and understanding for God alone is above and beyond the limits imposed by gradual advance, possessing, as he does, every perfection from everlasting.[29]

Like all the saints, Ambrose knew that faith is absolutely necessary to man's ascent to heaven. Each of us has the Kingdom of God within us, when the Lord approaches it is within our hearts that the gates have to be opened.

> For Christ stands at the door of thy soul. Hear Him speaking, "Behold, I stand at the door and knock: if anyone open to me, I will come in to him and I will sup with him and he with me" (Rev. 3:20).... He stands then—but not alone, for before Him go the angels saying: "Lift up the gates, O ye, the princes," what gates? Even those of which the Psalmist sings, in another place also "Open to me the gates of righteousness." Open then the gates of righteousness, the gates of chastity, the gates of courage and wisdom.[30]

The angels are part of Christ's glory and of his mercy. If we let him enter, the angels enter too, for they are always with him, and to ignore them is to ignore the very glory of God himself.

Ambrose, a great pastor, feared no power but that of God and cared for each of his flock with all-encompassing goodness, be it an emperor or a beggar. One of those who sat and listened to the saint and received Baptism at his hands was St. Augustine.

### 6. St. Augustine of Hippo (c. 354-430 A.D.)

Without St. Augustine's powerful intellect and profound spiritual discernment, Western theology would not have the form it possesses today. Although his viewpoint is completely Occidental, he emphatically belongs to the undivided Church and is one of its foremost exponents. He, like so many of his time, came late—and through overpowering conviction—to the Christian Faith. He, too, like so many other saints before and after him, was profoundly influenced by the example of a pious and saintly mother.

Augustine knew but little Greek and no Hebrew. Unlike Ambrose, he could not for himself study directly from the Fathers. Like them though, he assumes a common fall from original holiness, but is more drastic about the final damnation of all sinners, be they angels or men. Whereas the Eastern Fathers allowed all fallen creatures, through trial and tribulation, under the unchangeable loving and redeeming mercy of God to find their way back to him, Augustine, as he follows the history of the virtuous and unvirtuous on their two antagonistic ways, comes to the conclusion that eternal heaven is for the elect, eternal hell for the reprobate. He does not feel, like many Greek Fathers, that perfection must through countless ages finally be reached by *all* creation, so that "God may be all in all."

St. Augustine has very much to say about angels and he goes very thoroughly in discussion about them, especially in his greatest work, *The City of God*. In this book he discusses the origin, the progress, and, finally, the deserved destinies of the two cities into which he sees the world divided;

there is the City of God, and the city of the world. The angels constitute a large part of the Holy City, the most blessed part, since they have never been expatriated. St. Augustine holds that they were created during the six days and that "They are the light which is called day."[31] He draws attention that in the book of Genesis the creation of light was called day and stands by itself and is not numbered. Here Augustine's views accord with that of St. Basil who also maintained that God made all things at once.

Two cities, that of God and of the world originated, he believes, among the angels, the good and the evil; both have a common nature but their dissimilarity lies in their purpose, which itself has its root in the free choice they made by virtue of their independent will.

While some steadfastly continue in that which was the common good of all, namely in God Himself, and in his eternity . . .others, being enamored rather of their own power, as if they could be their own good, lapsed . . . from that higher and beatific good which was common to all . . .they became proud, deceived, envious . . . . Therefore, if when the question is asked why are the former [the good angels] blessed, it is . . .because they adhere to God . . .there is no other good for the rational or intelligent creature save God only.[32]

St. Augustine seems to see men as co-inhabitants of either one or the other of these two cities, and says:

it is not incongruous and unsuitable to speak of a society composed of angels and men together . . .two in all, one composed of the good, the other of the wicked, angels or men indifferently.[33]

He believes that in as far as we are of good will we come to resemble the good angels and so can be with them, live with them, and worship with them, though we cannot with our mortal eyes see them.

But it is not in locality we are distant from them, but in merit of life . . .for the mere fact of our dwelling on earth under the conditions of life in the flesh does not prevent our fellowship with them. It is only prevented when we, in the impurity of our hearts, mind earthly things . . .we are brought near to them by faith, if by their assistance we believe that he who is their blessedness is also ours.

Augustine is much concerned by the cause of evil. He differentiates between the cause of blessedness and misery in that the good angels cleave to him who supremely is, while the misery of the bad occurs because they have forsaken him and turn toward themselves alone. He asks what was the cause of their evil will in the efficient order, and reply can only be that there was none. For what is it that makes the will bad, when it is the will itself which he says makes the action bad. And so, the bad will is cause of the bad action, but nothing is the efficient cause of the bad will.[34] With Augustine there is no "out" for the wicked; but if drastic with them, he makes the blessedness of the good shine forth in endless happiness and glory.

### 7. St. John Chrysostom (c. 347-407 A.D.)

Equal to SS. Basil and Gregory Nazianzen is St. John the Golden-Mouthed, as among the Church's greatest doctors; he studied law but early felt the call to monastic life. An outstanding reformer of profound moral sense and intrepid spirit, his total honesty brought down upon him the ire of the powerful. They are forgotten, he lives forever, remembered in the Liturgy of the East that bears his name.

In several of St. John Chrysostom's homilies as well as other writings there are many very lovely passages about the angels. For him, too, they are first and foremost the servants of Christ. In fact, he says they can only know God's essence through his Son, Jesus Christ. Also, he unquestionably believes in their guardianship of us:

> Let us keep our vigil, beloved; we also have those that are eager for our success, if we will. Near each one of us angels are sitting; and yet we snore through the whole night. And would it were only this.[35]

The saint here comments on the sins of man performed under the cloak of darkness, and the subsequent chagrin of our guardians.

The angels themselves are supremely happy, says St. John Chrysostom, because they have no wants. "Therefore the less we need, the more we are on the way to them; the more we need, the more we sink down to this perishable life."[36]

> Are they not all ministering spirits, sent forth to minister for them who shall be heirs to salvation! See how he lifts up their minds, and shows the great honor which God has for us, since he has assigned to angels who are above us this ministration on our behalf . . .so that it is an angelic work, to do all for the salvation of the brethren. And we, though servants, are yet angels' fellow-servants . . .they are servants of the Son of God, and are sent many ways for our sakes, and minister to our salvation. And so they are partners in service with us.
>
> And yet the space between angel and man is great; nevertheless he brings them down near to us, all but saying, for us they labor, for our sake they run to and fro: on us, as one might say, they wait. This is their ministry, for our sake to be sent every way.

He then enumerates instances in the Old and New Testaments, especially the latter, and notes:

> Dost thou see that they minister to us on God's behalf, and that they minister to us in the greatest matters? Wherefore Paul saith, "All things are yours, whether life or death, or the world, or things present, or things to come" (1 Cor. 3:20).[37]

St. John Chrysostom is deeply imbued with things heavenly; otherworldliness is to him what we should always strive for so as to be ever conscious that heaven and earth are very close. He shows that we cannot easily distinguish the fine line that separates heaven and earth, as for instance, in the Sacraments.

> It follows then that our thoughts are in Heaven, and heavenly things are ours, even though they be accomplished on earth, yet they are called heavenly. And why do I say "appeared"? nay rather they dwell on earth as indeed in Paradise . . .and "Our conversation is in Heaven" (Phil. 3:20), and yet we live here.[38]

This, says St. John Chrysostom, is the teaching that is given us from above. It is, indeed, the only true philosophy of those Christians who are called to such zeal and study.

### 8. The Celestial Hierarchies of Dionysius the Areopagite

No study of angels can be complete without at least a rough knowledge of that mastermind of the fifth century who so powerfully influenced mystical theology in both the East and the West. We meet his thoughts and conceptions in his writings, though we never heard his name. Most of the great medieval scholars made extensive use of his writings. St. Thomas of Aquinas, the Angelic Doctor, quoted him abundantly. Dante Alighieri placed him in his *Paradiso*. The founder of St. Paul's School, John Colet, translated him with the aid of Erasmus. He inspired Tiepolo's and Fra Angelico's angel-crowded heavens, and his *Celestial Hierarchies* are re-echoed in Milton's verse. His spiritual descendents are to be found in every school of Christian mysticism, and his authority was all but final throughout Christendom. For ten centuries the Church at large and the Eastern Church especially, has always accepted him, though his way is not for all, even as he testifies. So entirely did he belong to God that he completely effaced himself. He gave himself the name of St. Paul's friend, "Dionysius the Areopagite," whose conversion by the Apostle is recorded in the Acts of the Apostles (17:34) and who is believed to have been the first bishop of Athens. Of course, our writer no place claims actually to be that great Apostle's Athenian convert.

Great as the influence of Dionysius was and is, no one knows to whom this enlightened mind belonged. Some authorities claim he was a pupil of Proclus or of Damascius, the last great teachers of the Athenian school, and a late convert to Christianity. Some say he was a Syrian monk, others a Greek bishop; but no one knows when or where he was born, lived, and died. All that is known for sure is that his influence began during or immediately after the fifth century. In fact, we know of him in his extraordinary intellect and in this sense only. If ever a pure mind, it is that of Dionysius. It is as if he had borrowed the celestial "intelligences," so assuredly does he speak. In his teachings one notes much Oriental wisdom. It may be that many of those who wander far afield, dabbling in strange cults, in search of the mystical, would have remained within the Christian fold had they studied Dionysius.

Like all great mystics, the Areopagite taught the method of contemplation which, turning away from outward things, concentrates into the center of one's being so that it becomes at once both simplified and unified. But the attainment of this is neither simple nor easy. It is only as we begin to glimpse the possibility of this inward perfection that we begin to understand something of the angelic nature that is the very essence of this undivided unity and utter simplicity. Because of this great equality, angels stand at the inception of the temporal order and are, of all created beings, the closest to God. Dionysius possessed, to a singular degree, the mystical gift of inner concentration which gave him access to the pulse of creation itself so that his *Celestial Hierarchies* has the power "of one speaking with authority."

Dionysius is very hard to follow: one gets lost in a world of metaphor and a spate of words that flow with bewildering plenitude. One could almost be tempted to lightly brush him aside, rashly judging him to be intoxicated with words, were it not that one is arrested by the stern core of sober reality in all that he says. Here is one who speaks with the confidence of an Isaiah, Ezekiel, or John the Divine. Yet with Dionysius there is a difference. He is a true thinker who attempts to describe the unknowable nature of God. He is neither prophet nor preacher. He rather, like a scientist, a mathematician, deals in facts. He appears to be calculating metaphysical equations, adding, subtracting, dividing, multiplying, and always coming to the same resultant sum total: *One.* His mind's eye saw clearly what others only dimly perceived. He uses the symbols of things we know to describe those things that are far beyond us. We stand before his writings like people congenitally blind, trying to comprehend a description of color. Nonetheless, when we have struggled with his remarkable choice of words, we gain an astoundingly clear picture of the *Undefinable.*

One senses that Dionysius had a difficult time with his involved sentences trying to put into words what so brightly illumined his mind; we battle from the other end, so to speak, trying through the mastery of his words to see the light.

As we read the Areopagite, we must always remember that he is continually contemplating God. He sees all things in relation to the tremendous fact that God is. And we cannot approach his study without first understanding something of his theology which he approaches from two different angles: the positive, *Via Affirmativa*, and the negative, *Via Negativa*. One affirms all that God is; the other by realizing that God cannot be contained by any one thing, reaches him by abstraction entering what Dionysius terms the Divine Darkness which outshines the light of all sensible things.

He says:

> For example, the mystical traditions sometimes celebrate the superessential ONE as Word and Wisdom and Essence, proclaiming the Intellect and Wisdom of God both essentially as the source of being and also as the true Cause of existence and make It equivalent to Light and call It Life.

> Now although such sacred forms are venerable, even so, they fail to express the Divine Likeness; at other times It is extolled, in the same writings [as] Invisible, Infinite, Unbounded, in such terms as indicate what It is, but what It is not. If therefore, the negation in the descriptions of the Divine are true and the affirmations are inconsistent with It, the expositions of the hidden Mysteries, by the use of unlike symbols accords more closely with that which is ineffable.[39]

The negative way does not mean ignorance or denial of knowledge; it affirms that no finite knowledge can hope to have full cognizance of the infinite. God alone can only be approached by that which is above knowledge, a transcendent, unknowing or super-knowledge beyond dialectic reasoning.

> It is necessary to distinguish this negative method of abstraction from the positive method of affirmation, in which we deal with the Divine Attributes. For with this latter we begin with the universal and the primary; but now we ascend from the particular to the universal conception, abstracting all the attributes in order that, without veil, we may know that Unknowing, which is enshrouded under all that is known.[40]

It is when we understand what God is not; when we have rid ourselves of all preconceptions and enter into the Divine Darkness that we have set our feet upon the true mystic way. The fourteenth century English mystic, deeply steeped in Dionysius, called it *The Cloud of Unknowing*. It is a concept of extreme purity and oneness that we can approach only by humbly realizing our ignorance and incapacity of understanding without symbols. But, when by symbols, we have grasped what they stand for, we have cast them aside, and worship God in spirit and in truth.

"Every good gift and every perfect gift is from above and cometh down from the Father of Lights." Thus, with a quotation from the Scriptures, Dionysius would appear to be writing a commentary on the text, but in reality he is composing a treatise of the *Celestial Hierarchies*. He begins with this quotation simply to set the scene in its proper light, so that we should never for one moment forget the One from whom all blessings flow. Even as the angelic host proceeds from God they also recall us to things above and gather us into the fold of the shepherding Father.

Calling, then, upon Jesus the Light of the Father, the Real, the True which lighteneth every man that cometh into the world by whom we have access to the Father, the Origin of Light—let us contemplate the Hierarchies of the Celestial Intelligences revealed to us, in symbols for our upliftment and admitting through the spiritual and unwavering eyes of the mind the original and super-original gift of light of the Father who is the Source of Divinity, which shows us images of the all-blessed Hierarchies of the Angels in figurative symbols, let us through them strive upwards towards its Primal Ray.[41]

Light cannot be deprived of its intrinsic unity, even when defused into a "manyness"; it unites, illumines and warms those creatures that it touches.

The divine light in pouring itself out in love, loses nothing of its entity; but uplifts, embracing to Itself all it falls upon. It abides eternally within Itself in changeless sameness, and elevates to Itself, according to their capacity, those who turn towards It.[42]

Dionysius takes great pains to show us that we can understand only insofar as enlightenment reaches us. We need material guidance to understand "those beauties that are seen to be images of hidden beauty."

So introduces Dionysius his subject. He makes clear that his words are but inadequate symbols describing the glory of God of which we are able only to catch a fleeting glimpse. The divine and celestial are revealed to us in symbols because we would not otherwise understand them. We should never confuse the idea with the symbol although the symbol does in a sense partake of the virtue of that for which it stands. "We must celebrate the Celestial Hierarchies as they are revealed in the Scriptures," seeking to understand the pure virtue they embody. Dionysius urges us not to think of them as lions, or that they are in reality full of eyes, have beaks of eagles, or feathers, but that they are strong and far-seeing, all-embracing and swift in movement, and that they hover over us protectingly. He goes on to say:

Theology does indeed use poetic symbolism, having regard to our intelligence—But someone may prefer to regard the Divine Orders as pure and ineffable in their own natures, and beyond our power of vision.[43]

The Areopagite considers his readers above believing that the heavenly regions could be inhabited by earthly-formed creatures, but that, nonetheless, we are incapable through "the feebleness of our intellectual power" to rise directly to contemplation, and that at the same time the sublime truth should be veiled and rendered difficult of access. "For, as the Scripture declares, not everyone is holy, nor have all men knowledge."

Dionysius claims no heavenly vision for himself. He bases all he says on the Scriptures. Nevertheless he seems to have an astounding insight which shows he saw and contemplated what is beyond us. He is very anxious to guard us from the error of thinking of angels as some "kind of golden beings, or shining men, flashing like lightning, fair to behold."[44] Yet he believes that seen in their true light all things can inspire us to higher thoughts . . . .

> no single existing thing is entirely deprived of participation in the Beautiful, for, as the true Word says, all things are very beautiful. Holy contemplation can therefore be derived from all things.[45]

After profound study of the two Testaments, Dionysius arranges the celestial beings into hierarchies:

> Hierarchy is, in my opinion, a holy order and knowledge and activity which, as far as is attainable, participates in the Divine Likeness, and is lifted up to the illuminations given it from God, and correspondingly towards the imitation of God . . . . The aim of Hierarchy is the greatest possible assimilation to an union with God . . .to become like Him, so far as is permitted by contemplating intently his most Divine Beauty.[46]

Dionysius saw the celestial intelligences as constituting three triads, forming in all, nine Orders, or Hierarchies, whose names stand for the Divine Attributes.

The choirs each successively reflect and channel the perfection flowing from the Godhead. The angelic orders impart the Holy Light one to another until it reaches us and enlightens us according to our several capacities. One could liken the choirs to a threefold waterfall falling in three consecutive cascades, bringing clear mountain water to the thirsting plain below. At the same time they can be likened to an ascending ladder by which we may reach ever higher even unto "Deification."[47]

The angelic beings have a direct interrelationship with each human soul. It is through their ministrations that the spirit of man is freed from material bondage and becomes aware of its true reason of being. The more enlightened the soul becomes regarding its real purpose the closer it draws to the ultimate attainment—the full Divine Likeness. Keeping this supreme goal in mind, we note Dionysius' divisions and qualifications of the Celestial Hierarchies, an arrangement which has governed religious literature and art through the ages.

The first choir is formed of Seraphim, Cherubim and Thrones. They stand closest to the Godhead, ever dwelling in the vestibule of Divinity, as Isaiah and Ezekiel saw them. The Seraphim, "the Burning, or Fiery Ones," are the channel through which divine grace flows. The burning intensity of their love consumes all that comes between man and God, enabling man to reach the heights of his own fulfillment. Their fire welds all activities of the soul into the unity that is with the Divine; pictorially, they are red in color. It is through the Cherubim's fullness of knowledge that comprehensive understanding is poured forth, transcending all ignorance and lifting man into union with Divine Wisdom, clarifying his vision and enlightening his soul. The Thrones inspire man to serve and unite his soul with the very essence of Divine Service.

Dominions, Virtues, and Powers are the second choir, and are the dedicated seat of ordered governance. They are true lords, free of harsh tyranny, as they are free of degrading servility. They mirror the higher perfection of the first choir.

According to Dionysius, Dominions epitomize freedom from worldly discord and all that is earthbound. Virtues signify the virility of Godlike energies, never weakening or falling away, but ever mounting Godwards. The Powers are co-equal with the Dominions and Virtues, and signify a regulated but unconfined order of intellectual power. This choir in its turn reflects its perfection in the third choir.

The third and last choir is the closest to us men and consists of Principalities, Archangels and Angels.

The Principalities combine divine lordship with perfect service. They guide the soul away from worldly pursuits towards the service of God. Ultimately, the soul may thus become a co-worker with the Creator's ministers.

The Archangels are the bearers of the Divine Seal, as we noted in our reflection upon the Book of Revelation, marking the soul with the living Word of God and, at the same time, enlightening it so that it may read and comprehend the Book of Life. The Angels, in turn, intimately minister to all men, uplifting and purifying them.

All the Celestial Hierarchies are the spiritual *hypostasis*, that is, the objective, or spiritual reality, of ordered creation, the stable patterns in which disruption is unknown. "This may fittingly be added, that each Celestial and human intelligence contains in itself its own first, middle and last powers."[48] On each level we have our own affinity, according to our capacity, with these Intelligences, and through them with God. Angels should never be thought of as standing between us and God, but rather as a luminous span bridging any distance between us and God. Dionysius is careful always to remind us that "there is one Sovereign and Providence of all." God shares his sovereignty with none. The guardian angel is given to us in order that we might "know through him the One Principle of all things . . .and that all the Angels who preside over the different nations lift up to that Providence as their own Principle as far as is in their power, those who willingly follow them."[49]

While reading Dionysius' writing, one's mind gets caught up in wonder. He never talks of visions, but one senses that he really *saw*. No "apparitions" dazzled his mortal sight, but eyes of the spirit saw with absolute clarity.

Jacob's ladder was of easy ascendance to him. His every word is pregnant with meaning; there is nothing lighthearted, superficial, or feigned. The voice of the Scriptures is detectable in his language, to which, like all orthodox authors, he always refers. He deals not in fanciful legends, but builds a road on solid rock, paves it with bricks that have been sought out with meticulous care. There are no loose ends to his arguments; he would not have us soar up to celestial heights, lost in a golden daze. Wooly pink clouds and golden harps are not part of his heavenly pictures, but only the dazzling light of Divine Darkness.

If we could conceive of tones issuing from no musical instruments, of notes unaccompanied by the timbre of a voice, or the twang of a chord, but only the pure sound itself: then we could catch the echo of heavenly music.

One might be tempted easily to speak in superlatives about Dionysius, but he would not have it so; he speaks always of realities, mystical realities, not to be tossed about with impunity. Only with sober mind do we approach his writings, and with a very real knowledge of the Scriptures. Without knowing the Bible, we will not comprehend Dionysius. One feels like saying with Shakespeare, in the Prologue to *Henry V*:

> Pardon, gentles all
> The flat unraised spirits that have dared
> On this unworthy scaffold to bring forth
> So great an object:

Who am I to fathom the mind hid beneath the name of Dionysius the Areopagite? His shadowy figure seems to disappear into the cloud of unknowing he loved so well. But, all said and done, he feels he did no credit to his subject, for so he closes his treatise on the *Celestial Hierarchies*: "the hidden Mysteries which lie beyond our view we have honored by silence." So may we take his leave, realizing few can follow in understanding things "veiled in the dazzling obscurity of the secret silence".

### 9. St. Gregory the Great (c. 590-604 A.D.)

St. Gregory the Great is the last of the chief four doctors of the Latin Church. His theology followed the teachings of St. Augustine though he put his thoughts in terms suitable to his own day. In the East he is known as *Gregorios Dialogos*.

Gregory I was the wealthy son of a Roman senator, but turned his back on these earthly advantages and chose the life of a Benedictine monk. He sold his vast possessions and divided the proceeds among the poor. In 590, he was chosen Pope of Rome, which office he accepted reluctantly and only after fierce inner struggle. The firmness and strength of his character, tempered by charity and deep personal humility, made him a truly great man. He came to the Roman See in troubled times. He was a warrior Pope and a capable administrator, indeed, the father of the medieval papacy. During his reign, England was converted to Christianity, due, as St. Bede tells us, to an encounter Gregory had had with fair Saxon slaves in the marketplace. As he looked upon the blue-eyed captives his heart was touched and he said, "Non Angli, sed *Angeli*,"* and sent St. Augustine, later named "of Canterbury," as missionary to the British Isles.

Gregory was a warrior, but also a visionary, and angels were most real to him. In one of his sermons, preached the third Sunday after Pentecost, he devotes himself entirely to angels. His kindly nature is reflected in the way he interprets the Biblical text, and the influence of Dionysius the Areopagite is seen in his angelology.

Commenting on the parable of the lost sheep, he says:

> See how by his wondrous divine design, Truth places before us a similitude of the tenderness a man might see within himself, but which however relates to the Author of all men.
>
> Since a hundred is the perfect number, He possessed a hundred when He created angels and men. But soon after one was lost, when man through sin forsook the pastures of true life.[50]

Gregory then shows how the Lord leaves the ninety-nine behind to save the one. He combines this parable with that of the lost penny, likening the woman's joy and her calling the neighbors to rejoice with her over her recovered treasure, to Christ's joy and that of his angels, as he returns with the repentant sinner.

> He who is signified by *the shepherd* is also signified by *the woman* . . . . And since there is an image stamped upon the silver piece, the woman lost the silver piece when man who had been made in the image of God abandoned through sin the image of his Maker . . . .
>
> The house turned upside down, the silver piece is found; for when the conscience of man is turned upside down the image of his Maker is again found within him . . . .
>
> . . .Since the Lord created the natures of both men and angels to the end that they might know Himself, and willed that they should endure forever, He made them without doubt to His own image. The woman had ten pieces; for nine are the order of the angels. To make perfect the number of the elect, man as the tenth was made: who, even after his sin was yet not destroyed by his Maker . . . .

Gregory loved metaphor, as we can see; he bases all on the Scriptures, proving that there are nine orders by quoting Ephesians, Colossians, Isaiah and Ezekiel.

St. Gregory's translation of Ezekiel 28:12 is noteworthy:

---

*"Not Angles, but Angels."

...the prophet says to the angel who was first created: "Thou wast the seal of resemblance full of wisdom, and perfect in beauty." And let us take note that he does not call him "made in the likeness of God" but the *seal of resemblance* so that it may be made clear to him that the purer his nature, the more clearly is the image of God stamped on him . . . .

and he continues, further quoting from Ezekiel,

"Every precious stone was thy covering." . . . Here nine names are given of precious stones because they are without doubt the nine orders of angels . . . . Among these orders he the first stood forth, clothed and adorned with beauty; for as he was placed over all the angelic host in comparison with the others, he was more gloriously endowed.

From these generalizations the great Gregory turns to the ministry of the angels to which he devotes several pages. He tells us that,

We must also know that the name *angel* refers rather to their office, and not to their nature. For these holy spirits of our heavenly fatherland are indeed always spirits, but cannot always be called *angels* for then only are they *angels* when by means of them certain things are announced . . . .

They who announce things of lesser significance are called *Angels* and they who announce the greater things are called *Archangels*.

St. Gregory believes that in heaven the angels do not need to necessarily be differentiated by names "for there, because of the Vision of God, they each enjoy perfect knowledge," but for us they take the name befitting their task.

Accordingly Michael is called "Who is like God," Gabriel is "The Strength of God," Raphael is called "The Medicine of God."

Gregory sustains his assertions with Biblical quotations, but of special note are his explanations of the various titles of the nine choirs:

Those spirits are called Virtues through whom signs and wonders are wrought from time to time. They are called Powers who, in their order, have received this gift more powerfully than the rest.

St. Gregory, strangely enough, considers that some of the activities of the Virtues are inimical to men and are our tempters, in which pursuit the Powers curb them:

They are called Principalities who are placed over the angels . . . . They are called Dominions whose powers surpass those of the Principalities . . . Thrones they are called upon whom the Omnipotent God is ever seated to give judgment . . . who are so filled with the grace of Divinity . . . through them [He] makes known His judgments . . . . Again Cherubim means the fullness of knowledge . . . . And their love is a flame: for the more vivid their perception of the glory of the Divinity, the more ardently do they burn with His love . . . .

But of what use is it to speak of these angelic spirits unless we see through them to derive some profit from them for ourselves? . . . For the manner of life of the different men clearly corresponds to the diverse orders of the heavenly hosts, and they are assigned to their order each in accord with the similarity of their devotion.

St. Gregory senses that those who are filled with most love for God and neighbor shall receive reward of their merits and dwell among the cherubim, for St. Paul says: "love is the fulfilling of the law" (Rom. 13:10).

In regard to the definition of angelic office, St. Gregory says that those of highest rank are never sent out upon a mission:

. . .to minister is one thing, to stand before Him is another. For those who minister to God come to us as messengers. They who stand before Him take their joy in His close contemplation . . . . And this also we firmly hold regarding the angels who are sent to us, that when they come they so outwardly fulfill their mission that never for a moment are they withdrawn from divine contemplation. They are therefore sent and at the same time they assist before God's Throne; for though the angelic spirit is circumscribed, the supreme Spirit of God is not.

This last sentence is most important, for it explains how our guardian angel can be with us and yet see the face of God. And, too, how this could be with the Holy Trinity in heaven, and Jesus Christ on the earth. This also helps our understanding of why the angels carry our prayers to God, joining their prayer to ours, in one single act of worship.

St. Gregory the Great was a visionary, but he was also eminently a practical man. His administration of the Church was wise and strong, and his steadfastness saw Rome thoroughly overcome the difficulties of one of her worst periods when the Empire was crumbling to bits as the plague ravished her, and the barbarians stormed her gates.

### 10. St. John of Damascus (c. 675-749 A.D.)

It is only right to conclude this portion of our study with the clear, perceptive and precise sayings of the great theologian known as St. John of Damascus. He had been a high dignitary at the court of the Caliph of Damascus. Born a Christian, he was impelled by his faith to lay aside all vainglory of court life and retired to the monastery of St. Sabas, located in the arid mountains between Jerusalem and the Jordan Valley, where he led a life of abstinence and total surrender to God and his purposes. He wrote many lovely hymns and theological treatises, the most famous his *De Fide Orthodoxa*, a comprehensive summary of the patristic teachings. Hence, no one better to hear than himself.[51]

Though so few read St. John of Damascus today, he laid the foundation of all theological *summae*, including that of St. Thomas Aquinas. His writings remain the clearest and most relevant. The Damascene espouses in angel-ology, especially, the views of St. Gregory Nazianzen of whom he was especially fond, and those of Dionysius the Areopagite.

St. John claims that God created the angels after his own image—an incorporeal race, a "sort of spirit or immaterial fire,"—that they are light itself, burning with sharpest keenness in veritable hunger to serve God and quite free of materialistic thoughts.

> An angel then, is an intelligent essence, in perpetual motion, with free will, incorporeal, ministering to God, having obtained by grace an immortal nature: and the Creator alone knows the form and limitation of its essence. Also all that is rational is endowed with free will. As it is, then, rational and intelligent, it is endowed with free will: and as it is created, it is changeable, having power either to abide or to progress in goodness, or to turn towards evil.

According to St. John, the angels cannot repent because they are incor-poreal. He asserts that they are not immortal by nature, but by grace. For all that has a beginning has an end; God alone is eternal. "He is above the Eternal: for He, the creator of times, is not under the dominion of time, but above time."

The intelligence of angels is secondary, because they have received it from that Light which is without beginning. They neither need the power of speech or of hearing. They can instantaneously communicate their thoughts to each other.

They, St. John says,

> are circumscribed: for when they are in heaven they are not on the earth: and when they are sent by God down to the earth they do not remain in heaven. They are not hemmed in by walls or doors, and bars and seals, for they are quite unlimited. Unlimited, I repeat, for it is not as they really are that they reveal themselves to the worthy men to whom God wishes them to appear, but in a changed form which beholders are capable of seeing.

But St. John comes back to the fact that they are limited in the sense that all created things are limited by God who created them.

> Seeing that they are minds—he goes on to say—they are in mental places, and are not circumscribed after the fashion of the body . . .but to whatever post they may be assigned, there they are present after the manner of a mind and energies, and cannot be present and energise in various places at the same time.

St. John of Damascus is not prepared to say if angels differ in essence from each other, but he is convinced that they differ in elevation and brightness. But if the elevation depends on their brightness, or if the inverse is the case, he again feels he cannot commit himself to affirm it, though he holds that they impart their brightness and knowledge to each other and irradiate it upon the lower orders.

He remarks:

> They are mighty and prompt to fulfill the will of the Deity, and their nature is endowed with such celerity that wherever the Divine grace bids them there they are found right away. They are the guardians of the divisions of the earth; they are set over nations and religions, allotted to them by their Creator; they govern all our affairs and bring us succour. And the reason surely is because they are set over us by the divine will and command, and are ever in the vicinity of God . . . .
>
> They behold God according to their capacity, and this is their food.
>
> They are above us for they are incorporeal, and are free of all bodily passion, yet are not passionless: for the Deity alone is passionless.
>
> They take different forms at the bidding of their Master, God, and thus reveal themselves to men and unveil the divine mysteries to them.

The Damascene then differs from the Areopagite's division of the heavenly hosts, three choirs of three hierarchies each. He also mentions the various opinions as to exactly when the angels were created and sums it up thus:

> . . .all are agreed that it was before the formation of man. For me, I am in harmony with the Theologian [St. Gregory Nazianzen, who held they were the first of creation and that thought was their function]. For it was fitting that the mental essence should be first created, and then that which can be perceived, and finally man himself, in wise being both parts are united.

The Damascene's opinion of Satan is the traditional one of the fallen angel.

> . . .[he] was not wicked by nature but good, and made for good ends, and received from his Creator no trace whatever of evil in himself. But he did not sustain the brightness and the honor which the Creator had bestowed on him, and of his free choice was changed from what was in to what was at variance with his nature, and became roused against God who created him, and determined to rise in rebellion against Him: and he was the first to depart from good and become evil.

With Satan fell the innumerable host of angels who were subject to him. They have strength only insofar as God has conceded it to them.

> All wickedness, then, and all impure passion are the work of their mind. But while the liberty to attack man has been granted them, they have not the strength to overcome anyone: for we have it in our power to receive or not to receive the attack . . . . Note, further, that what in the case of man is death is a fall in the case of the angels.

A strong believer that repentance for man was possible only here on earth during his material life, St. John concludes that " . . .after the fall there is no possibility for them [the angels] just as after death there is for men no repentance." St. John wrote in the *Octoechos* eight odes, or canons, to the angels and twenty-four verses of troparions, many of which we find distributed throughout this book.

With St. John of Damascus we take leave of the Fathers. Some have not, alas, been quoted or mentioned. It would also be fascinating to follow through into modern theology, but that is not our scope. Suffice it to study in the next chapters the angels in prayer and liturgy and art. Let us close with St. John of Damascus thus:

> He who creates and provides for all and maintains all things in God, who alone is uncreated and is praised and glorified in the Father, the Son, and the Holy Spirit,

enlighten our minds and make us ever thoughtfully aware of the angel at our side.

[1]*Discourse II Against the Arians*, Chapter XVII, 27, in *Nicene and Post-Nicene Fathers*, Series II, Vol. IV, p. 362.

[2]*Discourse III*, Chapter XXV, 12, 14, p. 400-401.

[3]Letter VI, 9, 11. Easter 335, p. 523.

[4]Jean Danielou, *Les Anges et Leurs Mission*. Editions de Chevetogne, p. 51.

[5]Robert Payne, *The Holy Fire*. New York: Harper and Brothers, 1957, p. 162.

[6]*The Hexameron*, Homily 1, 5, *Nicene and Post-Nicene Fathers*, Series II, Vol. VIII, p. 54.

[7]*On the Holy Spirit*, Chapter XVI, 38, p. 23.

[8]Homily II, 4, 15, p. 61-62.

[9]*On the Holy Spirit*, Chapter XVI, 38, p. 24 (italics mine).

[10]*On the Soul and the Resurrection*, in *Nicene and Post-Nicene Fathers*, Series Two, Vol. V, p. 444.

[11]*The Great Catechism*, Chapter VI, pp. 480-481.

[12]*On Virginity*, Chapter XII, p. 357.

[13]*The Great Catechism*, Chapter VI, p. 481.

[14]*Ibid.*, p. 482.

[15]*Ibid.*, p. 495.

[16]*Against Eunomius*, Book I, 23, p. 64.

[17]Oration XXXVIII, VII-IX, *On the Theophany or Birthday of Christ*, in *Nicene and Post-Nicene Fathers*, Series Two, Vol. VII, p. 346.

[18]Lecture XVI, 23, p. 121.

[19]Lecture XI, 12, p. 67.

[20]Lecture IV, I, p. 20.

[21]Lecture X, 10, p. 60.

[22]Lecture II, 10, p. 10.

[23]Lecture III, 3, p. 14.

[24]Lecture XV, 24, p. 111.

[25]Lecture XIII, p. 88.

[26]*On the Christian Faith*, in *Nicene and Post-Nicene Fathers*, Book III, p. 245

[27]*Ibid.*

[28]*Ibid.*, Book III, Chapter XIII, 106, p. 257.

[29]*Ibid.*, Book IV, Chapter I, p. 263.

[30]*Ibid.*, Book IV, Chapter II, p. 265.

[31]*The City of God*, Book XI, Chapter IX, in *Nicene and Post-Nicene Fathers*, p. 210.

[32]*Ibid.*, Book XII, Chapter I, p. 226.

[33]*Ibid.*

[34]*Ibid.*, Book XIII, Chapter VI, p. 229.

[35]*Homilies on Hebrews*, Homily XIV, in *Nicene and Post-Nicene Fathers*, Series One, Vol. XIV, p. 438.

[36]*Homilies on St. John*, Homily LXXX, p. 298.

[37]*Homilies on Hebrews*, Homily III, p. 377.

[38]*Ibid.*

[39]Dionysius the Areopagite, *Mystical Theology and the Celestial Hierarchies*, p. 33.

[40]*Ibid.*, p. 13.

[41]*Ibid.*, p. 29.

[42]*Ibid.*

[43]*Ibid.*, p. 31.

[44]*Ibid.*, p. 33.

[45]*Ibid.*

[46]*Ibid.*, p. 37.

[47]"Deification is a technical term in the Mystical Theology of both the Eastern and Western Church .... Purified souls being raised up to the heights of contemplation, participate in this Effluence and so are deified and become in a derivative sense divine ...." C.C.E. Rolt, (Introduction), *Dionysius the Areopagite*. London: S.P.C.K., New York: The Macmillan Co., p. 39.

[48]*The Mystical Theology*, p. 58.

[49]*Ibid.*, p. 57.

[50]Excerpts from St. Gregory's sermon are from *The Sunday Sermons of the Great Fathers*, Vol III, trans. and ed. by M. F. Toal. Chicago: Henry Regnery Co., pp. 201-210.

[51]All quotations are from St. John of Damascus, *Exposition of the Orthodox Faith*, Book II, Chapters III and IV, in *Nicene and Post-Nicene Fathers*, Series Two, Vol. IX, pp. 19-21.

# IV

## The Angels in the Holy Liturgies and Prayers

Lest we come to think of the angels as long since buried in the tomes of old theological treatises, covered over and musty with the dust of the long ages of our indifference, let us turn to our daily, and especially our Sunday worship. We will first cast a glance upon the Western tradition, and then steep ourselves in the Eastern.

Attention to the angels is drawn in many a prayer. The Angelus bell of the Catholics reminds us of the angelic salutation of the Mother of God. Alas, this lovely custom is dying out.

The Roman Catholics have dedicated the second of October to the commemoration of the guardian angels and keep a day of honor for the archangels Gabriel and Raphael. St. Michael had several feastdays over the centuries, but his feastday is now a festival in honor of St. Michael and all the holy angels on September twenty-ninth. He is, of course, the most popular of the archangels and his is the only feast the Reformers retained. We find this lovely collect in the Anglican Book of Common Prayer, originally taken from the Sarum Missal. It brings out the two most important attributes of the angels found in the Holy Scripture: their service of God in heaven, and their help and protection of men on earth:

O Everlasting God, who hast ordained and constituted the service of Angels and men in wonderful order; mercifully grant that, as thy holy Angels always do thee service in heaven, so, by thy appointment, they may succour and defend us on earth: through Jesus Christ our Lord. Amen.

In the Lutheran tradition angels are always thought of as messengers who are agents in the answering of prayer. Their prayer book also incorporates the foregoing collect for St. Michael and All Angels, as well as the *Te Deum* of Matins which in the Lutheran Prayer Book used this exclamation of the Ambrosian hymn: "To thee all angels cry aloud, the heavens and all the powers therein. To thee cherubim and seraphim continually do cry: Holy, Holy, Holy." And, too, their liturgy employs the time-honored *Sanctus*.

The general feeling among other Protestants is that although there is no reason why angels should not exist, we Christians no longer have need of them to carry our prayers to God. No Protestants, though, seem to object to the use of every angelic appellative in praise, and so these are found in many lovely hymns sung in almost every Protestant church; all churches in some way do mention angels, even where they regard this only as poetic license.

An angelic hymn common to several churches is The Great Doxology, or the *Gloria in Excelsis*, the opening words of which are those sung by the angels when they announced the birth of Jesus Christ to the shepherds at Bethlehem. The whole of it is a kind of shout of praise to the glory of God. Its form is not exactly similar in the East and West, but it is used by both. The Roman Catholics use it in the Mass, whereas the Orthodox use it in Matins with the text on Sundays and feastdays slightly different from ordinary days.

The angels are remembered and honored in many a lovely prayer in as many languages and by as many faiths. Here, for example, is a prayer used in Orthodox Lauds as also as a private prayer in the morning:

> Angel of God, my holy guardian, given me by God to protect me, I pray thee earnestly; enlighten me this day; from all harm shield me; toward good advise me; and on the path of salvation guide me.

How much more happily and confidently would we walk into the coming day were we aware that God has given us a special companion to guard, protect, and enlighten us. Our guardian is an objective reality, integrating God's particular love for us as individuals. He is an expression of God's fatherly care, a companion who does not fall asleep at night, and never leaves us alone or lonely in the dark.

> Angel of Christ, holy guardian mine, who covereth my soul and body, forgive me the wrongs of this day, protect me from the evils of the enemy, and pray for me, unworthy sinner though I be, that I may yet be worthy of the boundless goodness and mercy of the Holy Trinity, of the Theotokos, and all the saints (*Private Morning Prayers*).

There is also this very naive little prayer used by most Orthodox children:

> Angel, little angel mine, given me by God: I am small, you make me big, I am weak, you make me strong.

Roman Catholics have a votive Mass called the Mass of the Angels which has its own Gregorian music. There is also a prayer to St. Michael, previously recited after Low Mass and which can well give strength and hearten any soul:

> St. Michael the Archangel, defend us in battle, be our protector against the malice and snares of the devil. We humbly beseech God to command him, and do thou, O Prince of the heavenly host, by the divine power thrust into hell Satan and the other evil spirits who roam about the world seeking the ruin of souls. Amen.

Perhaps one of the most beautiful prayers of the Roman rite is that said immediately after the consecration, asking God to accept the Holy Sacrifice:

> We humbly beseech Thee, Almighty God, command these to be carried by the hands of Thy holy Angel to thine Altar on High . . . .

When the priest at Mass blesses the incense he prays:

> By the intercession of blessed Michael the Archangel, standing at the right hand of the altar of incense, and of all his elect, may the Lord vouchsafe to bless this incense, and receive it as an odor of sweetness. Through Christ our Lord. Amen.

These many prayers have the function of sustaining and continually reminding us that the angels never have ceased to have a very real part, an active part, in our worship and also, by invoking them we keep intact our union with them. This has strong Scriptural basis, especially in St. Paul's doctrine of the Mystical Body of Christ, in which all members have their particular office (Rom. 12:4-8) as "fellow citizens with the saints, and of the household of God" (Eph. 2:19). The angels' intermediary attribute of course goes back to the Old Testament.

We can be certain that the holy service of the Church would not integrate angels if they were but pious fiction, or belonged to a past era. Past and present in eternity does not exist, and time itself is of very small importance. People today accept, even without understanding, the overpowering pronouncements of science which envisage the possibility of a time when men traveling faster than light will instead of flying forwards actually go backwards to before now! Time for us is still bound by night and day; once we surpass the speed of light, time will, even in human calculation, lose its meaning. But, strangely enough, as we accept these speculations of science, we meanwhile shelve eternal truths! Moonshots make people interested in what lies out in space; the Christian must be interested in what lies beyond it—in the heavenly world.

God still is the central and focal reality of life, however we dodge and hide from him. His heavenly hosts surround him and open the ring to include us. This, without the aid of man-made spaceships, but by the quiet act of true prayer, by the giving of self to God, by the power of a love which is not earthbound, that has not its source in us, but in God himself. "Herein is love, not that we love God, but that He loved us" (1 Jn. 4:10). This is the mystery, the explanation of why man dares to believe that he not only may, but does, join his feeble voice to that of the heavenly host. The truth of this can be truly apprehended only by personal experience, not visionary, but inward knowledge.

Every Monday in the Eastern Orthodox Church is dedicated to the angels. In Sunday Vespers, interposed between the verses of Psalm 129 are three troparions or verses to the angels as Vespers introduces the coming day. At Matins the angels have an entire Canon, an ode composed of nine canticles. These were written by St. John of Damascus in eight tones. March twenty-sixth, following upon the Annunciation, is the feast of St. Gabriel and all the angels with its own Vespers and Canon at Matins. On November eighth we celebrate St. Michael and all the heavenly hosts in the same manner. For private prayers there is a Canon to the Guardian Angel and one to the Heavenly Hosts and All Saints. How lovely that what so many look upon as "blue Monday" can be heavenly as the first working day of the week, with the special prayer, addressed to our Lord Jesus Christ:

> . . .O Lord today I give Thee my soul and body and will: and pray Thee that Thou will be in me as Thou pleasest . . . . For this I call as intercessors upon Thy Holy Angels.
>
> O heavenly servers of God, guardians of men and foes of the devils, I bow before you, blessed spirits, and rejoice in your greatness. You stand never slumbering, with faith you watch and with haste serve the will of our God. Untiringly you strive and ever conquer, having no other care but to chase away the enemies of God and of His creation. Oh blessed guardian of men! I venerate you and thank you for the help which every day you give us, for your guidance, and for praying to God for us . . . . Above all I bless you for your care of me an unworthy sinner. O Holy Angel guardian of my soul, and thou Michael the Archangel, my help, do not be offended at me, do not leave me alone, but guard me day and night until I shall with true repentance give my soul into the hands of God my Maker . . .save me from all the enemies, seen and unseen, that I may not from now on, repeat my faults before God, so that upon my death I may be worthy of seeing you, that you will be standing around me to bring my soul to heaven, that it may worship before the face of God. Amen.

This prayer incorporates all that the angels are to us, their mission, our trust in them, their care of man from birth to death, and even after death. Altogether there is a deep ever-reverent respect for the angels that has found expression in countless beautiful prayers and hymns.

The Eastern Liturgy, which is the older Eucharistic rite, has frequent mention of the angels. For those who are not familiar with this Liturgy, some explanation is necessary. It is an extremely complete service which culminates with the *Epiclesis*, that is, the invocation of the Holy Spirit to consecrate the elements of the Holy Eucharist. Just as the life of Jesus was a gradual preparation for the Passion and Resurrection, so also the Holy Liturgy commemorates the whole life of Jesus Christ on earth. His birth, the hidden years, his ministry, the Last Supper, Passion and Resurrection. The Orthodox faithful live through the integral drama of the Savior's life, take intimate part in it, listen, learn, glory, bow down in worship, and rejoice over every incident symbolically brought forth in the service. The Liturgy is often interspersed with litanies. These are "universal prayers" because in them petitions are made for all our human needs. The Orthodox Christian, participating at the Liturgy, is not an individual standing alone and solitary. He takes part in the prayers of the Church and the Church prays for him and for the whole world. The Communion of Saints is ever present, for all worship together. There is no division, sinner and saint, beggar and king, layman and priest, the living and the dead and the entire heavenly host—all worship together, side by side in otherworldliness, before the Throne of God. The Christian finds himself in his true native land.

The Orthodox lay great emphasis on the senses of sight, sound, and even smell; upon each great moment: through word, song, incense and beauty of the candle-illuminated church. The service is divided into three parts: (1) office of Oblation in which the Holy Gifts are all prepared, and which represents the birth of Jesus and his hidden years; (2) the Liturgy of the Catechumens which represents the ministry of our Lord; and (3) the Liturgy of the Faithful which represents the Passion Week and the Resurrection.

We have seen how during his life on earth, the angels were ever close to Jesus. Thus in the Holy Liturgy they are with him and we know them to be in our midst.

Our first reminder of the angels, as we advance into the church is visual, for we immediately take notice of the iconographic images of Gabriel and Michael painted upon the doors on either side of the central Royal Doors. In the Orthodox churches, it should be noted, the altar is separated from the nave by an *iconostasis*, an altar-screen, and is pierced by three doors, the middle ones are double, and are called the Holy or Royal Doors, significant of the gates of heaven. Through the side doors pass the deacon and the acolytes who, because they serve, represent on earth the functions of the holy angels in heaven. Also, should the church have a dome on which Christ the Pantocrator is depicted, directly beneath we will find a row of angels.

In the Liturgy of the Catechumens, the Little Entrance takes place in which the Holy Gospel is carried in solemn procession about the Altar Table through the north door on the left side, upon which St. Gabriel is painted, while re-entering of the sanctuary is through the Royal Doors. This signifies the beginning of Christ's ministry. The deacon and altar boys carry candles; the deacon here represents St. John the Forerunner, the boys the angels. For this procession, and also in the Great Entrance which takes place during the Liturgy of the Faithful, the ripidions are carried. These are two metal discs representing the seraphim surrounded by six wings, that otherwise stand behind the Altar Table. They were originally used to keep flies away during the offering. Some churches are endowed with these, while others are not. It is the characteristic instrument of the deacon, and is handed to him at his ordination. Just before the procession begins, the priest says, in a low voice, the following prayer:

O Master, Lord our God, who has appointed in Heaven Orders and Hosts of Angels and Archangels for the service of Thy glory; cause that our entrance there may be an entrance of Holy Angels serving with us and glorifying Thy greatness for unto Thee are due all glory, honor and worship to the Father, and to the Son, and to the Holy Ghost: now and ever and unto ages of ages. Amen.

It is a plea to God to render the action not only symbolic, but to transform it into a spiritual reality. Although we cannot see them the angels flock into the church in attendance upon their Lord.

Following this prayer the choir sings the *Trisagion* hymn, or thrice-holy song, derived for the Liturgy from the angelic praise (Is. 6:3). While the choir sings "Holy God, Holy and Mighty, Holy and Immortal" four times, the priest prays:

O Holy God who resteth in Thy Holy Place; who art hymned by the Seraphim with the thrice-holy cry and glorified by the Cherubim, and adored by every heavenly power . . . .

The censing at this time is also reminiscent of the "Angel of the Censer" in heaven and the mounting fumes of incense are associated with the offering of the prayer as a symbol of the ascent of our worship to God.

At the end of his personal prayer, the priest glorifies God who sits upon the cherubim. It is in the presence of the angels with us in the church, and in heaven, that we listen to the Epistle and Gospel. The *Alleluia* sung between the two sacred readings is also an echo of angelic praise, meaning "Glory to Him Who Is." It is sung in the heavens by the assemblage of the angels and blessed.

The Cherubic Hymn is sung during the Great Entrance in the Liturgy of the Faithful. In this procession the Holy Gifts are carried from the table of oblation to the Altar Table, signifying the triumphant entrance of Jesus Christ into Jerusalem to commence his Passion; it also foreshadows the *Parousia*, that is, the Second Coming of the Lord, when Christ shall return in all his glory, surrounded by the heavenly hosts. The Cherubic Hymn is one of the most beautiful of all in Orthodox hymnology:

We who mystically represent the Cherubim, and sing to the life-giving Trinity the thrice-holy hymn, let us now lay aside all earthly cares that we may receive the King of Glory like a Conqueror upon a shield and spears, by His Angelic Hosts invisibly upborne, Alleluia, Alleluia, Alleluia.

Earthly care does indeed, at this moment seem far away and heaven so very close as the swelling song fills the church.

Heaven comes even closer at the great moment of transformation of the Holy Gifts. As this sacred moment approaches man becomes conscious of his own smallness and of God's boundless goodness in admitting him into the life-giving Mystery. The priest thus gives thanks:

> ...We give thanks to Thee also for this ministry which Thou dost vouch-safe to receive at our hands, even though there stand beside Thee thousands of Archangels, the Cherubim, the Seraphim, six-winged, many-eyed, soaring aloft, borne on their pinions, singing the Triumphant Hymn shouting, calling aloud and saying,
> [Here the choir breaks in with high notes of exultant joy.]
> Holy, Holy, Holy, Lord of Sabaoth; heaven and earth are full of Thy Glory; Hosanna in the highest; Blessed is He that cometh in the name of the Lord—Hosanna in the highest.

The *Sanctus* is, of course, sung in the Roman Catholic and Anglican Eucharistic rites, though in their rituals the preface varies according to feast or season. For all of us this majestic hymn of praise and thanksgiving is the expression of our exultant gratitude that flows from the depth of heart and soul. It is founded upon the angels' song heard by Isaiah (6:3) and also upon the hymn with which the Jews welcomed Jesus into Jerusalem (Mt. 21:9-15; Mk. 11:9; Jn. 12:13; and Ps. 117:26).

This, the greatest hymn of praise, is that of the angels; higher than this we cannot ascend, more we cannot express. If we but realized it, as our voices fill the church, we would be conscious that they are picked up by the myriads of angelic voices swelling the song to unearthly volume and carrying it to where the Holy Place of God is. Our voices are but a faint echo of that majestic hymn. The wonder of it is that we do participate in it. Lovely indeed is the inaudible prayer that the faithful may say at this time:

> The Hosts of Angels and Archangels together with all the heavenly bodies sing unto Thee and say: Holy, Holy, Holy, Lord of Sabaoth! Heaven and earth are full of Thy Glory, Hosanna in the Highest. Blessed is He that cometh in the name of the Lord. Hosanna in the Highest.
>
> Bless me, O King, from on High. Bless me and sanctify me, O Source of Holiness, for Thou upholdest this world, and the heavenly armies without number in fear and trembling worship Thee and unceasingly sing the thrice-holy song. Thou who sitteth in Eternal Light, before Whom every being trembles, as an unworthy servant, I pray Thee enlighten my mind, cleanse my heart and open my lips so I may also worthily sing unto Thee, Holy, Holy, Holy art Thou, O Lord, forevermore. Amen.

Worthily to sing.... How great a longing, what an unbounded desire! When are we ever truly worthy? Then only when the Holy Spirit inspires us: "...no man can say that Jesus is the Lord, but by the Holy Spirit" (1 Cor. 12:3). But the angels always are worthy and thus inspired, they sing with us, carrying our prayers before the Throne of God. They gather about the Altar Table of our humble earthly churches, they kneel with us before the Holy Sacrifice. For that great moment when the Incommunicable is communicated to us, when the intangible becomes tangible, the angels fill the sanctuary with their invisible presence.

After the consecration, the priest prays for all those on whose behalf the Gifts were offered: the living and the dead, the Saints, and especially the Theotokos, whereupon the great hymn to her is sung:

> More honorable than the Cherubim, and more glorious beyond compare than the Seraphim, Thou who without spot of sin bearest God the Word, and truly Mother of God: we magnify Thee!

Enthroned even above the heavenly hosts sits the one who alone of all human beings was found worthy to be Mother of her Lord: to whose act of faith we owe the Incarnation; before whom alone the Messenger of God is known to have bowed.

Before the Lord's Prayer, the litany of supplication is said in which we humbly ask for those things most needful to us: a peaceful day, holy and sinless, pardon for our sins, a Christian ending to our lives. At this time, too, we pray for: "An angel of peace, a faithful guardian of our souls and bodies."

During the recitation of the Lord's Prayer, the deacon crosses his stole over his back symbolizing the folding of the angels' wings in adoration before God.

And, so, perhaps if we only knew how to listen we would hear the rustle of the celestial wings as they fold . . . . Or, perchance, does the submerging in the Divine Light of the angelic pinions create instead a great and holy silence, an infinite peace . . . ?

# V

## The Angels in Christian Art

*1. Introduction*

Worthily to deal with the subject of angels in art, would require several volumes. Art has done more harm to our notion of angels than any other single medium of exposition. It is, in fact, the agent most responsible for our misconception about and disbelief in angels.

We have been deluged with sentimental pictures of wraith-like creatures levitating just above the earth's surface, protecting with flowing veils little children walking on the edge of a precipice. Another popular form is in the medal offered to infants, representing chubby-cheeked children with sprouting wings, expressing a sweet idea more than anything else, and utterly divorced from truth. Then there are the decorative angels holding balustrades or altar rails, rather like buxom lasses who lack the force and majesty of the pagan Winged Victory. In other portrayals, angels are made to look like insipid and not very commendable young men. No wonder popular belief turns away from them, and finally finds them without any credence at all.

If it is true that the holy angels have been misrepresented, it is also true of the devils who, depicted with horns and tails, are equally incorrect. No one would fall to the charms of such a creature! It is perhaps one of Satan's most wily moves to have himself so portrayed, so that looking at him we forget who he is: Lucifer—the fallen Son of the Morning!

The plastic imagery of religious doctrine is pre-Christian and comes primarily from Egypt. For the early Christian Church this art was not thought of as decoration, but was put to theological use. The artist expressed in pictures what the scribe conveyed by the written words of the Scriptures. Certain symbolic principles were adhered to in imagery, just as the rules of grammar and spelling were kept in writing. It was principally during the Renaissance that artistic fancy got the upper hand over theology, and religious scenes became subjects for the work of art, but no longer served to express theology. The angels suffered most from this transfer from religious to secular art. More and more, they became mere decoration and embellishment, and less and less did they resemble the descriptions of them found in the Scriptures.

We must always remind ourselves that angels are spirit, and therefore, being bodiless, sexless and ageless, no portrait of them is at all possible. We can only symbolically show what they are like, never what they are. Being the personification of God's attributes, when they have made themselves visible to man, it has always been as "The Man of God," strong and commanding respect and attention. Those who saw the cherubim and seraphim saw them as great winged creatures almost impossible to describe, certainly not as baby faces with wings tucked under their chins! The mighty visions could only be symbolically represented in their entirety—for wings alone do not make an angel.

> The modern prettification to which all of us are exposed at Christmas and Easter, would have shocked the ancient Church, and, if our religion is very sound this should shock us.[1]

The Church does not permit the use of angels as mere decoration. They were so placed as to illustrate some solemn and significant belief or teaching of the Church. Angels were second only to the Holy Trinity and preceded by the Evangelists. They were represented as surrounding the Godhead and the enthroned Mother of God. In fact, decoration as embellishment is always stylized curtains or plants. This was true of the Church both in the East and in the West. Today, alas, only the East adheres strictly to this rule.

Within their own tradition, the artists of the East and of the West in each age, had their particular and peculiar manner of seeing and depicting the angelic world, and in keeping with the vision and understanding of each period.

## 2. Byzantine Art

The Byzantine is the oldest Christian art and inextricably linked to the Orthodox Tradition. At one time it set the standard for all of the Christian world. Today, the Eastern Orthodox Church still follows the tradition of Byzantine art and is faithful to the early principles guiding church painting. Unfortunately, though, in some places out of ignorance these rules have been disregarded.

Byzantine Christian art is primarily concerned with teaching truth; it is a graphic portrayal of Orthodox theology. The churches are so painted that a man entering the building should become visually aware of the whole cosmos that surrounds him, a cosmos in which each prophet, saint and event has his, her, or its particular and appointed place. Thus from the moment of crossing the west threshold of the church, until he stands under the dome representing heaven, with Christ in the center, a Christian is confronted with every major theological event. We must always keep in mind that

Byzantine art is concerned exclusively with theology and is not even remotely interested in decoration. When there is a call for decoration, for instance around windows, over arches, and so on, geometrical forms are used, and occasionally stylized flowers and plants. The angels then have their own appointed place in the cosmos, and are accordingly depicted in church painting, and in holy pictures, the icons.

It is perhaps wise here to explain what an icon means to an Eastern Orthodox Christian. It is much more than a picture, a simple image of a holy person. The best simile we can draw is to say that as Jesus was the image or icon of God so also a holy icon conveys to the faithful the very selfness of the person it portrays. An icon becomes a sacred meeting place between the worshipper and the worshipped. An icon is completely non-sensual, and its spirituality rules out any form of naturalism. In a sense, an Orthodox Byzantine church is, all of it, an immense icon of God's Kingdom, both in heaven and on earth.

The Byzantine angels are never pretty or effeminate, but manly and strong. They are draped like the old Greek philosophers, because they are "divine intelligences," or they are robed in the vestment of deacons, for like the diakonos, the server, they are called to be servers of the Most High. Usually they carry a wand as a token of authority. Their hair is long and wavy, bound by a blue ribbon or diadem, the sign of spirituality. Their wings are strong and soberly colored, never overemphasized.

The Archangels Michael and Gabriel are painted on the two side doors of the iconostasis—the altar screen separating the sanctuary from the body of the church. Michael is upon the north, and Gabriel upon the south door. Upon the middle, or Royal Doors, usually the Annunciation is represented, the Archangel Gabriel on one panel, the Blessed Virgin on the other.

The angels are never shown as children or placed according to artistic fancy. Sometimes they seem to make strange contortions in the air so to fit into the picture. The cherubim and seraphim have stern, uncompromising faces, their six red and blue wings deployed in many angles. They are found only in the scenes of heaven and paradise.

Like every other figure in icons or on church walls, the angels always face toward us. This is to show that we are never excluded, but on the contrary are always being drawn into their activity, whatever it may be. Even in the picture of the Annunciation where the Virgin and Gabriel are primarily concerned with each other, they are also concerned with us. It is for us that all this happened, therefore they also face us. Only sinners are shown in profile. We do not gaze at the pictures, we reverently look upon them as they also look upon us, as a group of people would as they conversed together. This is sound theology, clarifying the communion of the saints. Man should always be made aware of his need to be moving toward his native estate, which is heaven; there these holy persons already stand, not indifferent to us, but recognizing the bond of Christ's making.

Satan is hardly ever represented, and, if so, only on the outside wall of the church in the scene of the Last Judgment. Orthodox Christian art is strictly Scriptural. There are no Biblical descriptions of Satan so how should we know his features? St. John in the Book of Revelation saw him as a dragon, St. Peter called him a roaring lion, Jesus likened him to a flash of lightning. None of these, in themselves, are ugly, but very frightening. Satan is strong, threatening, and fearsomely, wickedly beautiful. At a loss to portray him, and inspired by the New Testament Apocrypha, he was shown as the ugliest thing possible, that is, entirely fear-inspiring.

Somehow, the symbolism of East and West has failed to really translate Satan pictorially. Actually, Byzantine art very seldom tried to do so; this because it is much more concerned with heaven than with hell.

The Orthodox paintings of angels seek to convey strength, celestial power, serenity, swiftness and austere non-sensuality, though unquestionably masculine in character. The Byzantine angels, if they do not move us by their beauty, certainly inspire us with their strength and fill us with confidence. One would always feel safe, if not comfortable, in their presence. And that is precisely what their portrayal is meant to convey.

### 3. The Middle Ages

The Middle Ages have also been called the Ages of Faith. It was the time of the great cathedrals and abbeys, beautiful in their design and in their details. Many a work of art, crowning arches and spires were placed so high that the eye of man could not see them. It was enough that God saw them; they were, after all, dedicated solely to his glory.

In paintings and tapestries, in stone and wood, in silver and gold, in church windows and on fine parchment, holy stories were commemorated with infinite love and worship. Everywhere from the great soaring domes to the illuminated pages of sacred books, the angels abound.

It is far from simple to make an outline of art at this period in the West, then, indeed a melting-pot of culture. Yes, a great diversity of traditions, ranging from the Byzantine to the Viking. In the early part of the Middle Ages the artists were more skilled in design than in the representation of the human form.

Pope St. Gregory the Great had declared that images are useful in teaching the faithful the Word of God. The religious art of the West primarily had this in mind: to teach, whereas in the East, iconography had come to mean a great deal more; it was and is considered as sacred as the Scriptures. The medieval artists were not seeking to create a convincing likeness of nature or even to make things beautiful; they wanted to convey to their brothers in the faith the content and message of the sacred story. Their angels, therefore, are not particularly beautiful, but they leave no one in doubt of their strength and power. There is no flimsiness in these angels. They are to be found at first chiefly in manuscripts, for in the West, Italy excepted, the adornment of churches with frescoes and mosaics was not a general practice. The illuminations and miniatures were painted for Bibles, Missals, Diurnals, and Books of Hours. Their main purpose was to be used in the service of God. The angels as God's holy messengers had their rightful place among the other Biblical figures.

The Bible, except for Isaiah's and Ezekiel's visions, does not mention angels with wings. Men's imaginations seem to have endowed them with these. Wings are the angel's distinctive symbol, as a crown is that of a king. They are emblematic of spirit, power, and swiftness. The seraphim and cherubim are represented by heads with three pairs of wings, which symbolize pure spirit, informed by love and intelligence; the head is the emblem of the soul, of love and of knowledge.

The angels also usually bear a wand in their hand as a sign of office. St. Gabriel is represented with a lily; St. Michael with sword and armor; St. Raphael carries a staff and a wallet hangs from his girdle, and sandals appear on his feet. Angels also have a diadem or blue ribbon, the ends of their ribbon curl upward, the symbol of holy inspiration. The halo is never omitted from the angel's head, and is always, wherever used, the symbol of sanctity.

The title "angel" signifying "messenger" may be and is given to a man who bears important tidings. Thus we may see the Evangelists, especially St. John the Baptist, too, who, in this sense, is an angel, represented with wings. This symbolism was at first strictly adhered to both in the West and in the East. The West later discontinued many of these traditional emblems, as well as the angelic dress of the Greek philosopher's robe, or the stole and alb of the deacon; often all sorts of flowing draperies were substituted. In the early Middle Ages, however, there was no danger of this. The Church was militant, all culture was in her safekeeping, and art was held in bonds strictly Christian and orthodox.

Because the Annunciation was always a very favorite subject, pictures of it are found in the earliest manuscripts throughout the Christian world. The angels' draperies are the classical Byzantine; their feet are firmly planted on the ground. They were somewhat ungainly, and their wings protruded at odd angles to fit the picture. These paintings are full of naive beauty, as well as intense religious sentiment. They are painted with loving, painstaking care and precision. There is an enchanting illustration from a Swabian Gospel from about 1150. The angel is shown half-profile, his right hand extended, a gentle gesture which in medieval art signified the act of speaking. But there are so many of these charming pictures that it is impossible to do them justice in this outline.

Isaiah's vision was also a great favorite. An excellent example of this is a Reichenau miniature of the eleventh century. God is seen sitting upon the throne of glory surrounded by flowerlike rays of light and encircling him are the seraphim, deploying their beautiful reddish-pink wings, one of them grasping the red-hot coal with which he cleansed the prophet's lips. There is no question in this period of baby-faced angels with fluffy wings, nor was there to be until the Renaissance, a good four hundred years later. Cherub and seraph in the Middle Ages were clearly understood to be the greatest of God's creatures, the description of which is beyond the pen or the brush of man. Yet man had had the vision, and this he tried to convey, or rather, its message.

The first sculptured church decorations appeared in France, though properly speaking, decoration is the wrong word, for this was not the primary function of these early carvings. They were there to express a definite idea connected with the Church's teachings. Over the porch of the twelfth century church of St. Trophime in Arles we find our first stone angel. He is the symbol of St. Matthew, and we see him flying above St. Mark's lion on the right side of the enthroned Lord; on the other side are the eagle of St. John and the ox of St. Luke. St. Irenaeus, among others, perceived in these four-winged creatures spoken of in Ezekiel and the Book of Revelation, the four principal characteristics of the Savior. During the Middle Ages they became definitely recognized as the emblems of the Four Evangelists in both the East and the West.

From this time on, especially with the development of Gothic soaring architecture, the angelic figures multiply. They appear especially around the altar or in the choir, where it is that they rightfully belong. They are also at the church doors, guarding the Kingdom of God within. It must not be forgotten that the cherubim were the only permitted decoration in the Temple of Jerusalem, and that apart from those of the Mercy Seat of the Ark of the Covenant (Ex. 25:18-22), Solomon also "carved cherubim on the walls" and embroidered them upon the blue, purple and crimson Veil of the Temple (2 Chr. 3:7-14). The tradition of angelic imagery placed in worshipful setting is very ancient.

One of the most perfect examples of thirteenth century sculptured angels is the angel-pillar in the Strassburg Minster—a slim four-sided column, it mounts from floor to arch with a true upward sweep that lifts the gaze on high. The first four figures are those of the Evangelists, above them are four angels blowing the last trumpet, and above these are four other angels carrying the instruments of the Passion. The full figures are pure Gothic. The draperies fall in simple folds with a perfect economy of emphasis which is carried out also in the admirably stylized wings. Their majestic bearing has a tranquil and arresting gravity. The angel with the cross is rightfully famous. His face is, I think, the most consummate in angelic imagery. It is of beautiful proportions, strong and serene, and lacking in any sensuality. Here is, indeed, the Man of God in all his pure impersonal beauty, his eyes searching the infinite horizons with powerful thoughtfulness.

At the turn of the thirteenth and fourteenth century, we see a subtle change in the conception of angels, in which the profound change in men's standard of living and thinking is clearly mirrored. The angel becomes more humanized, blander of aspect, with indications creeping in of a certain sweetness. The old conception of God's messengers and warriors, of the angels' heavenly priesthood loses its greatness. Men had become less spiritual; the increase of industries, the growing up of towns, had made them, and has made them, more materialistic, and in fact, simply bourgeois-minded. Their imaginations could no longer reach the heights of the Scriptural accounts in which the heavenly host sing with one voice unceasing praises to God, praises in which the entire cosmos partook. They now placed earthly musical instruments in the angelic hands, and draped them in heavy fabrics of their own rich clothing.

In Italy, Giotto rediscovered a more realistic way of painting the human form. He leaped over the barrier that separated painting from sculpture. He owed much to the methods of the Byzantine masters and to the sculpture of the northern cathedrals. With Giotto a new chapter opens up in art. His angels, though, are not inspiring. The Siena school held on for longer than others to the Byzantine forms, but breathed new life into old standards. A perfect example is Simone Martini's and Lippo Memmi's picture of the Annunciation. A beautiful Gabriel against a glorious golden background kneels before a soberly draped Madonna. This altar piece has two rarely seen angels painted in white and gray, on the back of the side panels, that are of great beauty.

Thus, imperceptibly, the Middle Ages slipped into the Renaissance.

## 4. The Renaissance

The artists of the fourteenth to the sixteenth centuries, inspired by pagan sculptures and paintings, then just coming to light again, gave full rein to their fertile imaginations in a riot of glorious colors and masterful compositions. It was a time when art for art's sake was uppermost. A man was commissioned to paint rather for his talent than because of his religious fervor. Churches were decorated with religious scenes as a book might be illustrated. The human aspects of our Lord's life were brought out, the Bible as a whole offered endless material for illustration and artistic expression.

This is not to say that the painters were impious, far from it. Nonetheless, their attitude was secular. The Jewish iconoclastic tradition which greatly restrained the early Christians lay far behind, and the sophisticated man of the Renaissance saw with completely different eyes. From that time on up to the present day, art became more and more secular as it went through all the known phases. Religious subjects always remained popular and the adornment of churches important, but even when deeply inspired, the simple charm, the spirit of faith which emanates from the primitive picture and carving has hardly ever been recaptured.

The Renaissance was fantastically rich in paintings, sculpture and architecture. Men became ever more aware of their own capabilities. New discoveries were made on all levels, so man was preoccupied with himself and his ideas. He was inclined to see God in his image instead of himself in God's image. Yet, this period produced one of the most religiously inspired painters of all time—Fra Angelico.

Guido di Pietro was born in 1387 near Florence and as quite a young man he entered the Dominican monastery in Fiesole. He was professed as Brother Giovanni, but soon he became known as Fra Angelico, the angelic brother. The purity of his life, as well as the candor of the faces he painted, and the multitude of angels that came from his inspired brush, earned him this title. He worked first in Fiesole, where he painted his great miniatures in which golds and blues predominate. A perfect example of this, his first style, is the picture of judgment day. The colors are bright and clear. In a cloudless sky Christ is enthroned upon the glory of the angels. In the inner circle are the red-winged cherubim and seraphim, suffused in golden rays. The outer circle is composed of the multitude of heavenly hierarchies. Just beyond this circle the Virgin is placed on the right hand of Christ, and St. John on the left. The company of the blessed extend on either side into the azure sky. Immediately below, cutting the foreground in half, are the open graves of the resurrected dead. On one side the damned and hell are treated in a conventional manner. But on the other side Fra Angelico painted with true feeling the rejoicing saints being embraced and led in a happy dance by the angels all the way up to the gates of heaven. His angels are, it is true, decidedly feminine, but they are so pure, so lacking in sensuality that one cannot but be moved to wonder by the beauty of his vision.

When Cosimo de' Medici built the new Dominican monastery of St. Mark in Florence, he had Fra Angelico decorate each cell. These frescoes are soberly treated with wonderful economy; the colors are fluid and gentle, they express a very real mysticism. To walk down the quiet conventual passage and look into each small room, to gaze upon heavenly picture after heavenly picture, is one of the greatest spiritual and artistic experiences a person can have. As with many others, the Annunciation was greatly loved by Fra Angelico. There is one in particular which tells the sacred story most perfectly. The Virgin and the archangel are shown as equal in purity and goodness. He is pictured in the act of bending his knee to her, she crosses her hands upon her breast in submissiveness. In another painting, Gabriel stands before her. He is beautiful and grave; his robe of lilac blended with pink, falls in harmonious folds, while with his hands held to his heart he looks at her in silence, full of love and reverence. The Virgin kneels humbly before God's messenger. Fra Angelico always prayed before he began his work. Because he believed himself divinely directed, he never corrected his original design.

The purity and spiritual fervor of Fra Angelico was never surpassed by any of even the greatest masters. The angels of Giotto and Benozzo Gazzoli are feminine, and rather unconvincing. Leonardo's angels have a smile that could almost be called a grin, while those of Michelangelo never attained to wings. Titian's angels are lovely children. Those of Francesco Albani, Guido Reni and Caracci are attractive and elegant boys. Not even Raphael ever attained Fra Angelico's unearthliness, beautiful as his paintings are. Botticelli's angels still retained some of the old majestic quality; they are joyous, strong and grave. The faces of the angels in his Coronation of the Virgin taken singly have much loveliness. His St. Michael in the reredos of St. Bernard has a youthful gravity which is truly moving.

Why did this same period usher in the baby-faced, naked "angelette"— really indistinguishable from Cupid, except that the rest of the picture is unquestionably religious in tone? There is no real satisfactory answer, except the charm of the rediscovery of pagan art with its many enchanting frescoes of winged children and cupids were transferred by the Renaissance artist to his work with perhaps not much else in mind than simply pretty innocent decoration.

For the bodiless baby head, supported by insufficient wings, it is difficult to find any justification whatsoever. And still less for their being called cherubs, which is in itself a misnomer, as the plural of cherub is cherubim. Nor is it to be understood how the cherub, described by Ezekiel as many-winged and many-eyed, the greatest of all created beings, ever came to be so misrepresented.

The artistic portrayal of angels became less and less Biblical and finally lost the power to transmit any sense of reality to the beholder. As time went on, not even the frequent reading of the Scriptures could counteract the false impression made upon the mind by these fanciful paintings and carvings. Art had fallen into secular hands, and though not impious, certainly theologically unsound.

## 5. The Baroque Period

History and art are often closely interrelated. With the coming of the

Reformation, and the stripping of churches of all decoration on one side of the religious fence, the other side reacted by seeking to make churches all the more beautifully adorned. Whereas the Gothic reached toward heaven, the Baroque tried to bring heaven down into the churches. It was an age of extreme opulence and luxury, in which palaces were the size of small towns and richly embellished. If the homes of kings and bishops were so designed, it was impossible to do less for the House of God. Nothing was too good, too precious, too lavish to bring before the eye of man the joys of paradise, and raise his thought to heavenly praise. Golden clouds hung around ornamented and twisting pillars, over altars and from ceilings; over them, in them, below them, jubilant, scantily-draped angels flew with golden wings and played on golden harps. This was a far cry from the old austere conception, but it was nonetheless an expression of deep religious feeling. The Baroque angels certainly flew, and the musical instruments in their hands were multiplied and varied. The expression of theological truth was no longer taken into account; paramount was the desire to show that heaven was a much lovelier, happier place than earth. There is a small Austrian Baroque angel, full of delicate charm. He is a high basrelief, his gown is blue, his wings golden, his hair auburn; he seems to sing to the accompaniment of his mandolin, his head slightly tilted to one side.

Many of the angels of this time have a wonderful movement. They express real joy and worship. The cupid-like "angelettes" also abound over the place, in nooks and corners in ceilings, tumbling out of clouds or upholding garlands of flowers. One may not theologically approve, but one cannot help smiling and feeling carefree in the presence of so much jubilance. Here and there we come across a face of real spirituality, or a gentle presence, but the solemn awe-inspiring statues in the Strassburg Minster are found no more.

I do not know if El Greco is to be counted a Baroque. He expresses the same exuberance we see in the Baroque statues. His angels are full of upward-flowing movement. His pictures are those of a passionately devout and inspired man. His angels are not attractive, yet they have, in spite of very ordinary faces, a look of ecstasy and worship. They aspire upwards; their attention is all directed heavenwards; they are full of movement. They are not serene, but rather passionately worshipful.

Velasquez has two charming "angelettes" in his Coronation of the Virgin. They are just charming, enchanting children for the Queen of Heaven to rest her eyes upon. Zurbaran's angels are strong and solid, and have real poise. The one in the vision of St. Peter comes the nearest to the Biblical description. There is an element about this angel that carries conviction.

One period of art melts into the next, one cannot draw a definite line between them. History, philosophical viewpoints, different religious tendencies, all had their influence upon art and its various schools. Ruben's painting is opulent and fleshy, and his angels partake of this tendency. Murillo's are sentimental and unreal. They belong neither to heaven nor to earth. Rembrandt's angels, except his remarkably visionary picture of Jacob's dream, are not too inspiring, swathed as they are in what looks like over-long nightgowns. One fears they will be tripped up by their folds. Back in France Delacroix depicted angels with strength, but decidedly earthly in character. In England there appeared a great visionary, William Blake, who illustrated his mystical poems and had his peculiar conception. His theology, like his methods of painting was unorthodox, but his pictures have an other-worldly element, rarely met in his era.

### 6. Towards the Modern

The nineteenth century ushered in quite a new trend in art in which the angels' pictures fare less well than ever. One has the impression that the artist painted or sculptured them only for the sake of convention or decoration. It is as if most artists considered the angels, even in heaven, as so much decoration.

The Victorian era was prosperous and complacent, and also very romantic and sentimental. The Victorian artists reflect the prevailing notion about angels. They thought of them as womanly, gentle spirits, not far removed from fairies. In statuary they are placed leaning over fonts or weeping over graves. Even Daniel Chester French's angels, though grand and imposing, are allegorical figures. They represent an idea, not a spiritual reality. Once more we see that wings alone do not make an angel. The magnificent Victory of Samothrace has wings, yet no one would take her for an angel, but for what she is meant to be, the expression of victory. The man who conceived her transmitted his thoughts so clearly to the stone, that she has remained victorious through the ages. It is the belief of the artist which, coupled to his talent, gives him the power to transmit to the beholder the reality behind the symbol. French understood and believed in Lincoln. He evidently did not understand or believe in angels!

The Victorians generally lived conventional, stolid, unimaginative lives. God's messenger, strong and pure, faithful guardian of man, was never given a thought. Men relied upon their bank accounts, not upon God's angels.

Dante Gabriel Rossetti revolted against this attitude. Take his painting of the Annunciation in what is called pre-Raphaelite style. It is a lovely picture but it does not recapture the primitive, unsophisticated clarity. The Blessed Virgin looks more cowed than submissive, and the angel simply does not look like a messenger of God. This is not for his lack of wings, but because of his whole bearing. Georges Rouault painted a guardian angel; one would not recognize it as such were it not so indicated beneath the picture.

The guardian angel slowly became a pious fable to comfort little children with, and to enhance Bible illustrations. The strange part is, though, that the idea of angels haunts the human mind, and again and again they remain the subject of artistic endeavor. Every age, even our own very scientific and realistic one, has been irresistibly drawn to the painting and sculpturing of the heavenly beings. Christmas and Easter cards and pious leaflets representing wraith-like, bewinged ladies and chubby cherubs still flood the market. We cannot call these art, but their pictorial influence is too strong and harmful for us to ignore their impact upon the receptive minds of children, and upon our own skeptical intellectualizing. Between these pious horrors and the extravagance of much modern art, no wonder we get lost and that our belief in angels becomes doubtful.

The modern artist in his search for new expression, his desire for a more honest, if less exact, interpretation, had to return to symbolism. But this symbolism has not yet really found itself. It has no meaning for the uninitiated. In a revolt against "over-prettification" they have gone the other way: many of the contemporary angels are stark and ugly, and some are almost symbolized out of existence into the realm of simple kitsch.

Before World War II in Germany, Sulamith Wülfing gave her angels a true other-worldliness. They lack, perhaps, in strength, but they make up for it in spirituality. One can see the artist not merely designing, but really following an inner vision.

In an ultra-modern jewel I have found a contemporary angel that comes strangely near to true semblance. The angel's face consists simply of a pure pear-shaped diamond. Here is a visage, peerless, unemotional, clear-cut, which, featureless, transfers to the beholder the image of a faultless, luminous countenance.

It is perfectly justifiable to try and portray angels, but they never should be permitted to take on such corporeality as to remind us of anyone human. We may catch in some human face an expression that may suddenly remind us of an angel. But that glimpse lies not in the features but in the spirit reflected in them. Angels are pure spirits who have, and still do manifest themselves to us in such a form as we may comprehend. They are the messengers of God, the personification of his attributes. They are spiritual beings to be approached with reverence and humility. Whenever we seek to paint or carve them, we must preserve that attitude, for they are holy.

To those of us who have been nurtured in the Eastern Orthodox Church, the proper representation of Christ, his Mother, the angels and saints is only possible when the painter abides by the canons and Holy Tradition of iconography. These rules make it possible to translate into images for our eyes the semblance of those whose features are projected upon the screen of eternity, beyond space and time, bathed in a light that throws no shadow, in a life that knows no death. So that looking at these icons we look not so much at them as through them, to and at the reality they indeed stand for and represent.

[1]Edward West, Lecture, "Byzantine Religious Art," New York.

# Epilogue

# Epilogue

It was early morning, when I was seven years old, that I saw the angels. I am as sure of it now as I was then. I was not dreaming nor "seeing things"—I just know they were there, plainly, clearly, distinctly. I was neither astonished nor afraid. I was not even awed—I was only terribly pleased. I wanted to talk to them and touch them.

Our night nursery was lit by the dawn and I saw a group of angels standing, as if chatting, around my young brother's bed. I was aware of this, although I could not hear their voices. They wore long flowing gowns of various soft-shaded colors. Their hair came to their shoulders, and different in color from fair and reddish to dark brown. They had no wings. At the foot of my brother Mircea's bed stood one heavenly being, a little aside from the others—taller he was, and extraordinarily beautiful, with great white wings. In his right hand he carried a lighted taper; he did not seem to belong to the group of angels gathered around the bed. He clearly stood apart and on watch. I knew him to be the guardian angel. I then became aware that at the foot of my own bed stood a similar celestial creature. He was tall, his robe was dark blue with wide, loose sleeves. His hair was auburn, his face oval, and his beauty such as I cannot describe because it was comparable to nothing human. His wings swept high and out behind him. One hand was lifted to his breast, while in the other he carried a lighted taper. His smile can only be described as angelic; love, kindness, understanding, and assurance flowed from him. Delighted, I crawled from under the bedcovers and, kneeling up against the end of the bed, I stretched out my hand with the ardent wish to touch my smiling guardian, but he took a step back, put out a warning hand, and gently shook his head. I was so close to him I could have reached him easily. "Oh, please don't go," I cried; at which words all the other angels looked toward me, and it seemed I heard a silvery laugh, but of this sound I am not so certain, though I know they laughed. Then they vanished.

I was but a child when I saw my guardian angel. As time passed I still sporadically remembered and acknowledged his presence, but mostly, I ignored him. Paradoxically, it was evil and distress that brought me up short and cleared my vision.

Perhaps due to all I had witnessed and undergone in the War and under Communist occupation, I was, in the following years, plagued by demonic nightmares. My only salvation while in these dreams was to make the Sign of the Cross. I have always known that I was asleep; it was a conscious dreaming—but to drag myself out of sleep into wakefulness was torture.

One day, in looking through a collection of old icons, I came across one done in three panels representing the guardian angel; in the middle panel, he is defending his sleeping charge from bad dreams. Later, when plagued once more by one of my most fearsome of nightmares, upon wakening I suddenly remembered the icon, and with overpowering clarity I recollected that as a child I had seen my guardian angel.

With utmost certainty, at that instant, I turned to my guardian angel as I had not done since my childhood; and I knew positively as I did when I saw him, that he was standing by me to protect me. Reassured and at peace, I fell back into deep, restful sleep.

This, my own experience, stands both at the beginning and at the end of this book, for without it I would probably never have started upon my study. Also, without all I have studied this experience would have remained simply a remarkable experience (at least to myself), but unexplained and meaningless. Today, for me, it has a very real and uplifting significance and the angels have taken on a stupendous reality. Their activity among us has become to me a vital, positive reality. I no longer seek to see them, the knowledge of their presence is enough. To try to have a vision of angels or to hope or ask for such a thing is wrong. To seek intimacy with them by any other means than the grace of God is useless; Christ is our only way of union with the Father and with all his creatures.

Angels are pure spirit, but they do not necessarily lack a consistency, the nature of which is beyond our ken. When we see them we behold a reality. It would perhaps be wrong to call such an experience a "vision," if we mean by the word vision a trancelike state, and not simply a faculty of sight. What we see on such occasions, we perceive quite effortlessly, all in knowing that materially speaking there is nothing there to see. According to the records in the Scriptures, and also from the testimony of the saints, the emotion is described as one of joy and wonderment, sometimes fear, in which the mind remains perfectly clear and judgment is unimpaired. St. Simeon says that "those who are worthy . . .perceive, both by the senses and by intellect, that which is altogether above both sense and intellect."[1] St. Joan of Arc said in her trial that she grasped her vision of St. Catherine and St. Michael around the knees, but when asked what she held in her embrace she was unable to explain. I do not believe that the angels materialize in the physical sense of the word, yet they do have a spiritual concreteness. They are not transparent like ghosts, but appear to those who see them as completely substantial.

Our guardian angel is believed to be the spiritual image of all our true and good qualities; this renders him intensely personal and our very own specific angel. He is, accordingly, nearer or further from us, as we are nearer or farther from our true nature.

Even as our good characteristics are given us by God so is our angel given to us, to protect and foster these traits, until we grow into the full maturity of our God-given and God-like nature. He is indeed our guardian and our mentor, and beholds the face of God. He is incorruptible and always with us, but he may not always be able to reach us, because of our wilfull perversity. The evil angel, or demon, on the other hand, can only approach us as far as our bad qualities, or rather our indulgence in them, makes him our shadow. He too, upon occasion, can be seen or felt by the perceptive. But when I speak of him as a shadow I do not mean to imply that the Devil has no reality, for only those who have never resisted temptation, who, in other words, have not stood up to Satan, could doubt his existence, for they have not had occasion to feel his strength. It is just this experience of the tremendous power of temptation, that confirms my belief in the fallen angel.

The holy angels are immortal by the grace of God. They have a positive and dynamic selfness and existence independent of all else except God. They are far from will-less, but their will is completely attuned to God's will, because of their utter love and adoration of the Lord. The misery of time is unknown to them.

To worship the angels, in the heathen sense, is definitely wrong and forbidden by the Scriptures and the Church, but to pray for their help and to reverence them is quite Scriptural. Prayer is the great bond of unity, the welding substance by which all God's creation stands as one before him.

The holy angels of God guard us, shepherd us, lead us, tending us when we fall, cheering us upon our way. Our personal angel and also the guardians of our different nations, mingle their prayers with ours, carrying them to God on High, until we shall all stand before the Throne of God and know even as we are known (1 Cor. 13:12).

It is meet, right, and our bounden duty, that we should at all times, and in all places, give thanks unto thee, O Lord, Holy Father, Almighty Everlasting God.

Who, in the multitude of thy Saints, has compassed us about with so great a cloud of witnesses that we, rejoicing in their fellowship, may run with patience the race that is set before us, and, together with them, may receive the crown of glory that fadeth not away.

Therefore with Angels and Archangels, and with all the company of heaven, we laud and magnify thy glorious Name; evermore praising thee, and saying,

**HOLY, HOLY, HOLY, LORD GOD OF HOSTS,
HEAVEN AND EARTH ARE FULL OF THY GLORY;
GLORY BE TO THEE, O LORD MOST HIGH. AMEN.**

[1]*Works of St. Simeon*, Part II. Smyrna ed., 1886, p. 1.